The Field of
Life and Death

&

Tales of
Hulan River

THE FIELD OF
LIFE AND DEATH
&
TALES OF
HULAN RIVER

XIAO HONG

Translated by Howard Goldblatt

Cheng & Tsui Company
Boston

The Field of Life and Death & Tales of Hulan River

Copyright © 2002 by Howard Goldblatt

First Cheng & Tsui Revised Edition 2002

Published by

Cheng & Tsui Company
25 West Street
Boston, MA 02111-1213 USA
Fax (617) 426-3669
www.cheng-tsui.com
"Bringing Asia to the World"™

Library of Congress Cataloging-in-Publication Data

Xiao, Hong, 1911-1942.
[Sheng si chang. English]
Field of life and death and Tales of Hulan / Xiao Hong ; translated by Howard Goldblatt.
    cm.
ISBN 0-88727-392-0 (pbk.)
1. Xiao, Hong, 1911-1942—Translations into English. I. Title: Field of life and death ; Tales of Hulan. II. Goldblatt, Howard, 1939- . III. Xiao, Hong, 1911-1942. Hulanhe zhuan. English. IV. Title: Hulanhe zhuan. V. Title: Tales of Hulan. VI. Title.
PL2740.N3 S4813 2002
895.1'351—dc21

                                        2002003508

Quality Paperback ISBN 0-88727-392-0

20 19 18 17 16 15 / 4 5 6 7 8 9 10

Printed in the United States of America

Contents

Translator's Preface

Most will agree, I believe, that translations of significant literary works are as prone to becoming dated, in some respects at least, as the works themselves; the translations, however, can be given a second life (or, more exactly, third, since any translation extends the life of the original work). Sometimes, ironically, thanks to publishers who allow works to go out of print, a translator is given the opportunity to revisit his work and make it available to a new generation of readers. That is the case with Xiao Hong's finest works. My translations of *The Field of Life and Death* and *Tales of Hulan River* first appeared from Indiana University Press in 1979. *Tales of Hulan River* was reissued with minor changes in Hong Kong in 1988 by Joint Publishers. My thanks to both for releasing their rights to the works for the current revised translations.

Returning to these, my earliest full-length translations, has been an instructive and humbling experience. Happy to be able to apply more than two decades of experience to a "rewriting," and somewhat embarrassed by its necessity, I've mainly profited by the chance to reread the most important works of the most important Chinese writer in my career and one of Republican China's true treasures.

I have included translations of the original prefaces to both novels: Lu Xun, as Xiao Hong's patron and friend, bestowed immediate stature to *The Field of Life and Death*, not just by reading it before he had even heard her name and publishing it in his own Slave Series, but by putting his name up front on his Preface. His close friend and fellow literary mover and shaker, Mao Dun (China's Minister of Culture in the 1950s) wrote an emotional and predictably ideological preface to *Tales of Hulan River* for a 1947 Shanghai edition. Both works, with or without the prefaces, have appeared in China, Taiwan, and Hong Kong in a variety of editions.

The original translation of *The Field of Life and Death* was a collaborative project. I acknowledge the fine work of Ellen Yeung, who has not been consulted for this revision. I have, however, relied upon the sensitive reading of Sylvia Li-chun Lin, whose suggestions have proved invaluable to the re-translation of both novels.

Translator's Introduction

Xiao Hong wrote *The Field of Life and Death* in Qingdao, Shandong, in 1934; she was 23 years old. Six years later she completed *Tales of Hulan River* in Hong Kong. Within a year, at the age of 30, she was dead of a chronic respiratory infection. In strictest terms, these two novels cannot be considered the alpha and omega of her creative life, yet they were the high points of her writing career and, we can suppose, of her tragically short life.

In 1936, Xiao Hong was asked by the renowned journalist and China watcher Edgar Snow to write a brief autobiographical sketch for his short story anthology *Living China*. Though noticeably short on factual data, this piece goes a long way toward describing the author's emotional state at the time of its writing and her feelings toward her family and herself.

In 1911, in a small county seat I was born into a petty landlord family. That county seat is in what is probably the easternmost and northernmost part of China—Heilongjiang province—and so for four months of any given year there are snow flurries.

My father often gave up his humanity over greed. His relationships with servants, or with his own children, as well as with Granddad, were all characterized by his stinginess, aloofness, even hard-heartedness.

Once, over rent payment due on a house, my father took possession of a tenant's entire team of horses and his wagon. The tenant's family wept, pleaded, and prostrated themselves at the feet of Granddad, who then unharnessed two tawny horses from the wagon and gave them back.

My father quarreled with Granddad all night long over those two horses. "Two horses to us mean nothing, but to a poor man those two horses mean his very existence," Granddad said, but my father continued to quarrel with him.

When I was nine my mother died. My father changed even more; when someone would on occasion break a glass, he would shout and carry on until the person was shaking in his boots. Later on, even my father's eyes underwent a change, and each time I passed by him, I felt as if there were thorns stuck all over my body; he would cast an oblique glance at you, and that arrogant glance of his would shift from the bridge of his nose, down past the corner of his mouth and continue moving down.

So at dusk during snowstorms I stayed near the radiator and by Granddad, where I would listen to him read poetry and watch his slightly reddened lips as he read the poems.

Whenever my father beat me, I would go to Granddad's room and stare out the window from dusk to late into the night—the white snow beyond the window floated there like white fleece, while the lid of the water jug on the radiator vibrated, sounding like the accompaniment of a musical instrument.

Granddad would often place his wrinkled hands on my shoulders, then place them on my head, and my ears would ring with sounds of:

"Hurry and grow up! It will be fine once you have grown up."

The year I reached the age of twenty, I fled from the home of my father, and ever since, I have lived the life of a drifter.

I've "grown up," all right, but things are not "fine."

But I learned from Granddad that besides coldness and hatred, life also includes warmth and love.

And so, in my bosom there is a perpetual longing and pursuit to find this warmth and love.

According to Xiao Hong's second husband, Duanmu Hongliang, she was born on the day of the Duanyang or Dragon Boat Festival, which falls on the fifth day of the fifth lunar month. Local superstition had it that it was unlucky to be born on that day, so her birthday was moved forward to the eighth day of the fifth month.

Xiao Hong (her true name was Zhang Naiying) was born into what, by all accounts, was a wealthy landlord family. It is the family portrayed in chapters three through five of *Tales of Hulan River*. There seems little doubt that she led a cloistered and troubled childhood in Hulan County, where she was raised, and it is not difficult to reason, from her writings and the comments of her friends, that the source of the emotional and psychological problems she later experienced can be traced to these early years. Her first extended contact with the world outside of Hulan County came when she attended middle school in Harbin, some twenty miles away, in 1928. The initially pleasant and exciting nature of her stay in Harbin came to an end a few years later, when she began cohabiting with a local teacher, was expelled from school, and was subsequently abandoned by the man. Pregnant, destitute, and unwilling or unable to return home, she found herself with no one to turn to.

It was during this time, too, that the opening shots of the Sino-Japanese conflict were fired. On September 18, 1931, a minor anti-Japanese incident occurred near the southern Manchurian city of Mukden (Shenyang). Retaliation was swift and decisive and led to the formalization of Japanese control over all of Manchuria, with the establishment of the puppet regime of Manchukuo in early 1932.

A few months after this incident, Xiao Hong met and began living with a contributor of stories and poems to a Harbin newspaper who wrote under the penname of San Lang. Over the ensuing year and a half, Xiao Hong (who had adopted the pseudonym Qiao Yin—"Gentle Moanings") also contributed works to the newspaper. In August 1933, she and San Lang privately published a joint anthology of stories and essays entitled *Trudging* (Bashe); it was quickly proscribed by the Japanese and not reprinted until a century later.

By the spring of 1934, the Japanese occupation of Manchuria had become intolerable to patriotic Chinese youths. Following a brush with the Japanese authorities, Xiao Hong and San Lang fled to Shandong, where they stayed for six months before traveling on to Shanghai. During their brief stay in the city of Qingdao, the two writers worked on their first full-length novels. San Lang's *Village in August* (Bayue de xiangcun), which he wrote under the pseudonym Tian Jun, was not completed until after his arrival in Shanghai, in August 1935. It is the story of a band of guerrilla patriots and their anti-Japanese activities. Xiao Hong, on the other hand, completed her manuscript prior to her departure from Qingdao for Shanghai. It was sent ahead to Lu Xun, the most popular and influential literary figure of the time, with the hope that he would help get the work published. This novel, untitled at the time, was *The Field of Life and Death*. It was, in fact, published under Lu Xun's auspices, but not until late 1935, when Xiao Hong had been in Shanghai for over a year and had already had several short pieces published in Shanghai magazines. By then her relationship with her domineering husband, who had now adopted the pseudonym by which he is best known—Xiao Jun—was becoming strained. Fortunately for her, the unhappiness she was experiencing in her life with him was balanced by the intimate friendship she had formed with Lu Xun and his family.

Following the appearance of *The Field of Life and Death*, which made its author an overnight literary sensation, Xiao Hong published a long reminiscence of her life with Xiao Jun in Harbin from 1932 to 1933, entitled *Market Street* (Shangshi jie), and a collection of short stories and essays entitled *The Bridge* (Qiao). But in early 1936, when her treatment at the hands of Xiao Jun was growing unbearable, and Lu Xun was not only beset by physical ailments but was also embroiled in a heated battle over National Defense Literature, Xiao Hong left Shanghai for Japan. There, for the remainder of 1936, she licked her wounds, studied a little, and did some writing.

Lu Xun died on October 19, 1936; this was an unparalleled emotional blow to Xiao Hong, and it precipitated her return to Shanghai from Japan. She had now lost the second person in her life who had treated her with kindness, understanding, and warmth (her grandfather, of course, was the first). The death of Lu Xun was a prime reason why, over the next two years, Xiao Hong's literary output nearly ceased. But there were other reasons as well, on both the national and personal levels.

The full-scale opening of war with Japan in July and August 1937 drove large numbers of writers out of besieged Shanghai and into the interior. Xiao Hong and Xiao Jun joined the exodus, settling for a few months in Wuhan. There she met another writer from Northeast China, Duanmu Hongliang, who, for good or ill, was to be the most important figure in her life from that point on. In early 1938, following a one-month journey to Northern China (the stay there cut short by the approach of the Japanese army), Xiao Hong and Xiao Jun separated, and she eventually returned to Wuhan in the company of Duanmu Hongliang, with whom she lived, off and on, for the next four years. She was pregnant again, and she was left alone in Wuhan when Duanmu Hongliang traveled to the new capital of Chongqing. The accumulation of physical and emotional ills that beset her pushed her to the brink of despair. In September she, too, went to Chongqing, where she was delivered of a dead infant. Following her subsequent reunion with Duanmu Hongliang, her life returned to normal: she began to write again and slowly regained some of her health.

The war, from which Xiao Hong had been fleeing for most of her adult life, caught up with her again in Chongqing, so she and Duanmu Hongliang fled to Hong Kong in early 1940. A year or so later, her second novel, *Ma Bole*, was published. It is a humorous satire set in Qingdao and Shanghai and, though generally condemned by contemporary critics who were demanding wartime literature of a more strident, propagandistic variety, is an entertaining and rather successful novel.

In December 1940, Xiao Hong completed her manuscript of *Tales of Hulan River*, a work that was begun in Chongqing but whose origins go back even further, to one of the stories she had written in Japan in 1936. A sequel to this novel was planned, but she never had the opportunity to put her plan into effect. Her physical condition, which had been poor from as early as her days in Harbin and was adversely affected by her nearly nomadic and bohemian life throughout the first stages of the war with Japan, grew even worse during her stay in Hong Kong. Bothered by a recurring stomach ailment, tuberculosis, and complications during childbearing, in December 1941, she was forced into the hospital because of a respiratory condition.

On January 22, 1942, slightly over a month after the Japanese occupation of the city, Xiao Hong died in a temporary hospital set up by the Red Cross; she had not reached her thirty-first birthday. Her remains were cremated and buried in Repulse Bay, where they stayed until August 1957, when they were transferred to the city of Canton (Guangzhou) for permanent burial.

The Field of Life and Death

Xiao Hong's first novel has long been heralded by Chinese critics as one of the two most important early examples of anti-Japanese literature (Xiao Jun's *Village in August* is the other). Yet the anti-Japanese theme is not the dominant one. Rather, the novel is a grim and powerful portrait of the lives of peasants in Northeast China. The effect of the work on its contemporary readers was anger, pity, and a sense of outrage, outrage not only against the outside forces that so demeaned and brutalized the villagers, but also against the fatalistic, passive, conservative mentality of the peasants themselves. To readers of our generation, the forceful impact is lessened only slightly by the knowledge that the events portrayed belong to history. Humanity being what it is, we can never be assured that such suffering, cruelty, and ignorance are very far away.

The Field of Life and Death is not the story of any particular individual. Many of the characters we find in it are little more than stereotypes, and although the spotlight shifts from one individual or family to another, it seldom stops long enough to give much definition. It is the aggregate village that has the starring role, and with the author's skill, it comes alive.

It is unfortunate that this broad aspect and many finer points have escaped the attention of most critics in the years since the novel was first published, for by focusing only on the final portion of the work and its patriotic message, Xiao Hong's artistic skill and the subtle workings of her creative mind have gone largely neglected. There is, for example, the strong Buddhist flavor that runs through much of the novel: the villagers' fatalistic attitudes and repeated mention of the four distresses (birth, old age, sickness, and death) are unquestionable and, we can assume, conscious references to the Buddhist faith. Beyond this, we might ponder the possibility of Christian influences on the author (who lived in an apartment below a Catholic nun in Qing-dao and was friendly with several Russian émigrés in Harbin); the sac-rificial goat is but one possible manifestation of this influence.

The role of animals, generally, is yet another neglected aspect of this novel. Whether it is Mother Wang's old mare, Two-and-a-Half Li's goat (which both opens and closes the novel), the stray dog that shares Golden Bough's lodging in Harbin, or Zhao San's ox, animals are often used to heighten the dramatic effect of an episode or scene. Animal imagery, too, is a significant facet of Xiao Hong's descriptive art; in the first two chapters alone, the characters' appearance and actions are portrayed with the aid of animal images nearly twenty times. The vis-ual effect of this device on the reader is substantial.

Finally, the related themes of feminism and autobiography deserve detailed investigation. These two themes are most obvious in the chap-ters dealing with Golden Bough's liaison and subsequent marriage to Chengye, the horrifying chapter on births, and the episode concerning Golden Bough's adventures in Harbin. That Golden Bough is, in some respects and to some degree, a fictional representation of the author herself is hard to dispute. Her ambivalent and often contradictory view of men seems to parallel what we know of Xiao Hong's experiences in this regard. Xiao Hong's dependence upon men, her willingness to al-low them to exploit her for their own ends, and the anger that erupted when she was abandoned or mistreated are nearly exactly duplicated in Golden Bough. Beyond this, the agonies of childbirth and the de-meaning act of prostitution by an impoverished woman were also ex-perienced by Xiao Hong no more than two years before she wrote *The Field of Life and Death*.

All this brings us to the final portion of the novel and the introduc-tion of the anti-Japanese theme. When it is viewed in political terms (as it has been by most Chinese critics and literary historians), this portion of *The Field of Life and Death* makes it the important novel it is; but when it is viewed from a more detached literary perspective, this portion is the least well-integrated part of the work.

Upon further reflection and analysis, however, I believe there may be yet a third approach, one in which the true significance of this por-tion of the novel may be discerned. For with all its literary flaws and political overtones, it is here that we perceive the author's understand-ing of the burning issue of the day—Japanese aggression and ap-proaching war—and the force of her implicit message is clear. The un-characteristically (for her) sketchy, ill-defined descriptions; the abrupt, loosely connected transition from the first to the second parts of the novel; and the role of hearsay as regards the actions of the Japanese all point to a fragmented and clouded comprehension of events taking place around her. What Xiao Hong puts before the reader is not the idealized, patriotic-romantic view of war, but the isolated and extremely personal effects it has on real people in everyday situations. Rather than viewing the war in its broad historical sense, she has subtly yet forcefully described the individual tragedies experienced by people who, like the author herself, are brutalized by this violence they do not understand. The episodic and loosely connected nature of this portion in particular and of the novel as a whole makes one think of a series of individual photographs, each with its own clarity and significance. That is, after all, how Xiao Hong observed the lives of her villagers, before and after the advent of war. In this she may well be representative of the vast majority of her feminine contemporaries who, raised in a patriarchal society that relegated women to domestic functions, relied upon their men-folk and gossip for their knowledge and understanding of the world beyond their family circles. Signs of immaturity in the writing itself are offset by the maturity of Xiao Hong's worldview.

Tales of Hulan River

The careful reader of *The Field of Life and Death* and *Tales of Hulan River*, while acknowledging the almost totally disparate nature of the two novels, will find a great many similarities in style, themes, and specifics. The same issues, for the most part, were the author's concern in both works, written six years apart. The plight of the peasants, the role of women, the scenic beauty—all these are at the core of Xiao Hong's literary creations. In nearly every case, these themes are most powerfully and vividly drawn where they are inextricably tied up with Xiao Hong's personal experiences and observations. In other words, she is at her finest when she is most openly autobiographical, and *Tales of Hulan River* is an autobiographical novel. Regarding this type of work, Northrop Frye has written in *Anatomy of Criticism*:

> Autobiography merges with the novel by a series of insensible gradations. Most autobiographies are inspired by a creative, and therefore fictional, impulse to select only those events and experiences in the writer's life that go to build up an integrated pattern. This pattern may be something larger than himself with which he has come to identify himself, or simply the coherence of his character and attitudes.

Tales of Hulan River is not merely an exercise in nostalgia, nor is its purpose to feed the author's ego, for while recounting the experiences and images of her youth, it clearly captures her attitudes as an adult, her concerns about the society in which she lives, and her philosophical position. Her descriptions of the incidents, people, and scenery that made up her early life hold deeper meaning than is at first apparent.

Chapter Five, the tragic story of the child bride, is the author's most powerful indictment of the cruel and dehumanizing effects of traditional society. It is a tale of suffering, insensitivity, selfishness, morbid curiosity, superstition, and compassion made impotent in the face of more powerful forces. It is not an isolated theme, for the victims of this complex social order people many of the other chapters as well. The young women whose lives are the counterpoints to the outwardly convivial activities of the various festivals are sacrificed in the name of traditional morality and wisdom. This is not, as Mao Dun and others have suggested, merely a result of the author's melancholia in her final years, but, as we can see with equal clarity while reading *The Field of Life and Death*, it is an idée fixe with Xiao Hong. The effect is heightened by the way in which she deals with more or less commonplace events and contrasts the ostensibly serene and simple daily life of the town as a whole with the horrors experienced by the individuals whose lives are swallowed up in this grand design (in Chapter One she has given the reader a microcosmic view of this paradox in her description of the products of the ornament shops and the lives of the craftsmen themselves). As we have seen in the autobiographical sketch, however, warmth and love are irrepressible, if generally in retreat, in Xiao Hong's world; this is evident in *Tales of Hulan River*. Beyond the obvious figure of the narrator's grandfather, the people in this novel are eminently worthy of love and compassion, and goodness can be its own reward. The good will triumph, and the evil will suffer cosmic retribution (represented by the breakup of the Hu family in Chapter Five and the poetic justice meted out to its members).

Among the most striking features of *Tales of Hulan River* are the simple beauty of Xiao Hong's rhetorical style and the vivid quality of her descriptions. The unadorned and unpretentious style brings to the work highly evocative and intimate qualities. Her genius in capturing detail and nuance (the camera-like quality already apparent in *The Field of Life and Death*) makes this work appeal to the reader's visual as well as verbal senses. It should come as no surprise to the discerning reader that Xiao Hong was a budding artist in her youth and continued to paint for most of her adult life.

In the final analysis, *Tales of Hulan River* must stand as Xiao Hong's representative work; it is her most personal and artistic creation and is a lasting testimony to her artistic genius.

*... for those whose lives
are at Heaven's mercy,
who hasn't experienced
Heaven's wrath?*
Xiao Hong

Xiao Hong

The Field of Life and Death

Golden Bough — character arc/development

Preface to *The Field of Life and Death*

I recall it was four years ago in February that my family and I were trapped in the line of fire at Shanghai's Chapei district, and there I witnessed the extinction of the Chinese population as they fled or died. Later, with the assistance of a few friends, we gained entrance into the peaceful British Concession. Although refugees filled the streets, the residents there were living in peace and comfort. We were no more than four or five li, I suppose, from Chapei, and yet it was such a different world. How then could our thoughts have been on Harbin?

When this manuscript reached my desk, it was already the spring of this year. I had long since returned to Chapei, which was once again bustling with people. But in the manuscript, I was seeing a Harbin of five years ago, or even earlier. This is, of course, nothing more than a brief sketch whose narration of events and scenic descriptions are superior to its characterizations. And yet the tenacity of survival and the resistance to death forcefully permeate the pages. Keen observations and an extraordinary writing style add considerably to the book's vividness and beauty. Its spirit is robust. Even those who have an abhorrence of literature or those of a practical bent cannot help but be moved by this work.

Having heard that the Literature Society was willing to publish this work, I submitted the manuscript to the Publications Censorship Committee of the Central Propaganda Department. It was held up there for half a year; ultimately, approval was denied. Very often people become wiser only after an event, and on reflection, the outcome was never in doubt. The themes of tenacity of survival and resistance to death are, I'm afraid, contrary to the doctrine of "political tutelage" of the National Reconstruction Process. In May of this year, this haughty committee was suddenly and completely dissolved as a result of an article entitled "Short Talks on Emperors." This, then, is an application of the great object lesson of "using oneself as a model."

The offer of the Slave Society to use its meager, hard-earned funds to publish this book came half a year after our superiors had "used themselves as a model." I was asked to write a short preface. However, over the past few days, rumors have been circulating, and the bustling crowds of residents of Chapei are once again scurrying like rats. Constant streams of cars bearing luggage and pedestrians pass through the streets, while on both sides, foreigners, yellow and white, watch the antics of our civilized nation with amusement. Newspapers from publishing companies located in the safe zones call these fleeing people "commoners" and "fools." For my part, I consider them wise. At least they have learned, through past experience, not to trust the pompous, official-sounding pronouncements. They still remember.

It is now the night of November 14, 1935, and I have just finished rereading *The Field of Life and Death*. All around me there is a deathly stillness. Gone are the sounds of neighbors talking, which I've grown so used to hearing, and gone are the cries of the street vendors selling food. Now and then I hear the faint sound of dogs barking in the distance. I can imagine that a similar condition does not exist in the British or French Concessions, nor, for that matter, in Harbin. The residents in those places and I harbor different feelings and live in different worlds. But at this moment my heart feels like the stagnant water at the bottom of an abandoned well, devoid of ripples. In such a mood I have mechanically penned these few words. This then is the heart of a slave—and yet, if these words can stir the heart of the readers, assuredly we are not yet slaves.

But, rather than listen to these jeremiads uttered in comfort, you will do better to turn quickly to *The Field of Life and Death*, which follows. It will infuse in you the strength to persevere and to resist.

LU XUN

1 THE WHEAT FIELD

A goat gnawed at the exposed roots of an elm tree by the side of the road.

Elm trees had partitioned the long road out of the city into shady patches. Walking down it was like striding beneath a huge swaying umbrella that blocked out the sky.

As the goat began gnawing on the bark of the tree, threads of saliva trickled down its whiskers. Caught up by the wind, they looked like soap lather, or sluggish, floating strands of silk. The goat's legs were covered with them. Huge scabs on the elm tree bore witness to how badly scarred it was. Yet the goat lay down to sleep in the shade, the white pouch that was its stomach rising and falling.

A little boy made his way slowly through a vegetable plot. His straw hat made him look like a big mushroom. Was he hunting for butterflies? Stalking grasshoppers? Just a little boy under the midday sun.

Before long a limping farmer also appeared in the vegetable plot. The cabbage patch was about the same color as the goat.

Green-tasseled sorghum grew adjacent to the southern edge of the vegetable plot. The little boy wormed his way in among the sorghum, brushing against the tassels with his head and knocking them to the ground. Some of them struck him on the face. The leaves rubbed against each other, at times pricking his skin. He was in a world of verdant sweetness, a world obviously cooler than the one outside. Soon the little boy fought his way to the last stalk, where the sun began to scorch his crown; he quickly put his hat back on. Under a canopy of blue sky the sun sent its rays to dance atop the vegetable plot. Not a cloud to be seen. The little boy carried a willow switch tucked under his arm. He was so bowlegged and pigeon-toed that, as he walked, it almost looked as if he were holding a bowl between his legs. The limping farmer had long since seen that it was his son, and from a distance he hailed the boy in a raspy voice:

"Hey, Tunnel Legs! Didn't you find it?"

The name fit the boy perfectly. "No," he answered.

Wild vegetables fringed a short path at the edge of the vegetable plot. At the far end of the path was Two-and-a-Half Li's house, in front of which stood a poplar tree; the leaves were always rustling. Each day, as Two-and-a-Half Li passed beneath the tree, he stopped to listen to the rustling of its leaves and watch them move. So it was with the poplar day after day, and day after day he stopped. On this day, however, he abandoned his routine. His mind was a blank. His limp had become more pronounced, and with each stride he seemed to be stepping into a rut.

A fence of woven twigs and branches circled the mud house. Half of the poplar shade fell on his yard, and in this shade Granny Pockface washed clothes. In the fields the midday calm was broken only by butterflies waltzing among the flowers, unafraid that the sun would scorch their wings. Everything had gone into hiding. Even the dog had found a shady spot for its nap. Insects, too, were hidden and silent.

Sweat gathered on the face of Granny Pockface like pearl drops or peas, seeping into every crevice before flowing on down. Granny Pockface was not a butterfly, and could not sprout wings. Only pockmarks.

Two butterflies flitted by Granny Pockface, who swatted at them with a wet hand, bringing them down. One fell into the tub and drowned. As her body continued its fore-and-aft movement, sweat flowed down to her lips and was salty. When it stung her eyes, she rubbed them with her wet hands, but never stopped washing. Her eyes were soon red, as if she'd been crying, and her constant rubbing left absurd smudges behind. Seen from a distance, she looked like a comic stage figure. Scary big eyes, bigger even than those of a cow. A network of wrinkles crisscrossed her face.

The doors and windows of her house looked like holes. Granny Pockface stepped through the doorway. She was looking for something else to wash, but when she tried to pick up a shadow from the *kang* on which they slept, she knew that the sun had dazzled her eyes. It was like passing from light into pitch-blackness. After resting awhile, she felt much cooler. Then from beneath the straw mattress she pulled out a pair of her own pants, with which she dabbed her brow as she returned to her tub in the shade. Into the muddy water they went.

Before the pants had much of a chance to get clean, she hung them on the fence anyway. Maybe they were clean, hard to say. Granny Pockface's chores came one on top of the other. If necessary, before finishing one, she would lay it down and start on another.

Clouds of thick smoke surged from the chimney of a neighboring house. Scattered by the wind, the smoke filled the yard and clouded her vision. Realizing that her family would soon be home for lunch, she grew anxious. She grabbed a handful of straw from the corner and, with bits of it sticking to her muddy hands, began to cook. She never bothered washing her hands with clean water. Soon smoke curled out of her chimney, too. Then she came out for more straw. She gathered up an armful and, with half of it trailing on the floor and the other half dangling from her apron, lumbered back toward the house. With her hair falling down in front of her face, she looked like a she-bear. The she-bear carried the straw into her cave.

As the thick smoke obliterated the sun, the yard turned dark. Smoke hung in the air like clouds.

Water dripped from the clothes on the fence and turned into murky steam. The whole village was suffocating from stifling cook fires. The midday sun ruled over everything.

"Damn . . . must have been stolen."

When Two-and-a-Half Li limped badly, his buttocks stuck out, and always at the same angle. He rapped on the goat pen, but where was the goat?

"Damn, who'd steal my goat . . . the son of a bitch."

Hearing her husband swear, Granny Pockface walked out with bulging eyes.

"Are you complaining about lunch being late? I thought you weren't coming, so I did some washing."

She sounded like a pig when she spoke. Maybe she had a porker's vocal cords, for the sounds she made were definitely pig noises.

"Hell, the goat's gone. Why would I waste my time bawling out a stupid wife like you?"

When Granny Pockface heard that the goat was gone, she went over and began to dig through the stack of kindling; she recalled that the goat had hidden there once. But that had been in the winter, when it was trying to get warm, and it didn't dawn on her that only a goat as stupid as she would go into a stack of kindling for warmth in the middle of summer. But digging was easier than thinking. Her hair was covered with wisps of straw. Her husband tried to stop her, asking what she was doing, but she didn't answer him. She hoped her actions would produce a miracle, one that would make people respect her. In order to show she was not stupid, to show that her intelligence could rise to the occasion when necessary, she tired herself out the way a dog playing in a stack of kindling might do. Finally she sat down and picked at the wisps of straw in her hair. She sensed, to her surprise, that her intelligence had failed her; also to her surprise, she was disappointed in herself.

Before long the neighbors fanned out under the sun to look for the goat. The rice in Granny Pockface's pot was already steaming, but she too joined the search.

Two-and-a-Half Li wasn't far from home when Tunnel Legs came up to him.

"Papa, I'm hungry."

"Then go home and eat," Two-and-a-Half Li said.

But when he wheeled around, he saw his wife, looking like a bundle of straw, trailing along after them.

"What are you doing here, woman? Take him home to eat."

He turned back and limped off.

Only stubble remained on the yellow and nearly yellow patches of wheat, a sorry sight when viewed from a distance. At the edge of the field someone was drawing water from a well. Two-and-a-Half Li shaded his eyes with one hand and peered around before deciding to walk over to the well. When he got there he looked over the side. Nothing. He lowered the bucket to the bottom. Again nothing. Finally, he raised the bucket, leaned over the edge, and drank, the water gurgling in his throat. He sounded like a horse at the trough.

Old Mother Wang was resting on the threshing floor in front of her house.

"How's the threshing coming along? My goat's gone." Two-and-a-Half Li's pale face had grown even paler over the goat's disappearance.

"Baa-aa—baa-aa—" The bleating of a goat? No, just someone out looking for the goat.

A line of carts carrying bricks passed beneath the shade trees, the drivers' shouts waking the goat from its nap. Still half asleep, it scratched itself with its horns. The leafy green of the trees turned its coat a pale yellow. A roadside melon peddler was eating his own wares. The line of carts stirred up clouds of dust as it moved from the shade onto the road leading into town.

The goat was lonesome. It had finished its nap and its meal of bark, and was ready to go home. But no, it wasn't heading home. It passed under the trees and listened to each whispering leaf. Might it be heading into town, too? Yes, it trotted off toward the road leading into town.

"Baa-aa—baa-aa—" The bleating of a goat? No, just someone out looking for the goat. Two-and-a-Half Li was louder than anyone, but he didn't sound like a goat. More like a cow.

In the end, Two-and-a-Half Li came to blows with a neighbor. His hat, like a kite torn from its string, drifted down from his head and sailed off some distance away.

"How dare you step on my cabbages . . . you . . . you . . ."

The tall man with the red face looked like the King of Hell. Two-and-a-Half Li was beaten until he saw stars. He pulled up a sapling beside him, a defenseless, guiltless little tree. The tall man's wife came out and handed her husband the stirring rake for their bean vat. It was still dripping sauce.

When Two-and-a-Half Li saw the rake, he ran home carrying the small tree. His straw hat lay all alone beside the well, the hat he'd worn for countless years.

Two-and-a-Half Li swore at his wife: "Damn you, who wants to eat your burnt rice?"

He had the long face of a horse. Granny Pockface was frightened, and her movements grew clumsy. She knew the goat hadn't been found, and before long, she was weeping beside the rice pot. "My . . . my goat. I fed it every day . . . and it grew. I raised it with my own hands."

Granny Pockface was not the complaining type. When she was unhappy, or was being yelled at by her husband, or had a quarrel with a neighbor, or when the children were giving her trouble, she'd act like a pool of melted wax. She wasn't one to put up a fight. She seemed to be forever storing sorrow in her heart, which was like a piece of worn-out cotton. Racked by sobs, she went outside to bring in the clothes that were drying in the sun; she was too preoccupied to notice the goat.

As for the wandering animal, it scratched itself from time to time in the shed, nearly knocking down the door, which banged noisily.

It was already afternoon, but Two-and-a-Half Li was still sitting on the *kang*.

"Damn . . . if it's lost, it's lost. It's bad luck to have a goat around, anyway."

But his wife couldn't imagine how keeping a goat could bring bad luck.

"So, just let it wander off somewhere? I'll go look for it. It must be out in the sorghum field."

"You're going looking for it again? Don't bother. Let it stay lost."

"I know I can find it."

"Hell, looking for the goat can create other problems." His mind returned to the beating he'd sustained—his hat drifting down like a kite torn from its string, the rake dripping bean sauce. Quick, grab that little tree! Grab it! These unhappy thoughts kept running through his head.

Knowing nothing of what had happened, his wife headed off toward the sorghum field, which was alive with butterflies and other insects, and where farmers were working. She didn't stop to chat with the women in the fields; like a little crawling insect, she passed through the stubby wheat field. The sun's rays were weaker than they'd been at midday. The buzzing of insects grew louder and louder, as more and more of them took flight.

When she wasn't working, Old Mother Wang would recount the seemingly endless story of her life. All the while, she'd grind her teeth in an expression of indignation and suppressed anger. Under the stars, the wrinkles on her face seemed greener than usual, and her big, round eyes shone with a pale light. Sometimes, when she reached a high point in her story, she'd emit low grunts. Children from the neighborhood called her an owl, which usually set her off. How could she be such a hideous creature? That's when she'd start to spit and sputter.

The mothers would then beat their children, who would go off and cry. By this time, Mother Wang would normally bring her story to an end, so she could crawl through the window into the house for the night. But once in a while she'd ignore the children's sobs and, acting as if she couldn't hear them, continue her tale. She'd tell about the year when the harvest was so good she'd bought an additional cow; about how the cow had had a calf; and about what had happened to that calf. Her talks always had climaxes and anticlimaxes. And when it came to that cow, she never ran short of words. She'd describe its color, the amount of grass and water it consumed in a day, even the position it slept in.

But, on this particular night, no obnoxious children had come to her yard. Mother Wang dragged two neighbor women over to the pig's trough, where they sat and let their stories flow into the evening air like water.

Clouds skittered across the sky, and when they obscured the moon, they looked like smoke, or a mountain of coal ready to burst into flames. Before long, the moon was buried in the clouds. The women heard no croaking frogs, and saw only the twinkling lights of fireflies.

Loud snores emerged from the cave-like house and spread across the yard. Stars at the edge of the sky winked on and off. Mother Wang's story continued on like the passing clouds:

"The child was three when I let her fall to her death. If I'd kept her, I'd have been a wreck. That morning . . . let me think . . . yes, it was morning. Anyway, I left her on the haystack when I went to feed the cow. Our haystack was behind the house. When I remembered the child, I ran back to get her. But she wasn't there. Then I saw the handle of the pitchfork under the haystack, and I knew that was a bad sign. She'd fallen right on top of it. At first I thought she was still alive, but when I picked her up . . . aah!"

A streak of lightning rent the sky, and in that eerie light Mother Wang looked like an aroused phantom. The wheat field, the sorghum field, and the vegetable plot were all visible in the light. The women shrank back, as if something cold had brushed their faces. After the lightning passed, Mother Wang continued:

"Aah . . . I threw her back in the haystack, which was stained by her blood. Her little hands were trembling and blood was streaming from her mouth and nose. It was like her throat was cut. I could still hear a rumbling in her stomach. Like a puppy run over by a cart. I've seen that happen with my own eyes. I've seen it all. Whenever a family in this village decided not to keep a child, I'd take a hook, or maybe a garden tool, and I'd dig the child out of its mother's womb. The death of a child is nothing. Do you really think I'd moan and wail over that? At first I shook a little. But when I saw the wheat field out in front me, I had no regrets, and didn't shed a single tear. That year we had a fine harvest. I brought the wheat in and then picked all the grains up from the threshing floor, one at a time. That fall I worked like the devil, never stopping to pass the time of day or even catch my breath. Then came winter. When I compared my grains with the neighbors', mine were so much bigger. That winter I had terrible pains in the back from all that stooping, and yet I held those big, full grains in my hands. But when I saw how the neighbors' kids had grown, I suddenly thought of my own Little Zhong." Mother Wang shook her head and nudged the woman beside her.

"Her name was Little Zhong. I suffered for nights on end, couldn't sleep. What was all that wheat worth? Grains of wheat haven't mattered much to me since then. Even now, nothing much matters to me. I was in my twenties."

Flashes of lightning, one after another. The talkative phantom now sat mutely in the light. The neighbor women looked at each other, feeling somewhat chilled.

A snarling dog ran over from the wheat field. The cloudy night had nothing to say. Suddenly another flash of lightning, and the yellow dog ran with its tail between its legs to Two-and-a-Half Li. After the lightning, the dog returned to the haystack.

"Is Third Brother home?"

"He's asleep." Mother Wang retreated into silence again. Her response seemed to have come from an empty bottle or some other hollow vessel. She sat alone on the trough like a stone.

"Third Brother, have you been fighting with Third Sister-in-Law again? You'll never enjoy peace and harmony if you're squabbling all the time."

Two-and-a-Half Li, who was tolerant of his wife, measured others by his own standards.

Zhao San lit his pipe; there was a smile on his ruddy face. "I didn't fight with anyone."

Two-and-a-Half Li took his tobacco pouch from his belt and spoke slowly:

"My goat was lost, or didn't you know? But it came back. You've got to find a buyer for me. Keeping this goat will bring me bad luck."

Zhao San laughed, the lightning illuminating his big hands and ruddy face.

"Ha ha. You may be right. I hear your hat flew all around the edge of the well."

Suddenly Two-and-a Half Li saw the small tree beside him again. Quick, grab that little tree! Grab it! His illusions came to an abrupt end. He realized that news of his beating had spread. Lingering over the job of lighting his pipe, he defended himself:

"That couple was unreasonable. Who says you can't go looking for a lost goat? He accused me of walking all over their cabbages. So you see, I couldn't fight with him."

He shook his head, silenced by his humiliation. He sucked on his pipe, truly believing that the goat would bring him bad luck and a loss of face.

Lightning flashed again, and Zhao San, tall, husky, and big-handed, got up from the *kang* and rubbed his eyes with his palms.

"Looks like rain," he blurted out. "That's bad. The threshing isn't finished yet, and the wheat's piled up on the threshing floor."

Zhao San had the feeling that raising livestock and planting crops weren't enough for him, that he had to try to accomplish something in town. Each day he went there, until he'd begun to neglect the wheat. He was dreaming of something with a better future.

"That wife of mine, why isn't she taking care of the wheat? It'll be washed away by the rain." Zhao San took for granted that his wife would be sitting in the yard. Flashes of lightning came more frequently. Then came the sound of thunder and the sound of wind. The storm set the village astir.

"I'm over here. Get the straw mats from the shed and cover up the wheat!"

As lightning flashed above the threshing floor, their shouts seemed to be echoing off a body of water. Mother Wang shouted again: "Hurry, you good-for-nothing old man! All that sleeping has made you so soft in the head you can't even find the door."

Unnerved by the impending heavy rainfall, Zhao San didn't argue with her.

The sorghum field seemed to be collapsing, and the elm trees at the edge of the field began to whistle, producing an almost metallic sound. Flashes of lightning made the village appear one moment, and then quickly disappear back into darkness. The village was like a bubble on the ocean. From neighboring families far and near came the sounds of babies crying and adults shouting: "The sauce urn hasn't been covered!" "Round up the poultry!" And from the wheat-growing families came other shouts: "The threshing isn't done yet!" The farming community was like a chicken coop: throw in a match and the chickens go crazy.

The yellow dog began making a nest for itself in the haystack, pawing at the hay and tearing at it with its teeth. Mother Wang shook as she picked up a rake.

"Damn you! The threshing should have been finished by now. But once you go into town, you won't come back. The wheat's going to rot."

Two-and-a-Half Li approached his house under flashes of lightning. Raindrops made the leaves rustle. He reached up as the rain fell on his head and was reminded of his straw hat; he began to curse his goat again.

It was morning, and the rain had stopped. In the east a rainbow hung in the air. Wet-smelling clouds passed overhead. Above the sorghum in the east the sun trailed behind the clouds, sparkling like red crystal, like a crimson dream. Off in the distance the sorghum stood somberly, looking like a little forest. Villagers were taking advantage of the cool morning air to work in the fields.

In front of Zhao San's house a little boy was leading a horse onto the threshing floor. The young foal trotted after its young master, tail swishing in the air. The young foal loved to nuzzle up against a stone roller on the ground; pawing the smooth ground with its front hooves, then looking for something, it gave a slightly discordant whinny.

Mother Wang, dressed in a short jacket with loose sleeves, came out onto the threshing floor. Her hair was untidy and snarled. The morning sun made it look like tassels on ripening corn, all red and curly.

The horse's whinny brought out its master. It was waiting for the roller to be put in place. When that was done, it swished its tail. It was a docile, happy animal.

The straw mat was damp to the touch, so Mother Wang pulled it to the side. The boy came over to help her. Then, with wheat grains covering the floor, Mother Wang stood off to the side with her rake. The boy ran gaily into the middle of the floor and the foal started to trot in a circle. The boy turned round and round; like a compass, no matter how the foal ran, he remained in the center of the circle. Then the foal got a little wild; it galloped, playful as a child, causing the grain to spatter beyond the floor. Mother Wang hit it with the rake. But it soon tired of its antics and, like a puppy exhausted after playing and in need of rest, it stopped. As if possessed, Mother Wang swung crazily with the rake, and the foal lunged wildly, made a couple of turns around the floor, pulling the roller off the grain-covered floor while nibbling at the grain. The boy, who was holding its bridle, was soundly scolded.

"Why do you always try to sneak that animal in here? A horse like that can't help with the threshing, so get it the hell out of here and stop giving me trouble!"

The child led the horse away from the threshing floor and back to the trough, where he tethered it and went to fetch the old mare. The older horse had shed nearly all its hair, and the boy didn't like it; so he hit it with the reins to get it moving. But the old horse was immovable as a rock or a plant rooted to the ground. It was the foal's mother. It stopped and nuzzled at the open, bleeding cuts on the foal's belly, and when the boy saw that his beloved foal was bleeding, his eyes brimmed with tears. He couldn't really understand the love between a mother and her offspring, since he had yet to see his own mother; he was an illegitimate child. The old, nearly hairless animal was forced to leave its foal; with its nose smeared with blood, it stepped onto the threshing floor.

A train passed over the bridge across the river in front of the village, but no one saw it; they only heard the rumble. Mother Wang watched the black smoke spiral up into the sky. Some people from the village up ahead were taking cabbages into the city in a cart, and as they passed by Mother Wang's threshing floor, they threw down a few tomatoes, saying: "You people don't plant tomatoes. They're cheap, worthless things. Now wheat, that's what brings in the money." A husky youth driving the cart cracked his whip and moved on.

The old mare looked at the horse beyond the wall, but neither whinnied nor snorted. The boy picked up the tomatoes and began to eat one. It wasn't quite ripe; it was always the unripe ones that were picked.

The horse stood quietly, its tail hanging limp. It didn't nuzzle the roller, it didn't look off into the distance, and it didn't shirk its work. When there was work to be done, it worked calmly. When ropes and chains were fastened to it, it obeyed its master's whip, which rarely fell on its body. But sometimes, when it was too tired to go on, its steps slowed, and the master would have to beat it with a whip or a switch. Yet even then it wouldn't rear wildly, since it had been conditioned by past generations.

Gradually the grains on the floor were crushed out of shape.

"Here, lead the horse for a while, Ping'er."

"I don't want to be with the old mare. All day long it's like she's asleep."

Ping'er pocketed the tomatoes and retreated to one side to enjoy them.

"Aren't you the one?" Mother Wang scolded. "Well, I may not be able to control you, but there's still your daddy."

Ping'er ignored her and left the threshing floor, heading toward the east edge of the field, where flowers grew, gazing at the red flowers and eating his tomatoes along the way.

The old gray phantom was furious. "I'll have your daddy teach you a lesson!" And like a huge gray bird she left the threshing floor.

Early morning leaves. Leaves on the trees and on the flower stems glistened with dewy pearls. Sunbeams as far as the eye could see hung above the sorghum stalks. Families nearby were already preparing breakfast.

The old horse was grinding the wheat by itself, its reins dangling beneath its mouth. It neither nibbled at the grains nor strayed from its orbit. It made one round, then another, the rope and the reins chafing its hairless body with a regular rhythm. The old animal moved without sound and all alone.

The haystacks of wheat-growing families were piled high and higher. Fufa's was higher than the wall. His woman sucked on her pipe. She was robust but tiny. As smoke drifted from her pipe, she combed the grains on the ground with a rake. Her nephew, cracking his whip as he passed beneath the shady patch up ahead, quietly sang a lonely song.

Moved by the song, she paused in her raking. The song continued to come from the edge of the woods.

> Yesterday morning there was a light rain,
> The young maiden donned her rain cloak,
> The young maiden . . . gone fishing.

Golden Bough's development/story intertwined with tomatoes.

2   THE VEGETABLE PLOT

ripe
young woman—tomato.→picked and consumed.

Golden Bough pregnant.

Lonely tomatoes ripened in the vegetable plot. Young women filled their baskets with the bright red fruit. Other young women were picking turnips and carrots.   *talked about Golden Bough*

When Golden Bough heard the crack of the whip and the whistles, she stood up abruptly and left the vegetable plot nervously, basket in hand. At the eastern edge she paused beside a willow fence to listen. The whistling had grown fainter, and the cracking sound of the whip was moving away from her. She waited patiently. Presently the seductive whistling came again from behind. She was getting close to him again. Some of the women in the plot saw her and called out:

"Why aren't you over here picking tomatoes? What are you standing there for?"

She shook her braids, waved, and answered loudly: "I'm going home."

She pretended to be on her way home, circling round the neighbors' fences, evading the eyes from the vegetable plot, and headed toward the bend in the river. The basket hanging from her arm swung from side to side. The distant whistling urgently beckoned to her, and she was attracted to it like iron to a magnet.

The quiet bend of the river smelled damp. The man was waiting there.

Five minutes later, the young girl was still pinned to the ground like a helpless chick in the grasp of a wild animal. Mad with passion, the man clutched savagely at her body with his large hands, as if he wanted to swallow it, to destroy that warm flesh. His veins gorged with blood, he cavorted on top of what had become for him a pale cadaver. Her naked, shapely legs sought to coil around him, but could not. A chorus of sound erupted from these two greedy monsters.

Flowers trembled and swayed, and the long grasses beneath them were crushed. Not far off, an old woodcutter was cutting wild grass.

Having been interrupted, the husky young man left the sorghum field with the girl, like a hound with its prey. As they fled, his hand traveled under her clothes.

Whistling and cracking his whip, he felt that life was gentle and pleasant. His body and soul had been sated. As he drew up to his aunt, who had seen him from a distance, she said:

"You've been with that girl again, haven't you? Quite a nice girl . . . ai. . . ai!"

Seemingly troubled, she leaned up against the fence.

"Why are you sighing, Auntie?" her nephew asked. "I'm going to marry her."

"Ai . . . ai!"

She was overcome with anguish. *a preview of Golden Bough's life*

"Once you marry her, she'll change. She won't look the way she does now. Her face will turn sallow, and you'll put her out of your mind. You'll abuse her and beat her. It's only when they're your age that men carry their women in their hearts."

To show her distress, she placed her hand on her heart, as if to keep it from undergoing a change.

"She's probably pregnant by now," she continued. "If you want to marry her, do it soon."

"Her mother doesn't know yet. I have to get a matchmaker."

Fufa was returning with his cow. As soon as the woman saw her husband, she ran back into the yard, pretending to be restacking the firewood. Her husband went up to the well to let the cow drink, and then he left again, taking the cow with him. The woman looked up again, like a little mouse, and continued talking to her nephew:

"Chengye, let me tell you. I also fished by the river when I was a girl. One drizzly morning during the ninth month, I sat at the river's edge in my rain cloak. I never expected . . . I didn't want it to happen. I know it's a bad thing to sleep with a man, but your uncle, he led me from the river over to the stable, where everything ended for me. I wasn't scared, I was happy to be your uncle's wife. But look at me now; I'm afraid of him. He's as hard as a rock, and I don't dare touch him.

"You're always singing about drizzles and donning a rain cloak to go fishing. Well, I don't want to hear that song ever again. You young men aren't to be trusted. Your uncle sang the same song, but now he never thinks of the past. The past is a dead tree that can never be revived."

Tired of his aunt's ramblings, the young man turned and went into the house for a drink. Later, emboldened by the liquor, he told his uncle everything. At first Fufa could only shake his head.

"The girl's only seventeen," he finally said, "and you're twenty. How can a young girl like her help out around here?"

Instantly on the defensive, Chengye said:

"But she's so pretty, with those jet black braids. She's strong, she can do anything."

The uncle could tell that Chengye was getting drunk. So he said nothing more and just sat there musing for a while. Then he laughed and looked at his woman.

"Hey, we were like that once. Have you forgotten? Those days . . . I guess you've forgotten them by now. Those were the days. It's nice to think back to our youth."

The woman came over and held Fufa's arm. She fawned on him, but he didn't move, and she sensed that his smiling face was not the smiling face of long ago. Her heart was filled with his many angry faces. She didn't move either. She smiled but immediately wiped the smile from her face, afraid that if she smiled too long, he might scold her again. He told her to bring him a glass, and she obeyed. Soon her husband was lying on the *kang* in a stupor.

She tiptoed out, stopping in the doorway. The rustling sound of the paper in the window was in her ears. She felt completely drained of strength; a sense of grayness enveloped her. In the front yard, dragonflies buzzed among the sunflowers. But all this had absolutely nothing to do with the young woman.

The paper window gradually lightened, and slowly the window frame came into view. The girl who had gone down to the sorghum field was deep in thought and tearful. But she wept so softly she couldn't be heard above the rustling of the paper window.

Each time her mother rolled over, she muttered something, occasionally grinding her teeth. Afraid of being beaten, Golden Bough dried her tears in the dark. She felt like a mouse sleeping under the tail of a cat. The whole night passed that way. Each time her mother turned over, it seemed like an eruption as she cursed her daughter's pillow.

"Damn you!"

After that she'd spit. And it continued all night long. She spat, but not on the floor. She'd rather the spittle fell on her daughter's face. This time, however, when she turned over she neither spat nor cursed.

But in the morning, after her daughter had braided her hair and was on her way out to the fields, she snatched the basket from the girl like a crazed woman.

"You think you're going to go pick tomatoes again? Golden Bough, you're not made for picking tomatoes. You even left your basket behind. I don't think you have any brains at all. It's lucky the woodcutter turned out to be Granddad Zhu. If it had been anyone else, what chance do you think we'd have of getting it back? If anyone else had found the basket, your reputation would be ruined. Fufa's wife, didn't she come to ruin by the river? Even the children were talking about it. Ai! What kind of woman is that? After that no man would have her, and since she was pregnant, she had no choice but to marry Fufa. Her mother suffered such terrible shame she couldn't hold her head up in the village."

The mother saw Golden Bough's face grow ashen; the girl looked so vulnerable her mother took pity on her. She didn't notice the girl's hand steal under jacket coat to feel her belly. Golden Bough had a panic attack, feeling just like a girl with child.

"You go on now," her mother continued, "but don't go to the riverbank again with the other girls. Remember, stay away from the riverbank!"

The mother stood outside the door for a long while, watching the girl walk off. She didn't go inside until the girl's figure disappeared into the crowd of people working in the fields. She kept sighing as she cooked, as if her body were wracked with disease.

The farmers had to walk home each day for their breakfast. On this particular day, when Golden Bough came home, her mother saw her holding her belly.

"Stomach ache?" she asked.

Startled, the girl took her hand out from inside her coat. "My stomach's fine," she quickly denied, shaking her head.

"Are you sick?"

"No."

So they sat down to eat. But Golden Bough had no appetite, and after eating a little rice porridge, she left the table. Her mother cleared the table by herself.

"You didn't even touch the cabbage. You must be sick."

As Golden Bough walked out the door, her mother called to her:

"Come back and put on an extra jacket. You must have taken a chill, which is why you have a stomach ache." She handed her a jacket "Maybe you shouldn't go out. I'll go."

Golden Bough shook her head, turned, and left. Her mother's small jacket, which had been draped unbuttoned over her shoulders, flapped in the wind as she walked.

The tomato patch belonging to Golden Bough's family was the size of a courtyard. When you reached it, there was a pungent smell in the air, but no one could say what the odor was. The tallest tomato plant was about two feet high, its branches laden with the golden-red fruit. Every plant carried many fruits, including green and half-green ones. Of all the plots in the area, only theirs and one that adjoined theirs were tomato patches. In the ninth month many of the people were busy digging potatoes, while others were cutting cabbages and loading them onto carts to take into the city and sell.

Two-and-a-Half Li was one of those with a vegetable plot. Granny Pockface went back and forth loading cabbages onto the cart at the edge of the field. Tunnel Legs did the same, sometimes carrying two cabbages, looking as if he were carrying a couple of huge rocks.

Granny Pockface saw that the pumpkins in her neighbors' plot had turned red. She glanced around furtively, and when she was sure nobody was looking, plucked four large pumpkins growing alongside her plot. Two were as big as small watermelons. She told her son to carry them away, but Tunnel Legs strained so much his face turned as red as the pumpkins. He couldn't hold them any longer. His arms were weighted down. He'd just passed Golden Bough but hadn't quite reached the edge of the field when he had to yell for help:

"Daddy, I'm going to drop the waterme . . . watermelons. I can't hold them!"

In his anxiety he'd called the pumpkins watermelons. All the people out in their vegetable plots laughed. Sister Phoenix glanced over at Golden Bough.

"Would you look at that boy," she said. "Calling pumpkins watermelons!"

Golden Bough gave a perfunctory smile as Two-and-a-Half Li came over and kicked the boy, sending two of the big pumpkins dropping to the ground. Rather than cry, the boy stood off to the side, dumbstruck. Two-and-a-Half Li lashed out at him:

"You asshole, you little son of a bitch! I told you to load cabbages. Who asked you to pick pumpkins?"

Granny Pockface was right behind them. Seeing her son in trouble, she cleverly bent down and rolled the two large pumpkins in among the tomato plants. But since everyone saw what she was doing, she was the only one who thought she was being clever.

"Did you do that, you stupid insect?" Two-and-a-Half Li asked. "Don't tell me you . . ."

Granny Pockface mumbled, her speech more incoherent than usual: "I . . . didn't . . ."

From off to the side, the boy accused her shrilly: "Didn't you pick them and ask me to carry them to the carts? Don't deny it!"

Desperately signaling with her eyes, she blurted out: "I was stealing them, damn it! Not so loud, or we'll get caught!"

People nearby were usually too preoccupied with their work to watch a bit of fun, no matter what it was. But today even these impassive souls crowded around. Here was a martial arts opera with three members of one family performing on stage. Two-and-a-Half Li berated the boy:

"You goddamn nitwit! You can't help us make a living, but you sure know how to botch things up. Who asked you to pick pumpkins?"

Unwilling to stand there and take the blame, Tunnel Legs ran over and rolled the two pumpkins out from among the tomato plants. Everyone rocked with laughter, the sound of their hilarity ringing in the air. But Golden Bough was like a chick with a contagious disease. She blinked and crouched down among the tomato plants, not paying attention to anything. She had momentarily escaped from the world around her.

Two-and-a-Half Li was so furious he could hardly breathe. Not until he finally disclosed that he'd grown the pumpkins for the seeds did Granny Pockface heave a sigh of relief. She hadn't, after all, done anything wrong. For, as it turned out, they were her pumpkins. She raised her head and said to no one in particular: "There, you see. I didn't know. I really didn't know the pumpkins were ours."

Not caring whether that sounded funny or not, she elbowed her way through the crowd and laid the pumpkins on the cart. The cart then moved onto the road into town, her bowlegged son running lopsidedly alongside it. The horse, the cart, and the people gradually disappeared from sight.

The incident was bandied about in the fields. Rumors were also beginning to spread about Golden Bough.

"It's all over for that girl."

"I knew she was up to no good. Imagine, taking forever just to pick one tomato. And yesterday she even left her basket by the river."

"The riverside is not a place where decent folk go."

Two middle-aged women were sitting behind Sister Phoenix, digging for carrots. But they were also gossiping and at times using lewd language she did not quite understand.

Golden Bough's heart was pounding wildly. For her, time seemed to spin out as long as a spider's silken web. She was depressed, her expression frail and clouded, as if a veil had fallen across her face. The whistle she was expecting did not come. She could see the wall around Fufa's house, but the man of her dreams did not appear. So she continued picking tomatoes, even green ones, since she was oblivious to the colors; her basket was getting full. But instead of taking them home, she spread the different-colored fruits on the ground.

"She went to the riverside to be with the man," a woman said, her voice purposely raised. "Shameless. I wonder if he tore her pants off?"

Golden Bough ignored the sights and sounds around her. She pressed hard on her belly, so hard she could almost feel something moving inside. Suddenly the whistling came. She crushed a tomato as she stood up; it made a squishing sound like a squashed toad. She slipped, and the whistling stopped. No matter how hard she listened, she couldn't hear the sound again.

Altogether, Golden Bough was with the man three times. The first time had been two months earlier. She'd kept that a secret from her mother. It was only yesterday, when the basket had fallen into the hands of the woodcutter, that her mother had become vaguely suspicious.

Golden Bough was in torment. Her stomach had become a hideous monstrosity. She felt a hard object inside, and when she pressed down, it was even more apparent. Once she was certain she was pregnant, her heart shuddered as if retching. She was seized with terror. When two butterflies wondrously alighted on her knee, one on top of the other, she stared at the two wicked insects but did not brush them off. She was like a scarecrow in a rice paddy.

Her mother came. Even from that distance her heart reached out to her daughter. But she approached quietly. From afar, her body looked like a perfect square. Gradually her pointed feet could be discerned, working up and down and peeking out from under the hem of her sacklike dress. Among the old ladies of the village, what was her unique characteristic? Angry or pleased, there were always laugh lines at the corners of her eyes. Her mouth was also drawn up into the shape of a smile. The only difference was in the upper lip. When she was truly happy, the upper lip retreated, but when she was angry, it protruded, forming a tiny peak in the middle, like a bird's beak.

The mother stopped. The telltale sign was apparent—her entire face was smiling, all but the beaklike mouth. The sight of all those green tomatoes angered her. Deep in thought, Golden Bough suddenly received a kick from her mother.

"What's wrong with you? Have you lost your mind? I'll tear out your braids . . ."

Golden Bough offered no resistance. She slumped to the ground. Her mother pounced on her like a tiger, and soon Golden Bough's nose was bleeding. Her mother scolded her in a low voice. In her anger, her expression became even jollier, as the beak slowly took shape, with more and more lines gathering at the corners of her eyes.

"Well, young lady, you sure know how to spoil things. Did you decide to pick only green tomatoes? Are you upset because I yelled at you last night?"

Her mother had always been like that. She loved her daughter, but when the girl ruined some vegetables, she directed her love toward the vegetables. For farming people, one vegetable or a single straw is worth more than a human being.

Now it was time for bed. Incense was burning from a wire used for hanging hand towels by the door. There were no buzzing mosquitoes in the house. On summer nights every family lit incense; it burned slowly and for a long time. Like the joss sticks in a temple, the incense obliterated all sounds and lulled the people into slumber, and the artemisia fragrance wove its way into the weary souls' dreams. The fumes drove off the mosquitoes. Golden Bough and her mother were still awake when a man came to the window and coughed lightly.

The mother turned to light the lamp when they heard the door opening. It was Two-and-a-Half Li. But no matter how she tried, she could not get the lamp lit. The wick sizzled. She held a match in her hand and brought the lamp up to eye level.

"Not a drop of oil," she said.

Golden Bough went outside to get oil while the two elders discussed a matter she had not expected. Seemingly startled by what she heard, the mother shook her head resolutely, as if ashamed.

"That's impossible. My daughter cannot be married into that family."

Two-and-a-Half Li heard the girl replace the cover of the oilcan and stopped talking. Golden Bough stood at the threshold. "There's no more oil," she said. "Shall I put in some water?"

After Golden Bough had filled up the lamp, she set it down on the edge of the *kang* and lit it. She had no inkling that she was the cause of Two-and-a-Half Li's visit. He lit his pipe from the burning incense.

The mother, her hands pressing on the pillow, appeared deep in thought, knitting her brows until they nearly met. Her daughter stood beside her, facing the lamp with bowed head. The tobacco in Two-and-a-Half Li's pipe glowed when he sucked on it, the smoke mingling with the smell of artemisia, until the little room was as dark and depressing as a dungeon. He coughed a couple of times in embarrassment. Golden Bough replaced the cotton in her bleeding nose with a new piece. Owing to the absence of conversation, they were all fidgeting.

And so they sat. The lamp crackled again. The oil floating on the water had nearly burned out, and the lamp flickered. Two-and-a-Half Li left with a heavy heart. Having been rejected in his matchmaking mission, he went home feeling humiliated.

The Mid-Autumn Festival now past, the fields had become a bleak and desolate land. The sun's rays descended sadly from the sky, and a damp smell circulated in the fields. The sorghum in the south was all lying down asleep, and as you looked around, you saw soybean sprouts lying like ruffled hair on the ground. Some plots had been plucked bald.

The mornings and the evenings were the same. The fields continued to wilt while carts drawn by oxen and horses rumbled past, piled high with sorghum tassels and soybean stalks. Slobber drooled from the mouths of the oxen as the carts rumbled by.

Driving a dark green cart, Fufa's nephew was carting sorghum from their field, intentionally traveling a circuitous route. There was Golden Bough's door. She was so overwrought she felt her heart would burst. At last she heard the crack of his whip. Putting down the red peppers, she said to her mother:

"I have to go to the toilet."

So the old lady was left to string up the peppers by herself, her swift movements those of a weaver.

Golden Bough's braids were coming loose and her face was flushed. But her sickly condition made her look like a paper doll. As if blown by the wind, she appeared at the fence behind her house.

Are you ill? What's the matter? But Chengye was a country boy who didn't know what to ask. He threw down his whip and soared like a bird over the fence. Grabbing the feverish girl, he pulled her to the ground and fell on top of her. He had no interest in kissing her or saying sweet things. He was driven by animal desire. Golden Bough struggled.

"No," she protested. "My mother will find out. Why hasn't the matchmaker come yet?"

"Uncle Li came over, didn't he?" he said. "You mean you didn't know? He said your mother refused the match. He'll be back tomorrow with my uncle."

Golden Bough pressed on her belly to show him. She shook her head. "It's not that . . . it's not. Look what's happening to me."

The young man was unconcerned. Softly he said: "I don't give a damn. Whether she says yes or not, it's going to happen anyway."

His eyes glazed over. A man's instinctive craving demanded satiation.

The sound of her mother coughing came faintly through the wall. Beyond the fence the gossamer in the autumn air clung to the horns of the dark ox.

Mother and daughter were having dinner. All at once, Golden Bough vomited. Her mother asked:

"Did you swallow a fly?"

She shook her head.

"Then you must have caught a chill. How come you're always sick? You can't even eat your rice. You don't have consumption, do you?"

As she spoke she put her hand on her daughter's belly and felt all around through the jacket. She spread out her fingers on the belly and said pensively:

"You must have consumption. There's something hard in your belly. Only people with consumption have something like that."

Tears welled in the girl's eyes and threatened to brim over. They finally rolled down her eyelashes. Even at night Golden Bough had to get up to go outside and vomit. In her sleep, her mother could hear her daughter calling to her. Outside, the moon was bright as day. She could see Golden Bough, half of her body on the floor and half bent over the pillow. Her face was covered by her hair. When her mother took her hand, the girl sobbed:

"Ma . . . please marry me to Fufa's nephew. That thing in my stomach is not . . . I'm not sick. It's . . ."

At this point she should have started beating her daughter, but not this time. As if she herself were guilty of wrongdoing, the words numbed her. For the longest time she seemed not to exist. After a while she said in a gentle tone she hadn't used before:

"You want to marry into his family? Two-and-a-Half Li came the other day to arrange it, but I sent him away. What do I do now?"

Seemingly calmer now, her mother started to speak again, but tears stopped up her throat. She felt as if her daughter had strangled the life out of her. Because of her daughter she'd take this disgrace to her grave.

3   THE OLD MARE'S TRIP TO THE SLAUGHTERHOUSE

The old mare stepped onto the road leading into town. The illegal slaughterhouse was located east of the city gate. There the knife had been unsheathed in readiness for the frail old animal.

Old Mother Wang was not leading the horse. She was following behind, driving it ahead of her with a switch.

Yellow leaves swirled in the forest, rustling loudly. Seen from her perspective, the woods looked like a gigantic, half-opened umbrella. Subdued sunlight shone down on the naked trees. From the field you could see houses, some far, some near. The late-autumn fields stretched out like cold, tanned hides. Houses buried by vegetation in the summer were now exposed, as if they had recently risen out of the ground.

Late autumn brought with it yellow leaves and chased away the summer butterflies. A falling leaf landed on Mother Wang's head and lay there silently. She drove her old mare ahead, wearing a yellow leaf on her head; the old horse, the old woman, the old leaf—moved down the road into town.

Up ahead the blurred shape of a person came into view. Gradually she could see that he was smoking a pipe. It was Two-and-a-Half Li coming toward them, looking like a tame monkey because of his long face and swaying body. "Say, it's too early to be up," he said. "Have you got business in town? Why drive the horse there instead of having it pull a cartload of grain?"

She shook her sleeve and tucked some stray hairs behind her ears. "It's time," she said, her hands trembling. "Into the soup caldron it goes." Despondently, she watched the horse nibble at roadside leaves; waving her switch, she drove it onward.

Deeply saddened, Two-and-a-Half Li shuddered. But before long he turned and caught up with them. "It's not right to send it to the soup caldron. It's just not right. . . ." But what could he do? He was at a loss for words. Limping forward, he patted the horse's mane. It snorted in response, its eyes looking as if they were crying, all wet and glassy. Waves of pain stabbed Mother Wang's heart. In a choked voice she said:

"Forget it, this is how it has to be. If I don't send it to the caldron, it'll just starve to death."

The bare trees of late autumn, shaken by harsh winds, wailed like lost souls. The horse walked in front; Mother Wang followed behind. Step by step the slaughterhouse loomed nearer. Step by step the whistling wind ushered the old mare to its final rest.

Mother Wang wondered how a person could change so drastically. In her youth, how many times had she taken old horses and oxen to the slaughterhouse? She shivered at a horrible vision of the butcher's knife severing her own spine. The switch dropped from her hand. Feeling faint, she stopped by the roadside, her hair dancing in the air like a specter. When she picked up the switch again, the old mare had disappeared. It had gone ahead to the ditch for a drink. Probably its last drink of water. The old mare needed water, and it needed rest, so it lay down by the ditch, breathing slowly. Mother Wang called in a low, gentle voice: "Get up. Let's go into town. What else is there?" But the horse just lay there. Mother Wang saw it was nearly noon; she had to get back to make lunch. But no matter how she tugged at the reins, the horse wouldn't budge.

Angered, she began to beat the horse with the switch, but though this forced it to its feet, it wouldn't leave the ditch. Life's afflictions had made her irritable, and the switch snapped in two across the horse's back.

Now they were back on the road, passing deserted houses and dilapidated temples. In front of one of these small temples lay a dead infant, bundled in straw. Its head poked out from the top; its pitiful little feet stuck out straight. Whose child was it, sleeping in front of this wilderness temple?

They drew near the slaughterhouse. Now the city gate was directly ahead. Mother Wang's heart was in turmoil.

Five years ago it had been a young horse, but owing to farm work, it had been reduced to skin and bones. Now it was old. Autumn was nearly over and the harvesting done. It had become useless, and for the sake of its hide, its unfeeling master was sending it to the slaughterhouse. Even the price of its hide would be snatched from Mother Wang's hands by the landlord.

When Mother Wang saw a cowhide nailed to the wall, she felt as if her heart, too, were suspended in the air, about to crash to the ground. The street was lined with tumbledown houses. Women and children gathered in groups on both sides. Gray dust kicked up from the street surface covered the pedestrians' shoes and got into their noses. When children picked up dirt clods or garbage and threw them at the horse, Mother Wang cursed at them:

"Damn you, you damned bunch of brats!"

It was a short street, at the end of which double black doors stood open. As she drew near, she saw bloodstains splattered on the doors. She was frightened by the bloodstains, feeling as if she were about to step onto an execution ground. She strove for self-control so as not to be shaken by memories of what she'd witnessed on an execution ground in her youth. But the memories unfolded in spite of her efforts: a young man crumpling to the ground; then an old man; the executioner with his sword poised over a third man

As if struck by an arrow, as if seared by flames, Mother Wang did not see the children pelting the horse with their missiles. She'd forgotten all about cursing the little ruffians. On and on she walked until she stood in the center of the yard. Nailed to the walls around her were a great many hides. Near the eaves a crossbar was supported by two upright stakes, over which horse and ox hooves tied together with hemp in pairs were draped, neatly suspended in forked fashion; looped intestines also hung from it. Having hung there for many days, the blackened intestines had taken on the appearance of stiff ropes. Then there were the trails of blood running from the site where the leg bones had been dismembered.

Another stake rose up on the southern side near the fence, from which hung coils of steaming intestines drying in the sun. That particular animal had recently been slaughtered—its intestines were still warm.

The courtyard gave off an overpowering stench, and amid this world of stench, Mother Wang seemed to have turned to lead. She stood there as if weighted down, devoid of emotion.

The old horse, the tawny horse, stood next to the wooden fence, scratching itself against a hide nailed to the fence. At the moment it was a horse, but before long it too would be just another hide.

A man with bulging eyes and a fierce expression ran out, his coat opened at the chest. As he spoke, his chest heaved.

"So you brought it, did you? We'll talk about price after I've had a look at it."

Mother Wang said: "Give me what you think is fair, and I'll go. No need to fuss over it."

The man flicked the horse's tail and kicked its hoofs. What a torturous moment!

Mother Wang received three bills, enough to pay the rent for an acre of land. She gazed at the money and brightened up a bit. Then, with her head down, she walked out the gate. She was thinking she might use the extra money to buy some liquor to take home. She'd already crossed the threshold when a shout came from behind:

"Hey! Hold on there! The horse is leaving!"

Mother Wang turned and looked back—the horse was following her. Not knowing what was happening, it was heading for home as always. Several men with hideous faces came running out of the slaughterhouse to take the horse back in. Finally, it lay down by the side of the road and planted itself as if it had taken root in the earth. There was nothing Mother Wang could do but walk back into the courtyard, and the horse followed her. As she scratched its head, it slowly lay down on the ground, seemingly about to go to sleep. Then Mother Wang stood up abruptly and walked briskly out the gate. At the head of the street she heard the sound of a gate slam shut.

How could she have the heart to buy liquor? She wept all the way home, until her sleeves were soaked with tears. She looked as if she'd just returned from a funeral procession.

A servant from the landlord was waiting by the door. Landlords never let a penny go to waste on the peasants. The servant left with her money. For Mother Wang, her day of agony was all for naught. A life of agony was all for naught.

4 THE DESOLATE HILL

Winter. The women gathered together as easily as pine nuts. The *kang* at Mother Wang's place was occupied by women. Fifth Sister, who was making jute slippers, dropped her needle into a crack in the mattress while she was laughing, and presented a funny sight as she searched for it. Like a spry pigeon, she hopped about on the *kang*, shouting:

"Who stole my needle? Was it a little puppy?"

"No, a little husband!"

Lingzhi, a recent bride, loved saying things like that. Fifth Sister went over and made as if to slap her.

"Don't you dare slap me, or you'll get a pockmarked husband."

From the kitchen Mother Wang picked up the threads of conversation. She was usually moody and silent one minute and happy the next, which distinguished her from the other older women of the village. Her voice floated in from the kitchen:

"How many pairs of jute shoes has Fifth Sister made? You should make a few more for that little husband of yours!"

Fifth Sister made a face.

"Whoever heard of an old woman approaching fifty saying such things?"

"What do you youngsters know?" Mother Wang said solemnly. "Make a few more pairs if you want to hold onto your little husband."

They cackled with laughter, all but Fifth Sister, who didn't dare laugh out loud; but she was laughing inside. She lowered her head and pretended to be looking for the needle in the mattress. By the time Lingzhi finally returned it to her, the room had quieted down. Scraping noises made by Mother Wang, as she scaled a fish in the kitchen, merged with the sound of snow falling against the paper window.

Mother Wang washed the frozen fish with cold water, until her hands were carrot red. She walked over to the *kang* to warm her hands over the brazier. A recently widowed woman with freckles on her nose put down the small patch on which she was working and found an even smaller piece from the rag pile. She quickly sewed it on. She had a face a little like Mother Wang's—high cheekbones and glassy eyes set deep into the sockets. And like Mother Wang, she had a protruding brow ridge. Not appreciating such racy talk, she asked Mother Wang:

"Is your first husband still alive?"

The hands warming at the fire stank faintly of fish. A scale fell into the fire, crackling slightly and giving off a little smoke She smothered the smoke with ashes and slowly shook her head, but did not reply. The smoke from the seared scale had such an unpleasant odor that everyone wrinkled or rubbed her nose. The freckled widow regretted asking the question. Fifth Sister's elder sister sat in the corner, and as she sewed, the thread rubbed against the shoe sole, producing a dull sound. The kitchen door, crusted with ice, creaked in protest.

"Why did you buy these black fish?"

Everyone knew that Second Aunt Li from Fisherman's Village had arrived. From the sound of her voice alone one could visualize her tall, slender figure.

"Is it almost New Year's already? Do you really have the money to buy fish like this?"

Her voice rang out crisp and clear in the cold air. As soon as she stepped into the house and saw the *kang* full of people, she commented:

"All gathered here, eh, you good little wives?"

She was so thin the wind could seemingly snap her in two. Her breasts were high, like facing hills. But her belly wasn't flat. A middle-aged woman suckling a child near the wall said:

"Second Aunt, pregnant again?"

Second Aunt looked down.

"You think I'm like you, with one baby in my arms and another in my belly?"

She sidestepped the issue, but then confessed:

"It's the third month. Can't you tell?"

Lingzhi leaned over to touch her belly and gave a wicked chuckle. "How shameless! You probably had your arms around your old man all night long."

"Says who? That's for brides like you."

"Brides . . . ha! I don't think so."

"People like us, we're old. It's nothing to us anymore. But it's really something with you young ones. It's only your young husbands who get so excited."

Titillated by such talk, they began to fantasize. Each heart was pulsating; every face was hot. Even unmarried Fifth Sister sensed the mystery and began to fidget. Bashfully, she passed through the kitchen and went home, leaving behind only married women. Then the conversation grew saltier. Mother Wang sat with them but said nothing, merely joining in the laughter. Deficiency in lives

In the village, people remained forever ignorant. They could never experience the spiritual side of life; only the material aspects gave them sustenance.

Second Aunt Li asked Sister-in-Law Lingzhi in a low voice (actually, her whispers were clearer than her normal speaking voice):

"How many times a night?"

Lingzhi was, after all, a new bride. Overcome by shyness, she said nothing. Second Aunt Li, her breasts heaving, nudged her. "Say something. You're young. You must do it every night."

Just then Two-and-a-Half Li's wife entered the room. Second Aunt nudged Lingzhi again. "Go on, ask her then."

"How many times do you do it a night?"

She'd asked a foolish old woman who had trouble finishing a thought.

"Ten times or more."

The women roared with laughter till tears ran down their cheeks. The baby in its mother's lap woke up and began to wail.

Second Aunt Li was silent for a while before standing up and saying:

"Oh, I almost forgot: Yueying wanted to eat some pickles, and I came over to get some."

So Second Aunt Li left with her pickles, and Mother Wang went in to prepare dinner. The other women gradually got up and left for home, leaving Mother Wang alone in the kitchen to fry the fish. As the room filled with smoke, it didn't seem quite so lonely.

The fish was laid out on the table, but Ping'er had not come back, nor had his father. So in the deepening dusk Mother Wang ate alone, with only the steam to keep her company.

Yueying was the prettiest woman in Fisherman's Village. Her family, who lived next door to Second Aunt Li, was also the poorest. A gentle woman, no one had ever heard her raise her voice in laughter or in anger. She had been born with eyes so expressive that in earlier days anyone who met her gaze felt a pleasure and warmth that could be likened to sinking into a pile of down.

But those days were all in the past. Now Second Aunt Li heard heart-wrenching sobs from next door every night. On one severe winter night in the twelfth month, the moaning grew even more mournful.

Mountain snow blown by the wind seemed about to bury the little hillside house. Trees howled; wind and snow swooped down on the little house. A wind-swept tree on the hill toppled over. The winter moon, fearful of being shattered by all that pandemonium, retreated to the edge of the sky. At that moment, from next door came a pitiful plea:

"Won't . . . won't you give me a little water? I'm parched."

The voice trailed off weakly. "My lips are parched. Give me a cup of water."

After a while, since no reply was forthcoming, the quaking entreaties ceased. But the weeping and moaning resumed, and from next door it seemed as if the fall of each teardrop could be heard.

During the day children gathered on the hillside. They climbed the slope by hanging onto the branches, then slid down the icy path, using different styles for their descent: backward rolls and split swoops, not to mention the daredevils who slid down headfirst, feet in the air. Often they went home bruised and bleeding. Winter mistreated the village children the way it abused flowers and crops. Every child's ears swelled up; his hands or feet were frostbitten. The village mothers acted as if the children were their enemies. When they streaked out of the house with their fathers' woolen caps, their mothers chased after them, cursed and beat them, then snatched the caps back. Mothers persecuted their children mercilessly.

Mother Wang went with Fifth Sister to visit Yueying. Just as they were crossing the slope they saw Ping'er; he was wearing his father's big felt boots, without permission. He turned and fled up the slope, but the boots were like the paws of a great bear; he tottered and tumbled back down the slope. This poor child with the big, disproportionate black feet rolled down like a ball, his fall broken by a huge tree at the foot of the slope. Running like the wind, Mother Wang flung herself upon him like a ferocious beast seizing its prey. Finally, she retrieved the boots, and Ping'er had to return home barefoot. He dared not stop, even for a moment—walking on the ice was like walking on fire. Even after he was some distance away, Mother Wang was still grumbling:

"One pair of boots has to last three winters. If they're worn through, where will we get the money to replace them? Your dad won't even wear them when he goes into the city!"

When Yueying saw Mother Wang, she was so choked up with emotion she couldn't utter a sound. Mother Wang put the boots on the floor next to the *kang* and wiped her runny nose.

"Feeling better? I think you have a little color in your cheeks."

Yueying tried to push the comforter off, but it stayed draped around her shoulders. "I'll never get better," she said. "You see, I can't even push the comforter off."

She was sitting in the center of the *kang*. The hushed dark room seemed to have become a shrine, and Yueying was the bodhisattva sitting in her place. Surrounded by pillows, she'd spent a year like that. For an entire year she hadn't been able to sleep lying down, for she was afflicted with paralysis. In the beginning her husband had called upon the spirits for her, had offered incense, and had gone to the temples of the local gods for medicine. Later he'd even gone into the city temple to burn incense. But all the incense and prayers had done nothing to improve her condition. Finally he reasoned that he'd fulfilled his responsibilities, especially since her condition deteriorated month by month. Feeling quite heartbroken, he'd complain:

"What rotten luck to have gotten a wife like you. It's like being married to one of my own ancestors and having to make offerings to her!"

At first, when she argued with him, he beat her. But no more, for despair had set in. At night, when he came home from the city after selling firewood, he'd cook and eat his dinner alone. Then he'd lie down and sleep till dawn. The suffering woman sitting beside him would moan until daybreak. It was as if a human being and a ghost had been thrown together, each having nothing to do with the other.

When Yueying spoke, only the tip of her tongue moved. As Mother Wang drew close to her, the stench from a pile of fetid matter was overpowering. Yueying pointed behind her.

"See there," she said. "That fiend put these bricks here. He said that since I'm going to die soon, I don't need the comforter. So he propped me up with these bricks. I don't have a bit of flesh left on me. That heartless beast dreams up ways to torture me."

Outraged by the man's cruelty, Fifth Sister tossed the bricks off the *kang*. Yueying started up again, haltingly:

"It's all over for me. How can I possibly get well? I'm going to die!" The whites of her eyes had turned green, and so had her straight front teeth. Her hair stuck to her scalp, as if singed. She was like a sick cat, abandoned and devoid of hope.

Mother Wang placed a comforter around Yueying's waist.

"Look down there behind me," Yueying said. "It's filthy!"

With a stick, Mother Wang stirred up the brazier until it began to smoke, and then placed it behind Yueying. Pulling back the comforter, she saw that the woman's tiny pelvis was coated with excrement. Fifth Sister tried to lift her up by the waist, but she shrieked in pain:

"Oh Mother! Oh, it hurts!"

She sat there with her legs out straight, like two bamboo poles, a perfect right angle with the *kang*. Her body seemed to be nothing but a gathering of lines supporting a large head that sat on the torso like a lantern on a pole.

Mother Wang cleaned Yueying first with straw and then wiped her down with a wet cloth as Fifth Sister raised her up slightly from behind. While Mother Wang was cleaning her buttocks, little white things landed on her arm and began to crawl around. She held it up close to the fire to see what they were. Maggots. Yueying's buttocks were rotting away, infested with maggots. The rest of her body, too, would soon become caves for the little maggots.

"Any pain in your legs?" Mother Wang asked her.

Yueying shook her head. Mother Wang washed her legs with cold water. She felt nothing. The paralyzed lower part of her body seemed detached, something that didn't belong to her. Mother Wang handed her a cup of water and remarked:

"How did your teeth turn green?"

Fifth Sister borrowed a mirror from next door, and when Yueying saw her reflection, she began to wail. Yet not a single tear appeared. Then, like a cat that had been run over, she began to make horrible, harsh sounds. "I've become a ghost! Let me die soon! Or bury me alive!"

She tore at her hair, twisting this way and that, over and over, until, exhausted, she stopped. Her head sagged down on her shoulder, and she fell into a light sleep.

Carrying the boots with her, Mother Wang left the little hillside house. People walking along the top of the desolate hill were silhouetted against the sky. She was dazed by the bright light, by the stench of the paralyzed woman, by worries about birth, old age, sickness, and death. Her thoughts were blocked by all these waves of worry.

When Fifth Sister reached her door, she waved good-bye to Mother Wang. The long distance yet to go was thus left to an old woman who had more experience with life. Knotting the blue scarf tighter around her head, Mother Wang quickened her step. Underfoot, the snow also quickened its accompanying howl.

Three days later Yueying's coffin was borne swiftly across the desolate hill to be buried at the foot of the slope.

The dead were dead, and the living needed to figure out how to stay alive. In the winter, women made ready the summer clothes and men started planning the following year's crops.

One day Zhao San returned from the city carrying two goatskins over his shoulders. Mother Wang asked him:

"Where did those come from? Did you buy them? Where did you get the money?"

Preoccupied, Zhao San said nothing. He staggered past the stove and was briefly lit up by the bright flames. Then he went out.

Long after night had fallen, he still hadn't returned home, so Mother Wang told Ping'er to go look for him. But since Ping'er's feet hurt, she went to Two-and-a-Half Li's house. He wasn't there; he'd gone to Fishermen's Village.

Zhao San's loud voice came through Li Qingshan's paper window. Mother Wang could tell he'd been drinking. She opened the door and said:

"What time do you think it is? Come home and go to bed?"

The men in the house clammed up immediately, and Mother Wang sensed that something unusual was going on. Qingshan's wife wasn't home, and neither were the children.

"What are you doing here?" Chao San asked her. "Go back home to bed. I'll . . . I'll be along soon."

Mother Wang saw the look on Zhao San's face. She also saw that there was no place for her to sit, so she turned and went out. She wondered why Qingshan's wife wasn't home, and what those people inside were doing.

Another night. Zhao San put on a new goatskin jacket and went out. He didn't return home until midnight. The moon shone on him as he knocked on the door. Mother Wang was sure he'd been drinking, but when he lay down to sleep, she couldn't smell any liquor on his breath. What was he up to? Why did he always come back in such an ugly mood?

Second Aunt Li came over with her child. "Is the land rent going up?" she asked.

"Not that I've heard," Mother Wang replied.

But Second Aunt Li wouldn't be put off.

"You don't know? Third Brother comes to my place every night to talk with my boy's daddy. I think there's trouble brewing. Every night they plot. They keep secrets from me. Last night I stood outside the window and heard them say: 'Kill him! He's a curse!' Who do you think they're going to kill? That's murder!" She rubbed the boy's head, a look of pity on her face.

"Talk to Third Brother," she said. "If they get into trouble, how are we supposed to carry on, especially with the children still so young?"

Fifth Sister and the other village women arrived with their little bundles right on time. When they came in, they were all smiles, but their expressions changed when they saw Second Aunt Li and Mother Wang sitting there in silence. When they learned what was happening, they also grew dejected. Gone were their high spirits and the sounds of their laughter. Feeling very apprehensive, they fearfully asked a few questions. Fifth Sister's elder sister was the first to waddle out with her swollen belly. Then the rest of them left, forlornly, one after the other. They were like schooling fish: a hook had suddenly been lowered, and they scattered in all directions.

Second Aunt Li stayed behind. She was depending upon Mother Wang to sabotage the risky venture.

For days, Zhao San had seldom eaten at home; during that time Second Aunt Li had come over three or four times a day.

"Isn't Third Brother back yet?" she'd ask. "My child's daddy isn't either."

It wasn't until the afternoon of the second day that Zhao San returned. As soon as he walked in, he hit Ping'er. Owing to Ping'er's sore feet, a group of children had come over to play. In the center of the yard they'd placed a few grains of rice. Then a long plank had been propped up by a short stick, to which they'd attached a long piece of string. The string led back into the house. As sparrows pecked at the grain, the children crouching behind the door kept watch, and when there were enough birds, they'd yank the string. Many hungry sparrows perished beneath the long plank. The kitchen smelled of bird feathers, and the children feasted on sparrow in the kitchen.

Zhao San was in a bad mood. Seeing that a chicken had also been killed, he'd kicked over the plank. Once inside the house, he sat on the *kang* and lit his pipe. Mother Wang dished out some rice from the pot, but he said:

"I've already eaten."

So Ping'er came up and finished the leftover rice.

"How are your preparations coming along? If you're ready, you'd better do it soon."

That caught him by surprise. How could the news have leaked out?

"Oh, I know all about it," she said. "Not only that, I can get you a gun."

He never dreamed that his own wife possessed such courage. Mother Wang did in fact manage to get an old gun. But since Zhao San had never used one, at night, after Ping'er was asleep, she taught him how to put in the gunpowder and how to load the buckshot.

Zhao San began to feel a measure of respect for his woman, although he kept his secrets to himself.

Then, suddenly, five new sickles were discovered in the barn, and Mother Wang knew that the day was drawing near.

When Second Aunt Li and the other village women came swarming to her for news, Mother Wang simply lowered her head and said:

"It's nothing. They're only planning to go off a ways to do some hunting, hoping to bag a few skins and divvy them up."

On New Year's Eve something finally happened. At the edge of the northern boundary the snow was stained crimson. But what happened was not what should have happened. Zhao San, who had been acting a bit odd, had broken a thief's leg with a wooden pole. He sought out Two-and-a-Half Li to help him throw the thief's body into a pit and bury it with snow. But Li talked him out of it: "No, that's no good. When the snow melts in the spring and the body is discovered in the pit, the news will spread. The charge will be murder."

Hearing screams of pain, the villagers came out to investigate, only to see Zhao San running in circles, dragging the crippled body, unable to hide it. He was desperately hoping to find a well into which he could dump the body. His hands were soon covered with blood.

By then the whole village was aroused, and the village chief went to report the matter to the police in town.

So Zhao San was thrown into jail. Without him, the "Sickle Society" of Li Qingshan and the others languished and finally broke up.

By the end of the first month, Zhao San's landlord had interceded on his behalf and gotten him released from jail. His hair was long, his face was ashen, and he had aged. In order to pay compensation to the crippled thief, he took his only ox to the city to sell. He may also have sold his goatskin jacket, for no one ever saw him wear it again.

When Li Qingshan and the others came to see him that night, he was penitent.

"I did wrong. Maybe it was fate that brought this calamity to me. It was dark, and I'd been drinking, when I heard Ping'er yell that someone was stealing our firewood. A couple of days before that, Second Master Liu had come to say he was going to raise the rent on our land. I protested and said we'd band together to oppose the raise. He left. After a few days, he returned and said he had to raise the rent, and if we didn't comply, he'd kick us off the land. I said: 'We'll see about that!' Then his steward said: 'So, you want to start a riot, is that it? If you don't get out, your haystacks will go up in flames!' Well, I thought it was some guy coming to torch my firewood, so I grabbed a pole and ran out to let him have it. I couldn't have been happier about breaking his leg, until I discovered it was a thief I'd hit. Ha ha, that thief sure got his. Even if he recovers, he'll be a cripple."

Apparently, he'd forgotten all about the "Sickle Society." Li Qingshan asked him: "How do we get rid of that no-good rat, Second Master Liu?"

Here is what Zhao San had said earlier: "Kill the bastard!"

But that was a long time ago. Now he'd changed his tune:

"What will getting rid of him accomplish? When I was in trouble, it was Second Master Liu who interceded for me with the landlord. I was wrong before. Maybe that's why I'm being punished now."

The vigor and spirit he'd once displayed were a thing of the past. Now the look on his face was a mixture of contrition, embarrassment, and discomfort.

Sitting off to the side, Mother Wang was so indignant even the curls on the back of her head were seething. "I've never seen a man like this. At first he was like a piece of steel, but now he looks more and more like a lump of mud!"

Zhao San just smiled and said: "A man must have a conscience."

So Zhao San took his conscience into town every day, bringing a load of cabbage to the landlord one day and peanuts the next. Mother Wang got into terrible rows with him over these gifts, but he insisted on following his conscience.

One day the landlord's son came out and, standing in the doorway, lectured Zhao San:

"You're lucky I put in a good word for you, or you could have spent the next three years in jail. That thief's luck ran out. You watch, I'll take care of everything. I'll see to it you don't have to pay to have his leg fixed. We'll just let him die, and you can save the money from the sale of the ox. As landlords, we can never stand by and watch our tenants . . ."

He paused. When he resumed, he changed the subject:

"But this year we'll have to raise the rent. After all, the other fields in the area all had their rents increased. We've been landlord and tenant for many years, but we still have to . . . all right, we'll make it a somewhat smaller increase."

In a few days' time, the thief was carried out of the hospital. He died, and the incident was closed. Half the money from the sale of the ox was returned to Zhao San; the other half, according to the landlord, went for miscellaneous expenses.

It was the second month, and the snow that had accumulated on the mountain showed signs of thawing. People were already walking on the desolate hill. Soon they were delivering manure over the hill. The peasants, like hibernating insects, began to stir. Gradually the passage of carts delivering manure became a more frequent sight. Only Zhao San's cart was not yoked to an ox. Instead, the shaft was harnessed to a sweating Ping'er and his father.

And the rent increase became effective.

5 A HERD OF GOATS

Hired as a goatherd, Ping'er chased his flock up and down the slope. On the top of the hill small flowers appeared to bloom, first turning green, then red. Ping'er played tricks on children who were out picking wild vegetables. He'd drive a goat over to eat the vegetables in their baskets, and sometimes he'd mount a big goat and charge like a horseman. The girls were frightened to tears when they saw him coming at them, like a little monkey on a goat. Once his goatherd days began, Ping'er's talents found an outlet. He'd herd the goats into a lonely spot, then bring the village boys together to practice riding. Every day the goats, like pigs, which loathe action, were ridden all over the hillside.

On the way home one day, a sea of white stretched out before him. He rode the last goat like a general overseeing his army, and played with his whip, feeling very pleased with himself.

"Have you had lunch?"

Zhao San was much gentler now with his son. Ever since the incident he seemed to have mellowed.

Ping'er was clowning on the back of a goat. When it walked in through the front gate, it began to gallop, as if possessed, and Ping'er had no chance to jump down. This time he really did look like a monkey frolicking on the back of a goat. It was a rainy day, and as rider and mount passed through the front gate, they knocked down the master's little boy. The master picked up a rake used for gathering firewood and knocked Ping'er off the goat. And he didn't stop there. He kept beating the boy as if he were pounding a piece of lifeless meat.

That night Ping'er couldn't sleep. He tossed and turned, as his father patted him with his large hands.

"You've been running around all day. You must be worn out. Get some sleep, since you have to get up early to go to work."

Under his father's gentle hands, Ping'er sensed how badly he'd been abused.

"I got a beating. My backside hurts."

His father got up, took some red powder from a paper packet, and put it on the cuts.

Zhao San had aged a great deal, but his son was still so young, and he began to feel that life had lost its meaning. The next day Ping'er reported for work, but was sent home. Zhao San was sitting in the kitchen weaving chicken cages with grain stalks.

"Oh well," he said, "tomorrow you can come with me to sell cages."

Day was breaking when he woke the child.

"Get up. Come with Papa to sell cages."

Mother Wang prepared rice balls, which father and son stuffed into their pockets. These would serve as their lunch.

The first day they sold few cages, but in the evening they carried most of them home on their backs. Mother Wang banged on the rice barrel. "I told you we should save some rice for ourselves, but you insisted on selling it. What are we going to eat? Tell me that."

The old man reached into his shirt and took out some coins.

"I'm not worried about today," she said. "It's tomorrow that concerns me."

"Tomorrow? That's easy. I'll sell a few more cages."

They sold ten cages in one morning. Only three big ones remained in the pile. He counted the bills in his hand as Ping'er munched on a rice ball.

"There must be over a hundred here," he said. "Let's go get some soft bean curd."

They walked to a nearby stall and squatted beside it to eat the steaming food. Ping'er was served first, while vinegar was being added to his father's bowl. This was quite a novelty to Ping'er. How smoothly the bean curd coursed down to his intestines. With his eyes opened wide, he gulped down the whole bowlful.

"Shall I give the boy another bowlful?" the vendor asked.

The father was surprised. "What, finished already?"

The vendor lowered his ladle into the pot. "I'll only charge you half price for the second bowl."

Ping'er's eyes were glued on his father as he passed the bowl over. The boy drank noisily, but not Zhao San, who fixed his eyes on the spot where he'd left the cages and ate slowly; but eventually, he too had finished his.

"Ping'er, you can't finish all that, can you? Pour some into my bowl."

So Ping'er gave a tiny bit to his father. After paying, his father returned to the cages, while Ping'er stayed by the stall, lingering over the last drop. He tipped his head all the way back, until the bowl covered his face.

In the vegetable section shoppers strolled by, and whenever anyone showed the slightest interest in the cages, Zhao San would say:

"Here, buy one. Only ten coppers."

But no one bought the last three cages, so he took two and put the third on Ping'er's back. As they passed through the livestock market, Ping'er pointed and said:

"Dad, that's our ox over there!"

With the large cage swaying on his back, the boy went over to look at the dark ox. Zhao San smiled and asked the owner:

"Reselling it?"

For no particular reason, he felt an ache in his heart. When he got home, he said to Mother Wang:

"Saw our ox in the market."

"It belongs to someone else now, so forget it." Mother Wang had no time for patience.

Zhao San grew adept at bargaining for his chicken cages. Slowly he learned how to hawk his wares as he sat at the base of the wall. Often he'd buy bright colored hard candies for Ping'er, and eventually, they no longer even bothered to take rice balls along with them.

He handed coins to Mother Wang at the end of each day, but she was never pleased, and put them away without comment.

Two-and-a-Half Li made arrangements with another family for Ping'er to be taken on as an errand boy. The news angered the boy.

"I won't go. I can't go. They'll beat me." He was bewitched by the chicken-cage business.

"I want to go into the city with Pa."

Mother Wang insisted that the boy go to work as an errand boy.

"What do you do while your father's selling cages?"

"Let him be," Zhao San said. "He doesn't have to go if he doesn't want to."

Excited by the sight of the money, Zhao San stayed up nights making the cages.

"Why don't you learn how to do this?" he said to Mother Wang. "With a few more, we can make a good living."

But Mother Wang went to bed, as if she harbored a grudge toward his work, as if she disapproved of making chicken cages.

Ping'er sided with his father. He was willing and eager to carry the cages on his back. One more. He could carry one more. But his father said:

"No, that's enough."

But he did carry one more, and on his way out he picked up a small one to carry with him.

"Are you sure you can manage?" his father asked. "Put those two back. We can't sell them all."

One time they came back with some meat and had a proper dinner The village women all envied Mother Wang.

"Third Brother is really smart. He may have sold his ox, and can't do any more planting, but this is better. It brings in more money."

As they passed Two-and-a-Half Li's place, Ping'er took Tunnel Legs along into town with him. Ping'er asked for a few coins from his father and bought two fried buns for his little friend. Then they elbowed their way over to a tent where they heard gongs and spent a penny each to view the "Western peep show." It was a device with a small hole covered with a lens, just big enough for one eye. Inside was a series of magnified moving pictures. Men were fighting, brandishing their guns. The pictures moved very quickly as the man who operated the device sang and narrated stories:

"Now here are some foreigners fighting. Look at those 'hairy ones' taking the city. Oh, what action! See how many are being killed . . ."

Tunnel Legs protested that he couldn't see.

"You have to close one eye," Ping'er told him

But it was soon over, and the boys were taken away from the busy city they loved so much. Ping'er found himself back in the sleepy village, since the chick-hatching season had passed, and everyone had all the chicken cages they needed.

Since Ping'er didn't feel like tagging along anymore, Zhao San went into town alone and tried to sell the cages at a reduced price. But he couldn't move them at any price. Finally, even he stopped going, and the cages piled up against the kitchen wall. Previously, that sight would have given him pleasure. Now it only served to infuriate him.

So Ping'er went herding again on the back of a goat. But Zhao San had suffered a setback.

6 DAYS OF PUNISHMENT

Warm air rose from the haystack behind the house. Sunshine flooded the village; stalks of grain waved in the gentle breezes. Summer had returned, and leaves burst onto the trees. Blossoms also appeared on flowering trees.

On the haystack behind the house a bitch was giving birth. Its limbs trembled, its body shook. After a long time the puppies were born.

In the warmth of the season the village was occupied with the birth of its young. Sows led their litters of piglets squealing and running, while the bellies of others were still big, nearly scraping the ground, their teats virtually overflowing.

It was evening. Unable to hold off even a minute longer, Fifth Sister's elder sister went into her mother-in-law's room.

"Send for a midwife. I really don't feel well."

She went back inside, where she let down the window shades and the bed curtain. By then she could no longer even sit properly, so she rolled up the mat and crawled onto the straw. When the midwife arrived and saw how things were, she cocked her head and said:

"I've never seen anything like it. A well-off family like yours has to give birth on straw. 'Sit on straw and the money dribbles in.'"

Her mother-in-law gathered up the straw, stirring up clouds of dust. The naked woman squirmed on the *kang* like a beached fish.

Dusk had fallen, and candles glowed in the house. The woman, nearing her time, moaned softly. The midwife and an old neighbor woman supported her from behind so she could sit up and move a little on the *kang*. But the punishing child just would not come out. Half the night was gone, and the rooster outside had begun to crow. Suddenly the woman was in so much pain her face turned first ashen and then yellow. Her family was growing uneasy, and had actually begun to prepare her shroud. In the eerie candlelight they looked around for suitable garments, the entire household under the disturbing influence of the shadow of death.

The naked woman could no longer even crawl, unable to manage a final burst of effort in this life-and-death moment. Though it was getting light outside, fear lay heavily in the house like a corpse.

When news of her elder sister reached Fifth Sister, she ran over.

"Try to drink some water," she said. "When did she go into labor?"

A man stumbled in. He was drunk. Half his face was red and swollen; he came up to the curtain and snarled:

"Give me my boots!"

The woman could not reply. He tore at the curtain, moving his thick swollen lips as he said menacingly:

"Feign death, will you? Let's see how long you can keep that up!"

With that he took the tobacco pouch at his side and flung it at the corpse-like figure. His mother came up and dragged him out. Every year it was the same: whenever he saw his wife giving birth, that was how he showed his disapproval.

In the light of day, the pain subsided a little, and she regained consciousness. She sat behind the bed curtain covered with sweat. All of a sudden, the red-faced devil rushed in again. Without a word, he raised his fearful hands and flung a bucket of water through the curtain. Finally the people around managed to drag him outside.

The pregnant woman with her bulging belly sat in silence, her body drenched with cold water. She dared not move a muscle, for, like the child of a patriarchal society, she lived in dread of her man.

Once more unable to sit up, she was undergoing torment. The midwife changed her wet outer garment. Suddenly there was a sound at the door, and the young woman was gripped by panic. She was not allowed even a single moan. This poor woman—had there been a hole beside her, she'd have jumped in. Had there been poison beside her, she'd have swallowed it. Feeling hate and contempt for everything, she nearly kicked in the windowsill. She'd willingly have broken her own legs if necessary. Her body was being torn to shreds by the heat, as though she'd entered a steamer.

The midwife pushed down on her abdomen with both hands.

"Be strong. Stand up and walk around, and the baby will pop right out. It's about time."

After only a few steps, her legs began to quake and, like a sick horse, she collapsed, scaring the midwife.

"I'm afraid we're going to have trouble with this one," she said. "Better go fetch another one of the older women."

So Fifth Sister returned home to get her mother. But while she was gone, the child came into the world. It died immediately. As the people helped the pregnant woman up, the baby dropped onto the *kang* with a sickening thud. The woman lay in her own blood, soaking it up with her body.

Outside, the sun was shining; inside, the woman was exhausted by childbirth.

In the green world of the fields everyone was bathed in sweat.

In the fourth month, birds were hatching. Yellow-billed fledglings would swoop down, skipping and pecking beneath the eaves. Litters of piglets grew fat. Only the women in the village, like farm horses, grew skinnier in the summer.

The punishment descended upon Golden Bough. Her bloated belly was totally out of proportion to her short figure. She didn't look like a woman yet; she still had the appearance of a young girl. But her belly had swelled up, and she'd soon become a mother. The woman's punishment would quickly catch up with her.

She'd been married a scant four months before she learned how to curse her husband. She began to feel that men are heartless human beings, a feeling shared by all the village women.

She sat on the sandy ground beside the river, washing clothes. The red sun shone down on the river at an oblique angle, and gradually the reflections of the woods on the opposite bank grew fuzzy under the reddish ripples.

Chengye stood some distance behind her. "The sky's turned dark, and you're still washing clothes! You lazy wife, what were you doing all day?"

In the morning, before sunrise, Golden Bough felt her way in the dark to get dressed. Then in the kitchen this little woman with the big belly started to cook. When the sun came out, the workers in the field came home with their hoes over their shoulders. The living room was packed with people, and a din arose, produced by people gulping down their food and slurping their soup.

She had to cook at midday and again in the evening. She was so exhausted her legs felt as if they were broken; so when the sky grew dark, she lay down and rested awhile. Subconsciously she sensed that Chengye was home, and she sat up. With great effort she opened her sleepy eyes and asked weakly:

"Are you just now getting home?"

But there was no response, even after several minutes. She watched the man undress and knew she was in for a scolding. But there were no abusive words. On the contrary, Golden Bough felt a warmth on her back. The man was trying his best to talk to her in a gentle voice.

The man mesmerized Golden Bough.

Immediately after—disaster. Suffering came close on the heels of pleasure. Golden Bough was unable to cook a meal. The village midwife arrived. Writhing in pain in a corner of the *kang*, Golden Bough was taking her punishment. Mother Wang came to help, and the baby was born. Mother Wang shook her head knowingly. "That was dangerous. Last night you two must have carried on. You young people, don't you know anything? When you're pregnant, you're not supposed to do it. You could easily have died!"

After ten days or so, Golden Bough was out in the yard again, while Little Golden Bough cried for her mother in the house.

In their ignorance, cows and horses cultivated their own suffering. At night, as the people sat in the cool breeze, they heard odd noises coming from stables or barns. A bull that was probably fighting over a mate crashed out of the shed, breaking the fence. Chengye hurriedly picked up a rake to beat the crazed bull until it retreated peacefully back into the barn.

In the village, men and beasts were occupied in the business of living and dying.

Two-and-a-Half Li's wife and Second Aunt Li met at the edge the field.

"My, you can still bend down in your state?"

"How are you getting along?"

"I can't do a thing."

"When's it due?"

"Any day now."

It was drizzling. Suddenly Two-and-a-Half Li's house was in an uproar. Whenever his foolish woman gave birth, she created a scene, wailing and ranting against her man:

"I said I didn't want any more kids. You heartless . . . it's all your doing. If I die, my death will be on your hands."

Mother Wang turned her head to laugh without being seen. After a while, the foolish woman rolled over and cried at the top of her lungs:

"My belly's killing me! Get a knife and cut it out!"

In the midst of this clamor, the baby's head was visible. Just then Fifth Sister came through the door looking pale. Having seemingly lost the power of speech, she kept wringing her hands.

"She's stopped breathing! Miscarriage . . . Second Aunt Li's going to die!"

Mother Wang abandoned Granny Pockface and hurried to Fisherman's Village. Another midwife arrived to find Granny Pockface's baby crying on the *kang*, so she bathed this tiny infant, who could barely cry.

When Mother Wang returned, outside the window at the base of the wall, somebody's sow was giving birth.

7 THE SINFUL SUMMER FESTIVAL

The approach of the Summer Festival in the fifth month heralded two occurrences—the self-poisoning of Mother Wang and the tragic death of Little Golden Bough.

The crescent moon, like a sickle, pierced the treetops in the woods. Mother Wang, her hair hanging loose, headed toward the woodshed behind the house. There she gently opened the gate. Outside all was darkness and silence; not even the breezes dared disturb the black nocturnal picture. The cucumbers had climbed up the lattice, cornstalks rustled their broad leaves, no frogs croaked, and few insects were chirping.

Her loose hair hanging about her shoulders, a phantomlike Mother Wang knelt on the hay and held the cup to her lips. As a flood of enticing memories rushed into her head, she dropped down in the hay and, overcome by sorrow, wept bitterly.

Zhao San awoke from his dreams, totally unaware of what was going on. Once inside the woodshed, he was harsh with her.

"What's the matter? Are you crazy?"

He assumed she was feeling melancholy and had gone to weep in the woodshed. Then he stumbled on the cup in the hay, which brought an end to his thoughts. He ran back into the house, where, in the light of the lamp he noticed a black heavy liquid at the bottom of the cup. He touched it with his finger and then tasted it with the tip of his tongue. It was bitter.

"Mother Wang has taken poison!"

This was the cry that rang through the village the next morning. Villagers, sad and somber, came to pay their last respects. Zhao San was not at home, having gone out to choose a site for her in the potter's field.

There the living were digging a grave for the dead. Two-and-a-Half Li was the first to jump into the deepening pit. The wet earth piled up on the sides as the grave grew deeper and larger. Several more people jumped down. The spades never stopped digging. Soon the grave was waist high, while on the sides the earth was piled higher than a man's head.

The graveyard was a dead city; there was no fragrance of flowers, no humming of insects. Even if there had been flowers and insects, they'd have been singing a song of farewell to accompany the eternal solitude of the dead.

The landlord had donated the field as a final resting place for impoverished peasants. But in life the peasants were constantly hounded by that same landlord. Shouldering their bundles and carrying their children, they were driven from ramshackle houses into even more dilapidated houses. Sometimes they were even banished to the stables. There the children cried and fretted at their mothers.

Zhao San went into the city, weakened by this unexpected blow. On the road he met up with a cart from Fisherman's Village carrying vegetables to sell in the city. The driver was in a complaining mood:

"The price of vegetables has dropped and the currency is worthless. Even grain isn't worth much." He flicked his whip and continued:

"Cloth's the only thing that's expensive. That and salt. Soon a family won't be able to afford salt. With the rent going up, how can a farmer make a living?"

Zhao San jumped onto the cart and sat on the shafts with his head bowed. His weak, tired legs dangled over the side, swaying with the movements of the cart as it rumbled down the road.

In town the main street was crowded, and the marketplace terribly noisy. The people around the meat stall sounded as if they were quarreling. Young boys hawked their wares, carrying colorful gourds that danced in the air. It was the madness of the Summer Festival.

But Zhao San saw none of this. It was as if all the pedestrians had disappeared, and the street was deserted.

"It's festival time," said a little boy who was following him. "Buy one of these for your kid."

Zhao San ignored him, but the boy selling gourds chased after him as if he were an adult, not a child. "It's festival time. Buy one of these for your kid."

The colorful gourds hanging from the willow branch like butterflies tied with ribbons followed Zhao San.

A coffin shop. Red ones and white ones were placed at the entrance. He stopped there. The child stopped following him.

Everything was in readiness. The coffin rested in front of the house; the spades had stopped their digging.

The window was opened so that the dying could take a last look at the sun. Mother Wang's heart was still beating and breath lingered on her lips. The bright light from the window illuminated her simple shroud. They had outfitted her in a pair of black cotton pants and a light-colored jacket, and except for the purple color of her face, there was nothing unusual about her deathbed. People were beginning to clamor:

"Lift her up! Lift her up!"

But she was still breathing slightly; a little froth gathered on her lips. Just as she was about to be lifted up, Ping'er called urgently from outside:

"The Feng girl is here! The Feng girl!"

But the meeting between mother and daughter came too late. They would not see each other again. The girl approached slowly with her small bundle. She took a close look, and when her face nearly touched her mother's, a shriek burst from her lips and her bundle fell to the ground.

There wasn't a dry eye among the people gathered round, for who could smother the unbearable sense of loss evoked by the girl? Even people who weren't related mourned with her.

That included a newly widowed woman, who wept the loudest, she being the most sorrowful. Imagining that she was weeping for her husband, she had deluded herself into thinking that she was seated in front of his grave.

The men clamored again:

"Lift her up! We have to get this over with. You can weep some more later."

The girl sensed that this was not her home, and that there wasn't a single loved one by her side. She stopped crying.

The poisoned mother's eyes were still open, but she did not recognize her daughter. She did not recognize anything. As she lay on a plank in the kitchen, with froth on her lips, her heart continued to send out a weak pulse.

Zhao San sat on the *kang* and lit his pipe. The women found a strip of white mourning cloth and tied it around the girl's head, while Ping'er tied a white sash around his waist.

After Zhao San left the room, the women began to question the girl.

"Your father, the one named Feng, when did he die?"

"Over two years ago."

"What about your real father?"

"He went back to Shandong."

"Why didn't he take you with him?"

"He was beating my mother, so she took my elder brother and me to Uncle Feng's house."

The women asked about Mother Wang's early days, and were moved by what they heard.

"Why isn't your brother here?" asked the widow. "Go home and get him to come see his mother."

The girl with the white cloth band around her head turned toward the wall. Her face was once again wet with tears. With an effort she bit her lips, but they parted immediately, and she was crying once more.

Emboldened by the kindness of the women, she went up to her mother and tightly grasped her icy fingers. She also carefully wiped the froth off her mother's lips, as if wanting not to disturb her. The bundle she'd brought with her was trodden underfoot. Again the woman said:

"Go home and get your brother."

The word "brother" nearly started her crying again, but she managed to control herself.

"Isn't he home?" the widow persisted.

Finally, covering her face with the white cloth, she gave rein to her grief. She could only speak of her brother as she sobbed.

"My brother died the day before yesterday; he was shot by officials."

She tore the strip of cloth from her head. This lonely, half-crazed girl then buried her head in her mother's bosom and wept.

"Mother . . . Mother."

There was nothing else she could say. After all, she was still young.

The women by then were talking to one another:

"When did her brother die? How come we never heard?"

Zhao San's tobacco pipe appeared at the door. They were, he could tell, talking about Mother Wang's son, and he knew that the young man had been one of the "Red Whiskers." How had he died? Mother Wang had taken poison after hearing that her son had been shot, hadn't she? Only Zhao San knew this, and he didn't want others to learn that his wife's suicide was related to an act of banditry. He felt it was disgraceful to be a bandit, no matter what the circumstances.

His stiff voice rang out as he motioned with his pipe for the girl to leave:

"Why don't you leave? She's dead. There's nothing left to see, so go back to your home."

This girl, abandoned by her father, her brother shot as a bandit, had brought her bundle along, intending to live with her mother, But now her mother was dead. And if her mother was no longer there, with whom could she stay?

Stunned by this realization, she forgot her bundle, and with just the white mourning strip, she left. As she walked out the door, she seemed to be leaving her heart behind, embarking on a long journey.

Because he was old, Zhao San silently condemned the young man:

"Keeping a woman, huh? If you're rich, you can do it. But without money . . . I've never seen anything like it. When festival time came around and that whore was unable to celebrate, she made him go out to steal. And just like that, a young man threw away his life."

When he looked down at his dying wife, he hated the young man who had been shot. Yet, when he recalled how Mother Wang had come back with a borrowed gun the winter before, he couldn't help but feel admiration for the boy:

"At least no one dared bully him while he was a bandit."

The women kindled the firewood, and soon the pot began to steam. Zhao San fingered his tobacco pouch as he paced back and forth. After a time, he looked down at Mother Wang again; she hung on tenaciously. As if growing impatient waiting for her to die, he leaned up against the wall and dozed off.

The prolonged threat of death began to lose its grip on the mourners. So they turned their attention to the food and drink. At that moment Mother Wang made a sound at their feet. Her purple face had turned several shades lighter. They put down their cups, saying that death had been turned away.

But that was not so. Suddenly from the corner of her mouth black blood trickled out between lips that seemed to be moving. Finally she howled twice, and everyone began to whisper that she was breathing her last. Even as they stared wide-eyed, she moved as if trying to sit up. The frightened women ran outside, and the men reached for the poles they used to carry water, saying that her body had been taken over by a spirit.

Zhao San, who had downed some wine, said boldly:

"If we let her get up, she'll die with her arms around a child, or a tree. She'd even have the strength to do that to a grown man!"

So with his large red hands he greedily pressed down hard on her with the pole as if it were a knife laid across her waist. Her stomach and chest expanded like a fish bubble; her eyes grew round, as if they were about to emit sparks. Her black lips moved; she seemed to be speaking, but no sound came out. Blood spurted from her mouth, drenching Zhao San's jacket.

"Don't press so hard," he shouted to the man on the other end of the pole. "I'm getting blood all over me!"

Everyone assumed then that she had drawn her last breath, so she was put into the coffin waiting by the door.

Two homeless old men stood at the entrance to the temple in the rear village. One carried a red lantern and the other a water jug as they led Ping'er in performing the rites. They circled the temple three times, then returned via the narrow path, the old men reciting the usual litany. On his way home, the red lantern accompanied the boy with the white sash around his waist. Ping'er didn't shed a single tear. After all, he recalled, he'd gone through the same routine that year when his own mother had died.

But Mother Wang's daughter could not go with them.

The news of Mother Wang's death had spread throughout the village, and women sat crying beside the coffin. They blew their noses and howled with grief. They were weeping for their children, for their husbands, for their own fates. In short, whatever suffering they'd endured, that's what they were crying for now. Whenever one of the old villagers died, they—the village women—always acted this way. *utter selfishness*

The coffin was about to be carried out to the potter's field, and it was time to hammer in the nails.

But Mother Wang did not die after all. She was cold, and she was thirsty.

"Give me some water," she said softly.

But she did not know where she was lying.

It was the Summer Festival, and each family had hung a gourd over its door. From Two-and-a-Half Li's house came the sound of a wailing baby, but his foolish wife was crouching by the door, grooming the goat with a metal brush they used for the horse.

Two-and-a-Half Li limped along. The festival always made him happy. In the cabbage patch he saw several heads of cabbage that had been eaten by worms. Ordinarily he'd have cursed the worms or, in a fit of temper, kicked at the cabbage. But it was festival time, and he was happy. He felt it only proper that he be happy. At the edge of the plot he saw that the tomatoes were not yet red, and the thought occurred to him that maybe he should pick a few green ones for the boy. After all, it was festival time.

The entire village celebrated this holiday. The vegetable plots, the wheat fields, no matter where, every place was quiet and tranquil. Even the insects sang more sweetly than usual.

The festive feelings affected the soul of Two-and-a-Half Li. He passed by his house but did not go in. He just threw the tomatoes in for the boy and walked on, for he wanted to take advantage of the happy occasion to meet some friends.

All the neighboring doors were fastened with paper gourds. He noticed a green one swaying above the door of Mother Wang's house as he passed. Farther on was Golden Bough's house. There was no gourd outside, and there were no people inside. Two-and-a-Half Li stared a long while at the billowing diaper hanging by the stove.

Little Golden Bough had been in the world barely a month when her father dashed her to the ground. Why had the baby even been brought into such a world? So she could leave filled with resentment? Such a very short life, it had lasted but a few days.

The little baby now slept among the dead. Wouldn't she be afraid? Her mother was getting farther and farther away, until soon the mother's weeping would be heard no more.

It was dark. Even the moon did not come out to keep the baby company.

During the few days before the Summer Festival, Chengye had gone into town many times. And each time he returned home, he'd fought with his wife.

"The price of rice has plummeted," he'd said. "The rice bought in April now sells at a loss. What we get isn't even enough to pay off our debts. But if I don't sell it, how can we celebrate the festival?"

And little by little he'd lost his love for Little Golden Bough. When she woke him at night, he'd complain:

"Go on, scream! Scream to your heart's content!"

The day before the festival there had been no preparations at his house. They hadn't bought an ounce of flour, and when it was time to cook, the oil container had turned up dry as a bone. Chengye had come home angry, to begin with, and when he'd seen the bare table, he'd roared:

"So! Someone like me is supposed to starve to death! Since there's nothing to eat, I'm going back to town, going back."

The baby had been suckling at Golden Bough's breast.

"I'll never see good days again," he'd complained. "You two have become a burden to me. I can't even go out and be a bandit."

With her head bowed, Golden Bough had laid out the dinner, as the baby cried off to the side. Chengye had looked at the pickled vegetables and the gruel on the table. He'd thought for a moment and couldn't resist adding:

"Go ahead, cry! You family wrecker. I'll sell you to pay off our debts."

The baby had kept crying while her mother was in the kitchen sweeping the floor or tidying up the firewood pile, and that had thrown him into a frenzy.

"I'll sell the both of you! What's the use of having you two noise-makers in the house?"

In the kitchen the mother, like a struck match, had flared up:

"And what kind of father are you? You come home, and all you do is fight. I'm not your enemy. You want to sell us? Well, go ahead!"

He'd thrown a rice bowl; she'd jumped up in anger.

"I'll sell, all right! But I'll kill her first. Then, I'll show you what I'll sell . . ."

So ended a tiny life.

When Mother Wang heard about the death of Golden Bough's baby, she wanted to come see what had happened. But though she was able to stand with the aid of a cane, she had to lie down again immediately. Her legs had been affected by the poison, and she could hardly move.

After three days, the young mother went to the potter's field to see her baby, but what was there to see? The wild dogs had already torn her to shreds.

Chengye saw a pile of bloodstained straw, which he fancied to be the straw used to wrap Little Golden Bough's body. The two parents wept, back to back.

No one will ever know how many tears of grief had dried on this potter's field. Not even crows would land on this eternally pitiful area.

Chengye saw another open grave; a skull was once again exposed to the light of day.

As they left the field, all the coffins, all the clusters of graves, and all the dead silent images made them quicken their steps.

8 BUSY MOSQUITOES

Her daughter had come. Mother Wang's daughter had come.

Mother Wang was now able to sit beside the river with her fishing pole. There were neither more nor fewer wrinkles on her face, which proved that she hadn't changed much. She still had to go on living.

At night the croaking of the frogs by the river was deafening, while ranks of buzzing mosquitoes set out from the grass at the edge of the river, invading every family. In the daytime the burning sun scorched everyone's skin. In the summer the peasants cursed the sun as they would an evil tyrant. That great fireball rotated in the sky above all the fields.

But Mother Wang always welcomed summer because of the plump green leaves and teeming orchards, not to mention the nocturnal gatherings that inspired poetry in her heart. This was the time for her once again to tell her stories to the summer night. But this summer she did not talk at all. She lay huddled against the window, facing the remote, distant sky.

The croaking of frogs shattered everyone's solitude; the mosquitoes disrupted their rest.

It was the sixth month, just like any other year; this time last year it had been wheat harvest time. But Mother Wang's household hadn't done any planting this year, and that made her even sadder and more silent. Whenever she passed by the waves of wheat, she'd busy herself winding up the line on her fishing pole. Looking up into the sky, she'd pass through the wheat fields without giving them so much as a glance.

Her temper grew worse, and she began to drink. She went fishing every day, no longer tending to the mending and the laundry. All she did every evening was cook the fish she'd caught, drink until she was drunk, and run around the house and the yard. Gradually her wanderings even took her out to the woods. Sometimes, when she raised her wine cup, she'd remember her former husband and feel sorry for the lonely daughter at her side. As a rule, after she drank, she'd think worrisome thoughts.

Now she was on the verge of becoming a laughingstock, as she fell like a stone in the middle of the yard. She'd gotten used to sleeping in the yard at night. When she slept there, she was pestered by throngs of mosquitoes that acted like an army of ants swarming over a rotting fly. But she had no interest in them; she'd lost all interest in life.

Mother Wang was attacked by mosquitoes until her face was covered with red blotches and her skin turned puffy from their bites.

As she gulped down liquor she recalled the day her daughter had come and how the girl had lain in her lap.

"Oh, Mother, I thought you were dead. You were frothing at the mouth and your fingers were icy cold. My brother was dead, and now Mother was, too. Where could I go to beg for food? When they chased me out, I left my bundle behind. I wept . . . I wept till I lost my senses. Mother, they're evil. They wouldn't even let me take one last look at you."

Finally the girl stood up and said meaningfully:

"I hate them all! If my brother were alive, I'd have him kill them." Then she wiped her tears dry. "I must be like Elder Brother."

She bit her lip.

Mother Wang wondered how the girl could have such strong feelings. Maybe she'd turn out to be worth something, after all.

Mother Wang abruptly stopped drinking. Every evening she instructed her daughter in the woods. In the quiet woods she said solemnly:

"Revenge. You must avenge your brother's death. Who killed him?"

The girl thought for a moment. "The officials killed my brother."

Then she heard her mother repeat herself:

"You must kill the people responsible for your brother's death."

After mulling this over for ten days or so, she said to her mother somewhat hesitantly:

"Who were the people who killed my brother? Mother, take me into town tomorrow to search out our enemy, so that when I see them, in the future I can kill them."

A child speaking childish words. Her mother laughed, but with an aching heart.

The night that Mother Wang quarreled with Zhao San the southern river overflowed its banks. People shouted:

"Flood! Flood!"

They milled by the side of the river. Inside his house Zhao San was shouting:

"Tell her to leave. She's not my child, and I won't take care of another man's daughter. I mean now!"

The next day, every family took its grain to the threshing floor. At harvest time each year the peasants feasted and drank to celebrate. This year Zhao San had done no planting, and so his house was quiet. When others asked him to join in the merrymaking, he sat down at the tables, listening to the happy chatter about him and watching other people bring in the harvest. His large red hands looked conspicuously out of place. He kept wringing them, but no one really paid him any attention. They were too busy talking with one another.

After the river waters receded, the mosquitoes returned in hordes. Even the croaking of the frogs at night was drowned out by the loud buzzing. In the daytime, too, they flew. Only Zhao San kept very quiet.

9 EPIDEMIC

Corpses were strewn about the potter's field. With no one to bury the bodies, the wild dogs were busy at their work.

The sun was blood red. From dawn till dusk clouds of mosquitoes and fog filled the sky. Sorghum, corn, and all the vegetable crops lay abandoned in the fields and plots, for every family was sick. Every family was on the verge of extinction.

The village fell silent. There were no breezes to rustle the plants. Everything was steeped in fog.

Zhao San sat at the southern edge of the field trying to sell five unused sickles, left over from the days of the "Sickle Society." As he gazed at the relics, sad memories stirred within him. An old woman from the village said to him:

"I say it's a celestial sign . . . but what kind of sign is it? Is the sky going to fall and the earth open up? Does Heaven want us all to die? Ai!"

She walked away from Zhao San, her hunched back disappearing in the fog; but her voice floated back from a distance:

"Heaven wants to destroy mankind . . . should have done it years ago. People know only how to rob and kill. Man has brought this all on himself."

As she moved farther off, the faint, distant braying of a donkey could be heard. Was it on the slope of the hill? Or was it by the side of the ditch?

Nothing to be seen; only sounds. Just then Two-and-a-Half Li's woman could be heard, muttering unhappily in her raspy voice. Zhao San, worried by the sickles, sat in the fog, full of resentment against them.

"I've already sold the ox," he thought, "and I can no longer work the fields."

He wasn't aware that the woman was speaking to him. She tripped on a dirt clod and got up, a little frightened. But because of the fog, it was hard to see just how frightened she was. The sound waves emanating from her like a fine net were akin to the buzzing of mosquitoes.

"Third Brother, are you still sitting there? I'm worried that the 'devils' are coming. They give shots even to little babies. You see, I've brought my child with me. I won't let them stick a needle in him. I'd rather see him die first!"

Granny Pockface left Zhao San and vanished in the fog, holding a baby who, though still alive, could no longer even cry.

Overhead the sun had become a big, dull red circle. Buried in the stunned village below were the seeds of a natural calamity, and slowly those seeds were germinating.

The epidemic spread like wildfire, and it flourished.

Stepping on dead toads, Zhao San walked ahead. Some people bearing a coffin suddenly materialized and slipped past him. A woman with a twisted face and bound feet followed behind, sobbing quietly. Again he heard the donkey braying. Shortly afterwards, the donkey also passed, bearing a sick old man on its back.

The Westerners, called "foreign devils" by the people, came in their white smocks. The following day, after the fog had dissipated, a woman in a white smock appeared outside Zhao San's window. Wearing a white mask over her mouth, she said in barely understandable Chinese:

"Your . . . sick people you have? I make sickness all good again. Come, chop-chop."

The older, heavier man with her waggled his beard and poked his head in through the window, looking around with eyes like a fat pig.

At first Zhao San lied and said that no one in his family was sick, but in the end he gave permission for Ping'er to be injected.

As the old "devil" spoke to the young "devil," the white mask covering his mouth moved. Then tubes, vials, and shiny knives emerged from his bag. Zhao San got a pot of cold water from the well, as the "devil" began to polish his glass tube.

Ping'er was placed on a plank in front of the window, his eyes covered with a piece of white cloth. Neighbors from across the yard gathered round to find out how the "devils" cured disease, to see what horrible methods they used.

The glass tube was inserted into a spot about an inch below the navel, leaving only half of its five-inch length shining outside. People held the boy down so he couldn't thrash around. Then one of the "devils" lifted up the pot of cold water while the other one lined the spout up with the funnel at the end of a longer rubber tube. It looked as if they were fixing some sort of machine. The spectators collectively drew in their breath, which made it seem as if they were shrugging their shoulders. The little boy could only utter short cries: "Ah! Ah!" Soon the entire pot of water had been drained. Finally, some yellow medicine was rubbed on the bulging abdomen and a piece of white gauze was snipped off with a small pair of scissors and put over the puncture. After that the white-clad "devils" took their bags and left nonchalantly to go to another household.

Another sunny day. The epidemic had reached a crisis. Women held their half-dead children, still afraid of the injections, afraid that the white-clad "devils" would pump water into their children's bellies. They did not have the heart to look upon those inflated bellies.

Terrifying news traveled far and wide.

"The whole Li family has died!"

"They've sent people from the city to investigate. Anyone with symptoms is being taken into the city in carts. Even old ladies . . . children, too . . . to be injected."

Gradually the sounds of mourning ceased, as quietly the corpses were wrapped in straw or placed in coffins to be rushed off to the potter's field, one by one, endlessly . . .

After midday, Two-and-a-Half Li's wife took her baby to the potter's field. There she saw the corpses of children, their white faces covered by hair. Some had been torn apart by wild dogs, but others were lying there whole.

At a safe distance, the dogs gnawed noisily on the bones. They were content, no longer mad with the lust for food, no longer having to chase people.

All through the night Ping'er vomited yellow and green fluid, while the whites of his eyes became covered with red lines.

Zhao San went out the door, mumbling. Although the village had lost quite a few people, and the fields lay barren and neglected, he was still obsessed with selling his sickles. As long as they remained in the house, they were thorns piercing his heart.

10 TEN YEARS

The hill in the village and the stream at its base remained the same as ten years before. The water flowed gently, and the slope changed its garb with the seasons. In the village, the cycle of life and death went on exactly as it had ten years earlier. endless warfare

The same number of sparrows congregated on rooftops. The sun was just as warm. At the foot of the hill a young goatherd sang a nursery rhyme, the same tune that had been sung ten years before:

> Autumn nights are long,
> Autumn winds are strong.
> Whose mommy left him when he was young?
> Whose mommy left him when he was young?
> The moon in the west window hears my song.

Everything was just as it had been ten years before. Even Mother Wang seemed unchanged. Ping'er, however, had grown up. Both he and Tunnel Legs had grown up.

Mother Wang, her hair blown by the wind, stood beyond the fence and listened to the nursery rhyme drifting across the slope.

11   THE WHEEL OF TIME TURNS

One snowy day a flag never before seen by the villagers was raised and began to flutter under the open sky.

Silence reigned over the village. The only sound came from the fluttering Japanese flag raised in front of the temporary garrison on the hill.

The villagers were wondering: What is happening now? Has the Chinese nation had a dynastic change? *Too indulged in their own survival. Not knowing the outside world*

12   THE BLACK TONGUE

A banner proclaiming the "Kingly Way" arrived, bringing with it dust, smoke, and clamor.

Motorcars roared down the wide, tree-lined roads.

In the boundless fields the squat seedlings were a light green. But this was no longer a quiet, somber village. The people had lost the equilibrium in their hearts. The motorcars whizzed across grassy fields, creating clouds of dust, after which scraps of red and green paper fell like scattered seeds. The scraps covered the roofs of nearby thatched huts, they covered the branches of the trees by the wayside, and they whirled and whistled in the wind. From the city more motorcars traveled in their wake. Imposing Japanese, Koreans, even Chinese, were standing in the cars, and as the wheels flashed by, the flags the men were holding in their hands snapped loudly, giving the impression that the people in the cars had sprouted wings and were airborne. The flag-wavers with their phony smiles vanished down the road. The handbills proclaiming the "Kingly Way" fluttered over to the slope and down to the riverbank.

torment of hardship

As Mother Wang stood in her doorway, Two-and-a-Half Li's goat lowered its bearded head and walked gently over to a spot beneath a luxuriant tree. It no longer searched for food. It was tired and so old its coat had turned a dirty color. Its eyes were dim and teary. It looked comical yet pitiful as it walked toward the low ground, its beard swaying from side to side.

Facing the low ground and watching the goat, Mother Wang traced the sad, bygone days. She longed to recapture the past, because the present was proving to be even worse. The ground remained uncultivated; farther up the hill wheat fields lay fallow. She dwelled on her memories with a sad heart.

A Japanese airplane passed overhead with a roar, and the sky was filled with dancing scraps of paper. One landed on a branch above Mother Wang. She took it down and, after glancing at it, threw it to the ground. The airplane flew by one more time, leaving behind even more handbills. She ignored them, crushing them underfoot as she paced back and forth.

After a time, Golden Bough's mother passed by, holding two roosters in her hand. She remarked to Mother Wang:

"We can't go on like this. How can we? These are my last two roosters. I'd better sell them fast."

"Are you going to sell them in town?"

"Where else could I find a buyer? There aren't many chickens left in the village." Then, dropping her voice, she confided to Mother Wang:

"Those Japs are nasty! All the village girls have fled. Even the young married women. I hear the Japs kidnapped a thirteen-year-old from Wang Village. They took her in the middle of the night."

"Rest awhile before you move on," Mother Wang urged her.

The two women sat beneath the tree. All over the land the insects were silent. Just two women, talking dejectedly. The roosters kept flapping their wings. As the sun moved overhead, the shadows of the trees grew round.

There were new sights in the village: Japanese flags, Japanese soldiers. And the topics of conversation had turned to "The Kingly Way," "the bonds of friendship between Japan and Manchukuo," and "the coming of the true Prince of Heaven." Under the "Kingly Way" the number of abandoned plots was on the increase, and people wandered dispiritedly in the square.

Just before leaving, the old woman said:

"I've spent these past few years raising chickens. Now I don't have a feather left. I can't even keep a rooster to announce the dawn. What kind of times are these?"

She shook her sleeves somewhat hysterically before standing up and striding across the abandoned field that stretched in front of her. The field seemed diseased, and under her feet the short grasses, sorry-looking and rigid, were trodden flat.

Even after she'd gone quite a distance, it was still clear that she was holding the two roosters in the hand hanging by her side and wiping her face with the other.

When Mother Wang lay down to rest she vaguely heard a woman scream. She opened the window to hear more clearly. After listening for a while she heard shrill whistles and gunshots. Who were the devils who had broken into that distant house?

"You have people in the house or not?"

That night Japanese soldiers and Chinese policemen conducted a search of the village. They came to Mother Wang's house.

"Who do I have? Nobody."

With their hands covering their noses, they took a turn through the house and went out, the flashlights in their hands sending out criss-crossing blue rays. As they stepped over the threshold, a helmeted Japanese soldier said in Chinese:

"Bring her along."

Mother Wang heard what he said.

"Why are they taking away the women too?" she thought. "To shoot us?"

"Who needs an old hag like her?" the Chinese policeman said.

The Chinese laughed at this, and so did the Japanese, although they didn't understand what the words meant. But since others were laughing, they joined in. 像猫咪记

They did, however, take one of the other women and led her away, bent over like a pig. In the faint glow of the flashlights Mother Wang couldn't tell who she was, but before they'd even passed the fence, she saw they were already having fun at her expense. She even saw the hand of the helmeted Japanese soldier give the woman's buttocks a quick pat.

慰药

13

DO YOU WANT TO BE EXTERMINATED?

Mother Wang thought it was another mock raid to camouflage their search for women in the village, so she didn't associate it with anything particularly sinister and slept on soundly. Zhao San, who was getting old, came home and went right to sleep without disturbing her.

The next day, Japanese military policemen tapped on the door. The one who came in looked Chinese. His high boots were damp with dew. He took a handkerchief from his pocket, calmly sat down on the *kang*, and leisurely polished his boots. Then the interrogation began.

"Did anyone come to your house last night? Don't be afraid, just tell the truth."

Zhao San had just gotten up. Still drowsy, he didn't know what was going on. So the military policeman gave his hat a violent shake, his manner no longer gentle or casual. "You damn fool! What do you mean you don't know? Wait till I take you in, then you'll know!"

Despite his threats, he took no one in. Mother Wang, who was buttoning her clothes, answered for her husband:

"Who is it you're asking about? Last night some officers came by on a search, but they left when they couldn't find anyone."

Directing his attention to Mother Wang, this man with the airs of an officer said cordially:

"Please tell me, old lady. You'll be rewarded."

But Mother Wang didn't bat an eye.

"We're looking for bandits," the man said. "You villagers are their victims too. Didn't you see the car that came yesterday to proclaim the Kingly Way? The Kingly Way wants people to be honest. Come on, old lady, tell us. We'll reward you for it."

Mother Wang turned toward the red glare on the window and said:

"I don't know anything about that."

The officer was on the point of screaming, but he managed to restrain himself, explaining in measured tones:

"Manchukuo wants to exterminate all those bandits who harm the people. Anyone who has information about the bandits but refuses to divulge it will be shot." Then the man in the high boots looked at Zhao San with an insulting leer. At that point he stopped speaking and waited for an answer. But none was forthcoming.

It was not yet midday when three more corpses appeared in the potter's field. Among them was that of a woman.

Everyone recognized the body: it was the "girl student" who had been discovered in a widow's house in North Village.

Zhao San heard others mention that the student had belonged to some "party," but he wasn't sure just what a "party" was. That night, after getting drunk, he confided what he'd heard to Mother Wang. He didn't know what sort of secret business the girl student was involved in or why she had died, but he sensed that this thing, which was not to be talked about, was something secret. Yet he felt he had to talk.

Mother Wang didn't feel like listening. Since all this had happened, she'd been worrying for her daughter, afraid she'd share the girl student's fate."

Zhao San's beard had grown white and sparse. After a few cups of liquor, his ruddy face turned even redder, and he simply flopped down in a corner of the *kang*.

Ping'er brought home a bundle of grass that, when dried, would serve as kindling. He laid it out in the middle of the yard. After walking into the house, instead of eating right away, he took off his sweat-drenched undershirt and put it down beside him. He seemed angry, slapping hard at his own muscular shoulders and breathing deeply. After a long time his father said:

"You young people should have more courage. This is no life. The country is lost. We can no longer plant wheat, and even the animals have to be killed off." *Is it the animals or the humans?*

When the old man spoke, it sounded as if he were quarreling. Mother Wang, who was darning Ping'er's undershirt, was moved by what she heard. As she thought about the loss of the country, she made a mistake in her darning, She'd sewn the two sleeve openings together.

Zhao San was like an old bull that had lost its youthful vigor. Now he could only fall back on memories of the "Sickle Society."

"You were just a kid then," he said to Ping'er. "Li Qingshan and some others and I formed a Sickle Society. Now that took guts. But I suffered a setback and ran into big trouble. Your mother had come home with a borrowed gun, but who'd have thought that before I could even use it, I'd take a man's life with a mere pole? From then on my luck was all bad. Each year has been worse than the last, up to this very day."

"A dog can never become a wolf. After your father got into trouble, he lost interest in the Sickle Society. That was the year we sold our black ox."

Mother Wang's comments brought Zhao San humiliation and anger. He wondered how he could have been so despicable back then. His heart flared up for an instant, and he spoke of things that gave him pleasure:

"Well, even the master is no longer master now. With the Japanese around, not even a master can do anything."

Feeling flushed and lightheaded, he went out to walk in the woods. There the treetops traced an arc against the blue sky, a lovely, symmetrical arc that billowed like clouds. A curtain of blue sky hung straight down before him, the treetops hemming it with a scalloped border. Butterflies flitted to and fro, even though the wildflowers were not yet in bloom. Spread out before him were isolated thatched huts, some left only with sections of walls standing in the sun, and some with the roofs carried off by bombs, while the main parts of the houses remained intact.

Zhao San puffed out his chest and inhaled the fresh air of the fields. Not wanting to leave, he paused at the edge of a barren field where wheat had once grown. But after a while he grew agitated as he recalled his own wheat field, which had been destroyed by gunfire. Under the Japanese military occupation, it would not be cultivated again, and he carried the sadness of the wheat field with him as he passed by a melon patch. The melon grower was absent from the patch, which was now overgrown with weeds, but the little hut where the keeper kept watch was still there. Starting to feel drowsy, Zhao San dropped down among the short grass by the hut. Just before he dozed off, he saw some Koreans emerge from the woods. Viewed from his prone position, they seemed to be walking at the edge of the horizon.

Had it not been for the houses sprouting up from the ground, Zhao San would have thought he too was sleeping at the edge of the horizon.

His eyes dazzled by the sun's glare, he could not see very far, but he could hear the village dogs barking aimlessly in the distance.

It was such a desolate wilderness that even wild dogs stayed away. Only Zhao San, whose heart was fired by liquor, came prowling around; but he lacked a purpose and wandered at will where his feet carried him. As he passed the countless bare fields, he experienced a sense of waste; shaking his head and throwing up his hands, he walked back home, sighing heavily.

The number of widows in the village had increased. Three of them were walking ahead of him, one leading her child by the hand.

The dead leaving the living behind. A land of desolation.

Just as the red-faced Zhao San reached the door of his house, he took a detour. With sorrow beckoning him, he roamed aimlessly. Suddenly he stepped into a hole in the road, but he didn't seem to notice. He proceeded as if he must finish a long journey. There were more holes where bombs had exploded, but he was not deterred, for the vigor of youth, aided by liquor, urged him on.

In a dilapidated house a cat was suckling a litter of kittens. He couldn't bear to watch the scene and walked on without running into any of his acquaintances. He continued on until the western sky glowed with color and he found himself, with a heavy heart and misty eyes, in front of the graves of his youthful companions. Having brought no liquor to pay his respects to the dead, he just sat silently before his friends.

Zhao San, who now lived in an occupied country, missed his brave, dead comrades. Those who survived them were old and could know only grief and indignation; they could never again be adventurous. Old Zhao San could not afford to be adventurous again.

It was a starry night. Li Qingshan seemed fired by the passion of a madman. His raspy voice added mystery and excitement to his speech. This was their first mass meeting. They gathered at Zhao San's house, solemn and hushed, as if for a grand ceremony. Everyone seemed to be suffering from a lack of air. No one even sniffled. Since the lamps were not lit, the people's eyes were like those of cats at night, shining with a phosphorescent light.

Mother Wang's pointed feet paced outside the window. She held a broken lampshade in her steady hand, prepared to smash it at any time; she was the mouse keeping watch during the night, looking out for the cat. She went out the gate and took a turn around the fence. Then she stood beyond the fence and listened to the rise and fall of the voices from inside the house. Was there any danger? Not for a single moment did she forget the lampshade in her hand.

Inside the house Li Qingshan's persistent and heavy voice continued:

"It's only been over the past couple of weeks that I realized how ineffective the People's Revolutionary Army is. If you join them, you're in for trouble. They're a bunch of Western educated students who can't even mount a horse without someone giving them a boost up. All they know is how to yell 'Retreat.' On the night of the 28th it was drizzling outside. Ten of us comrades were eating when our rice bowls exploded in our faces. Two men were sent to investigate the origin of the bomb. Just think about it—sending out a couple of Western students! Men, that hapless pair was chased by the enemy and, in the process, they even lost their caps. Those students often get killed by the enemy."

Tunnel Legs cut in:

"The Revolutionary Army can't compare with the Red Whiskers, can it?"

Moonlight shining in through the window was too faint for anyone to notice the funny expression on the boy's face.

Li Qingshan resumed his speech:

"Oh, but the discipline of the Revolutionary Army is really something. Do you understand what discipline is? Rules and regulations. Their rules are really too harsh for us. For example, you can look at the village girls but you can't . . . ha ha. I got into trouble over that once, and the comrades gave me ten whacks with the butt of a gun."

Here he stopped and laughed, but not loudly. Then he went on with what he was saying.

Unable to generate any interest in these matters, Two-and-a-Half Li dozed off. Zhao San nudged the politically apathetic Two-and-a-Half Li with the bowl of his pipe.

"Listen up, you! Pay attention!" he said unhappily. "What times are these that you can still sleep?"

They heard crunching sounds made by Mother Wang's shoes, but no smashing of a lampshade, and they knew there was no danger of Japanese soldiers suddenly appearing. And yet a grave atmosphere settled over the room. Qingshan solemnly announced his plan.

Since he was a farmer, and had no idea how to approach the issue, what he said was:

"The young men of the village must unite to save our country. Those students with the Revolutionary Army can't do it. Only the Red Whiskers are brave enough."

Rather than light his pipe, Old Zhao San threw it down on the *kang* and clapped his hands with a note of urgency. "Right, muster the young men," he said. "We'll call them a revolutionary army too."

Actually Zhao San had no idea what he was talking about, for he'd never heard of a revolutionary army. He was simply content. In his euphoria he rubbed his beard with his large hands. For him, all this planning aroused the same excitement he'd experienced with the forming of the Sickle Society ten years earlier. It had also been in a dark room, and there had been the same muffled speeches. He was so happy he couldn't sleep a wink, but kept gesturing all night long with his hands.

But anyone standing outside Two-and-a-Half Li's house could have counted the rhythmic snores.

In the countryside the Japanese were hard at work trying to poison the villagers' minds. They talked about reinstating the Manchu Dynasty and said that everyone should strive to be loyal subjects, filial sons, and chaste wives. Meanwhile the opposing force was gathering support.

As soon as it grew dark, a man climbed over the wall to hide in Mother Wang's house. Returning night after night, this black-bearded man had become a familiar sight to Mother Wang. While eating a meal in her house one night, he told her:

"Your daughter was quite a woman. She could scramble up a hill with a rifle slung over her back. But . . . she's already . . ."

Ping'er crouched beside the *kang*, puffing on his father's pipe. A tinge of jealousy crept into his heart. He ostentatiously knocked the pipe against the door and went out. The night was pitch-black, and he lost himself in the darkness. When he returned, still depressed, Mother Wang was in tears.

That night old Zhao San came home very late. He'd been talking to everyone he met about the loss of the country, about saving the nation, about volunteer armies and revolutionary armies . . . all these strange-sounding terms. That was why he'd come home so late. It was nearly time for the rooster to crow—except there was no rooster in Zhao San's house. In fact, the crow of a rooster couldn't be heard anywhere in the village. Fading moonlight shone through the windows. Orion's Belt was not visible in the sky, so he knew it was nearly dawn.

Rousing his son from his sleep, he proudly told him about his propaganda work: how a widow in East Village had sent her children back to her mother's house so she could join the volunteer army, and how the young men were planning meetings. Acting like an official in a magistrate's office, the old man swayed from side to side as he spoke. His heart too was swaying, and his soul was taking giant strides. After a momentary pause, he asked Ping'er:

"Did that man come? The one with the dark beard?"

Ping'er had fallen back to sleep, in spite of his father's spirited energy. He slept on, his father's words like the meaningless buzzing of mosquitoes in his ear. Zhao San was furious, sensing there was no one to carry on his glorious deeds. Raising such a useless son had been a waste of time, he figured. He was terribly disappointed.

Mother Wang didn't make a sound, pretending to be asleep.

The man with the black beard showed up the next morning.

"Did you see the girl die?" Mother Wang asked him a second time.

"Old lady, why won't you understand?" he answered her craftily. "Didn't I say from the very beginning: If you die, you die! Anyone who joins a revolution should not be afraid of dying. It's an honorable death . . . better than staying alive as a slave of the Japanese dogs!"

Mother Wang often heard people like him talk about living and dying. Death seemed right to her too. So she calmed down and, her eyes red from the previous night's tears, studied the changing expressions on the face of this man whom she was getting to know so well. In the end she accepted what he had to offer. She accepted all the pamphlets he took from his knapsack and the sheets of paper crawling with black dot-like words. He also gave her a small, shiny pistol. He was in a hurry to go, but Mother Wang couldn't keep from asking one final question:

"Was she shot to death?"

He opened the door and made a quick exit, in too great a hurry to pay any attention to Mother Wang.

Normally Mother Wang knew no fear, and she often took the pamphlets others brought her and hid them in the kitchen. Sometimes she'd just toss them under the mattress. But today she lacked that courage. She was thinking that if those things were discovered, she'd know what it felt like to be stabbed by a Japanese bayonet. Apparently, she assumed that her fate would be the same as her daughter's, especially when she held the pistol in her hand. She grew so terrified she began to tremble. Her daughter must have met her death by a gun like that. Finally she put a stop to such thoughts, as the seriousness of the current situation began to dawn on her.

Zhao San came home with panic written all over his face. Ignoring him, Mother Wang went out to where the firewood stack had once been located. But things were different now, and the firewood had all been used up. A sparse few purslane flowers grew on the flat ground. Just as she began to dig a hole, she heard the frenzied barking of village dogs. Flustered, she couldn't even muster the strength to pull out the sickle she'd stuck in the ground. She felt as if she were going to fall, subjected to a force that threatened to tear her body apart. After an unbearable, swooning second, she went to call her old man. But when she reached the door, she turned back. She recalled some advice she'd been given:

—Don't divulge anything important to anyone, not even your husband.

She also recalled what Black Whiskers had said to her:

—Don't tell Zhao San. That old man is like a child sometimes.

Once she'd finished burying the contraband, a dozen or so Japanese soldiers came over. Most of them had just thrown on their helmets; they hadn't even had time to lace up their boots, and the villagers knew they were coming for women again.

Mother Wang had lost her powers of observation: involuntarily, she retreated behind Zhao San. She didn't even recognize the Japanese officer with the smiling face who came so often to search her house. As he left, he said goodbye to her, but she said nothing in reply.

The blare of a bugle signaled the time to move out. Housewives were packing clothes, shoes, and socks for their men.

Li Qingshan sent men to each household to look for a rooster, but they found none, so someone suggested sacrificing Two-and-a-Half Li's old goat. It was right then in front of Li Qingshan's house, cooling itself, or perhaps just too tired to move. Its horn was wedged in a crack in the fence. The young men lifted it up, but couldn't free the horn.

And yet, when Two-and-a-Half Li passed by, the goat freed itself and followed him home.

"If you want to kill it, go ahead," he said. "Sooner or later the Japs will get it anyway."

Second Aunt Li commented:

"The Japs would never take it. It's too old."

Two-and-a-Half Li said:

"Even if they won't, it'll die of old age soon enough."

The day of oath taking arrived. Since no rooster was found, it was decided to use the old goat as a substitute. The young men lifted it up and hung it by its legs from a pole. It bleated pitifully. Two-and-a-Half Li, looking comical in his sorrow, limped behind the goat as if he were stomping holes in the ground. He traveled like an undulating wave, faster and faster. His wife tried to drag him back but could not. Thus distracted, he walked for some distance. The goat was carried along a winding path over the slope and placed on a square table with a red cloth in the center of the yard.

The widow from East Village knelt in front of the table and prayed for a while. Then she lit two red candles on the table. That done, Two-and-a-Half Li knew it was time to kill his goat.

Except for old Zhao San, the men milling around the center of the yard were young. They bared their chests and arms, looking powerful and savage.

Zhao San kept speaking to the widow from East Village—he'd begun propagandizing to her the moment he saw her. Now, whenever anything happened, he no longer puffed greedily on his pipe. And to show he was really serious, he no longer wiggled his beard as he spoke

"The time to save our country has come. No hot-blooded person would ever submit to being a slave to the invader. No, he'd rather die by a Japanese bayonet."

Zhao San knew only that he was Chinese. No matter how many times people explained things to him, he remained unsure as to what class of Chinese he belonged. Even so, he was considered progressive. In fact, he represented the progress made by the entire village. In prior days he hadn't understood what a nation was. In prior days he could even have forgotten his own nationality. He stopped talking and stood quietly in the center of the yard, waiting for the grand ceremony to begin as an expression of grief and indignation.

More than thirty people formed an impressive assembly. Zhao San's heart stirred. Even his whiskers seemed to sense the solemnity of the occasion and would not bear to be touched.

The April sky streamed down the ridges of the hill. Around the house, tall trees stood bowed beneath the midday sun. Bright daylight joined in the oath taking with the human beings.

At a command from Li Qingshan, the widows and single men who had lost their families knelt beneath the sky. Daylight fell on the back of the goat; the red candles burned before the heads of the silent crowd. Li Qingshan stood tall and erect in front of the table. "Brothers, what day is today? Do you know? Today is the day we dare to die . . . it is decided . . . even if all our heads swing from branches of village trees, we will not flinch, right? Isn't that right, brothers?"

Response came first from the widows: "Yes, even if we're cut into a million pieces!"

The shrill voices stabbed like an awl at the heart of everyone present. For a brief moment, sorrow swept through the crowd of bowed heads. The blue sky seemed about to fall.

Old Zhao San stood in front of the table; even before he spoke, his tears began to flow:

Chinese/manchuria under Jap suppression. Japs taking women.

"The nation . . . the nation is lost! I . . . I am old, too. You're still young, you go save the nation! My old bones . . . useless! I'm an old nationless slave, and I'll never see you rip up the Japanese flag. Wait till I'm buried . . . plant a Chinese flag over my grave, for I am Chinese! I want a Chinese flag. I don't want to be a nationless slave. Alive I'm Chinese, and when I'm dead, I'll be a Chinese ghost . . . not a nation . . . nationless slave."

The concentrated, irreducible grief caused even the trees to bow down. Standing before the red candles, Zhao San knocked hard on the table twice. In unison, the crowd directed their supplications and tears toward the blue sky. The crowd fell to weeping and wailing.

A loaded gun was placed before the assembly. By turns, everyone walked up to it and knelt to take the oath.

"If I am not sincere, may Heaven slay me; may this gun end my life. The bullet has eyes, is all-knowing and sacred."

Even the widows took their oaths with the gun aimed at their hearts. But Two-and-a-Half Li did not return until after the oath taking, when the assembly was about to kill the goat. He had managed to find a rooster somewhere. He was the only person who did not take the oath. He didn't seem particularly distressed about the fate of the nation as he led the goat home.

Everyone's eyes, especially old Zhao San's, angrily followed his departure.

"You crippled old thing. Don't you want to go on living?"

14 TO THE CITY

On the eve of her departure, Golden Bough sharpened a pair of scissors on the rim of the water jug. Then she cut her dead baby's diapers into strips. The young widow was now living with her mother.

"Do you have to leave tomorrow?"

Light from the lamp awakened her mother, who was sleeping beside her. Filled with infinite tenderness, the old woman sought comfort in her already determined fate.

"No, I can wait a couple days more," Golden Bough replied.

After a while, the old woman woke up again, no longer able to sleep. Seeing that her daughter was not beside her, but was doing some laundry, she sat up and asked:

"You're not leaving tomorrow, are you? Can't you stay on a few more days?"

It had been during the night, when Golden Bough was packing her things, that her mother realized she intended to leave.

"Ma, I'll only be gone two days, I'll be back. Ma . . . don't worry."

Seemingly groping for something, the old woman said nothing in response.

The sun was already high in the sky, but Golden Bough was still nestling against her ailing mother, who said:

"Do you have to go, Golden Bough? I guess if you must, you must. Go earn some money; I won't hold you back." There was sadness in her voice. "But behave yourself and don't copy other people. And stay away from men."

The women no longer felt any enmity toward their husbands. The girl wept.

"It's all the doing of those little Japs? Those damned Japs! If I stay, I'm just asking to be killed."

Golden Bough had heard from the old folks that a woman traveling alone should make herself up to look old or ugly. So she girded herself with a belt, from which she hung an oilcan and a little bucket holding rice. Then she stuffed a bundle of needles, thread, and rags into the bucket. To make herself resemble an old beggar woman, she smeared her face with dust until it was dirty and streaked.

Before she set out, her mother removed the silver earrings from her own ears and said:

"Take these with you. Put them in your bundle, and don't let anybody get their hands on them. I don't have any money to give you, but if you find yourself with nothing to eat, you can sell them for food." As the girl walked out the door, she heard her mother say:

"And if you run into the Japs, hide yourself among the mugwort stalks."

Even after Golden Bough had walked quite a distance and was heading down an incline, her mother's words continued to ring in her ears: "Buy some food." Her mind cluttered with disconnected thoughts, she didn't notice how far she'd gone. To her it felt like running away from home; she walked swiftly without looking back. The narrow, overgrown path slowed her down a bit.

Just then a horse cart carrying Japanese soldiers, cigarettes dangling from their mouths, came down the road. Golden Bough began to quake. Remembering her mother's warning, she quickly lay down in the weeds. After the soldiers had passed, she stood up with a pounding heart and looked around apprehensively. Where was her mother? Her home was far behind her. Soon she came to an unfamiliar village and began to feel as if she'd passed through countless worlds.

The red sun had reached the edge of the sky, and the shadow she cast was as long and thin as a post. After crossing a small bridge, she wouldn't have much farther to go.

Through the haze she saw the chimneys of Harbin factories rising up into the clouds.

She drank from the river, then looked back in the direction of home. It was completely out of sight. She could see only the hilltops. There, at the foot of the hills, was that smoke, or was it trees she was seeing? Her mother was there, amid the smoke or the trees.

How hard it had been to leave the hills of her home. Her heart seemed to have flown out of her breast, torn out and cast aside. Not really wanting to continue on, she forced herself to cross the bridge and walk down a small path. There, in front of her, the city of Harbin beckoned, while behind her the hills of her village bade farewell.

There was no tall grass growing on this path, so what would she do if Japanese soldiers came? Hide in the cracks in the ground? She kept a wary eye, but, owing to her flustered state and sweaty face, she was ultimately stopped by Japanese soldiers.

"You there . . . halt!"

As if shot, Golden Bough rolled into a ditch. The soldiers approached and took a look at her dirty appearance. Then, like fat ducks, they made little quacking noises and waddled away without paying her any attention. Long after they'd gone, she still hadn't gotten up. Finally the tears came. Her bucket lay there overturned; her little bundle had rolled out. She started walking once again, her shadow growing thinner and longer, like a fine thread. *Vampirism— consumed.*

That first night in Harbin, Golden Bough slept on a drainage-ditch cover near a street inhabited by workers and rickshaw pullers; nearby there were small restaurants and the lowest class of prostitutes, the latter appearing frequently in the doorways of the small houses clad in red pants. Men with nothing better to do had that special look in their eyes as they chatted and joked with the girls in red pants. Then they went into the houses and, after a while, came out again. None of them paid any attention to the ragged-looking Golden Bough. She might as well have been a garbage can or a sick dog curled up there.

There weren't even policemen on this street, where old beggar women exchanged insults with waiters from the restaurants.

The sky was covered with stars, but they were too remote to have anything to do with Golden Bough. After midnight a small dog came up to her. An abused animal, perhaps? The stray dog crept inside the wooden bucket to sleep. When Golden Bough awoke, the sun had still not risen, and the sky was still covered with stars.

Vagrants bunched up in front of the restaurants waiting for hand-outs. Golden Bough's legs ached so badly they felt broken; she didn't dare stand up. But finally she squeezed in among the beggars, where she waited in vain for a waiter to come out with some food. Having slept in the chilled May air, she couldn't stop shivering. Embarrassed by the stares of all the people, she went back to where she'd spent the night, despite her hunger.

What sort of world is a street at night? Golden Bough whimpered softly for her mother, her body knocking incessantly on the drainage-ditch cover as she shivered. Despair. Tears. Yet, like the little dog sleeping in the bucket, she was ignored. To the rest of the world it was as if they didn't exist. When day dawned, she didn't feel hungry, only empty. Her head was a void. Beneath a roadside tree she met an old woman who did mending.

"I'm new here," she said. "I just came from the countryside."

Noting her distressed state, the old woman paid no attention to her and moved away, her face white in the clear, cool morning. The curly-tailed little dog snuggled up against the bucket as it would its own mother; the morning air was probably too chilled for it.

Gradually people began going in and out of the restaurant, and a stack of steaming hot buns appeared in the shop window.

"Old Auntie, I'm new here from the countryside. May I go with you to earn a few pennies?"

This time Golden Bough was successful, for the old woman took her along. As they passed down noisy, foul-smelling streets, Golden Bough began to understand. This was definitely not the countryside; here there were only alienation, barriers, and insensitivity. As they traveled, except for the displayed chicken and the fish, and the aromas coming from the restaurants, she saw and heard nothing.

"This is how you darn socks."

In front of a place that boasted a gold sign reading Opium Specialty Shop, Golden Bough opened up her bundle and, after snipping a corner off a piece of fabric, mended the socks of men she didn't know. The old woman gave her some good advice:

"You have to work fast. Never mind if it's well done or not. Just sew up all the holes."

Golden Bough had no strength left. She wished she could die then and there. No matter how hard she tried, she couldn't keep her eyes open. A motorcar whizzed past. Then a policeman came and ordered:

"Move over there! Do you think this is a place to be frequented by the likes of you?" *Cruelty of Chinese → IA I hate the Chinese.*

Golden Bough looked up. "Mr. Soldier, I just got here from the countryside, and I don't know the rules yet."

In the countryside she was accustomed to using the term "Mr. Soldier," and that is how she addressed the policeman, since he looked imposing and packed a gun at his side. The passersby laughed at her. So did the policeman.

"Pay no attention to him," the old seamstress admonished her, "and there's no need to talk, either. If he says anything to you, just move on, that's all."

Golden Bough realized she was blushing. Looking down at herself, she saw that her clothes were different from other people's. Developing an instant dislike for an old jug she'd brought from the village, she aimed a kick at it.

The socks were mended, but the empty feeling in her stomach had not gone away. If she could have managed it, she'd have gone somewhere—anywhere—to steal some food. She rested her needle for a long time as she stared at a boy eating a biscuit on the street corner. She was still watching him even after he'd crammed the last piece into his mouth.

"Hurry up. When you finish, you can have some lunch. Have you had breakfast?"

Golden Bough experienced a feeling of such warmth she felt like crying. She wanted to say: *insensitivity*

"I haven't had anything since last night, not even a drop of water."

When noon came, they walked with the lost souls who emerged from the Opium Shop. The women's shelter had a particularly dead atmosphere, which reminded Golden Bough again that this was not the countryside. But it wasn't until after lunch, when everyone was washing up, that she noticed their lackluster eyes and sallow faces. The shelter was no more than five yards in length, with no dividers. The walls were smeared with the blood of bedbugs; the surfaces of the walls were spotted here and there with black and purple bloodstains. Dirty, moldy bundles were strewn about in heaps. The motley group of women laid their heads down on the bundles, as if they were all sick, and talked.

"The mistress at my house treats me real nice. I eat the same food they eat. Why, even if they eat buns with meat stuffing, that's what I eat, too."

The others listened with envy. After a while, someone said she'd been pinched on the cheek by one of the servants at her residence. She said she was so upset over this that she'd fallen ill. After that, she continued with some meaningless chatter. Golden Bough understood none of these bits and pieces of conversation; she was still trying to figure out what a "residence" and a "mistress" were. She exhausted her reasoning before asking a woman with short hair who was smoking beside her:

"Doesn't mistress mean old woman?"

The woman didn't answer her. Instead she laid down her tobacco pipe and vomited. Golden Bough remarked that she must have swallowed a fly when she was eating. Laughter rose from the city women up and down the long *kang*, which irritated Golden Bough. They rocked back and forth, so tickled by this countrywoman they were slapping each other on the shoulders. Some laughed until tears ran down their cheeks, as Golden Bough sat quietly off to the side. At night, when it was time for bed, she spoke to the old woman who had befriended her.

"I think Harbin's a lot worse than the countryside. The sisters there are kind. But you saw how these women laughed at me today."

As she spoke she rolled her bundle tighter—inside she had secreted the two ten-cent bills she'd earned. Using her bundle as a pillow, she went to sleep among the bedbugs of the city.

Golden Bough earned quite a bit of money. After sewing a little pocket into the waistband of her pants, she put in a two-dollar bill, and then sewed up the opening. When the woman from the shelter came to collect her fee, she said:

"I'll give it to you in a few days, all right? I haven't earned anything." She couldn't very well repeat her earlier excuse of, "Let me pay it tonight. I'm new from the countryside."

This time the woman refused to be put off. She stuck her hand under Golden Bough's eyes, palm up. The women began to gather and formed a circle around Golden Bough. It was almost as if she were performing tricks to attract spectators. Among them was a fat woman in her thirties whose hair had fallen out and whose pink shiny scalp stood out in the crowd. Her neck was seemingly set on springs; she could rotate and shake her shiny head with ease and at will.

"Come on, pay up," she said to Golden Bough. "How can you say you don't have any money? I even know where you hid it."

This so angered Golden Bough angry that right there in front of everyone she tore open her pocket. She was about to lose three-quarters of her earnings. When that was snatched away from her, she only had fifty cents left.

"How can I give Mother a measly fifty cents?" she thought. "And how many more days will I have to work to earn another two dollars?"

She went out into the street and worked till very late. That night the squashed bedbugs were nauseating. Golden Bough sat up, itching all over, and scratched until she bled. Upstairs she heard two women quarreling. Later she heard a woman weeping. Then the children began to cry.

"Has Mother gotten over her illness? Is she able to gather firewood for herself? When it rains, does the roof leak?" Gradually her thoughts turned morbid: "If Mother were to die on the *kang*, no one would ever know.

Golden Bough was walking along when a bicycle, its bell ringing, sped past. Her heart quickened as if a motorcar had just missed her. She ceased fantasizing.

Golden Bough had learned how to earn a living: several times a day she went to the single men's dormitory to sew bedcovers.

"How old is your husband?"

"He's dead."

"How old are you?"

"Twenty-seven."

A man wearing slippers, his pants unbuttoned, glanced at Golden Bough with a strange look and moved his strange lips:

"Well, well, a young widow."

She was too naive to understand the significance of his remark. When she finished the sewing, she took her money and left. On one occasion, as she was leaving, a man called to her:

"Come back here . . . come back."

The urgent call set off an alarm; Golden Bough knew she had to leave at once and not turn back. That night as she lay down to sleep, she asked Zhou Daniang:

"After I finish sewing and am leaving with my money, why do the men call me back?"

"How much money do you charge them?" Zhou Daniang asked.

"For a bedcover they give me fifty cents."

"No wonder they call you back. Why else would they give you so much? Normally, a bedcover is only worth twenty cents."

The worn-out Zhou Daniang had but one more thing to say:

"No poor sewing woman can escape their clutches."

The bald woman with the shiny scalp on the opposite *kang* shrieked and came up to Golden Bough. Twisting her fingers as if she wanted to pull out her hair, she said:

"Ah, my fine young widow, you're in luck. You'll have both money and pleasure."

Other women in the room, awakened by the bald woman's loud voice, began to curse her:

"You damned wild woman. You're not afraid of a hundred men. In fact, a hundred men wouldn't be enough for you!"

The women cursed and talked among themselves. Some were laughing loudly as one of them kept repeating:

"Talk about being afraid—even a hundred men wouldn't be enough!"

Finally, like a swarm of noisy bees that has calmed down, the women stopped buzzing and drifted off to sleep.

"Talk about being afraid—even a hundred men wouldn't be enough!"

Who said it that time no one knew, for it fell on deaf ears. It traveled around the room once and dissipated on the moonlit window paper.

Golden Bough stood outside the screened window of a Russian pastry shop. Inside, displayed on shelves, were all kinds of creamy yellow pastries, sausages, ham, and little chicks. All those delicacies lay there glistening with oil. Eventually she noticed an entire fat piglet on a long tray, its ears standing straight up. Around it were placed cabbage leaves and chili peppers. She felt like walking up, grabbing the platter, and taking it home to show Mother. But, of course, she couldn't do that. Her hatred for the Japs flared up again. If not for the Japs wreaking havoc in the village, her own sow would long ago have given birth to piglets. The bundle hanging from the crook of her elbow slid slowly down her arm as she stood fidgeting in front of the shop. The street grew more crowded, and she began bumping into other pedestrians. A lovely Russian woman came out of the pastry shop; Golden Bough no-

ticed her painted toenails peeking out from her sandals. She walked
very fast, faster than a man, and was soon out of sight.

From the pavement came loud noises: *clomp clomp*. A troop was
passing by. As soon as Golden Bough saw the helmets, she knew they
were Japanese soldiers, and walked quickly away from the pastry shop.

She met Zhou Daniang, who said to her:

"I couldn't find work at all. This jacket's the only one I own. I can't
save up enough to buy a few feet of cloth. Every ten days I have to pay
a fee to the shelter—one-fifty each time. I'm old and my eyes are weak,
and since I'm so slow at my work, no one ever asks me to come to his
place to do any sewing. I'm a month behind in my board payments.
Fortunately, I've been here many years. If I was a newcomer, they'd
have kicked me out long ago." She walked a block before continuing:
"That newcomer, old Mrs. Zhang, was sick, but they still sent her
away." *insensitive, cruel, cold Chinese women*

They passed a butcher shop, and Golden Bough found herself lingering there. If only she could buy a pound or so of meat to take home,
she'd be content. "Mother hasn't tasted meat for over six months."

The Sungari River—its waters flowed on. Since it was too early for
travelers, the boat operators sat around chatting and exchanging wise-
cracks. As she sat at the river's edge, Zhou Daniang was silent for a
second, then she wiped her eyes. Her tears flowed for the final days of
her life, while the river water lapped gently against the bank.
? People commit suicide?

Golden Bough, however, was unmoved. She'd just arrived in the city
and didn't know it well enough yet.

For the sake of money, for the sake of her livelihood, she cautiously
followed a single man to his room. As soon as she stepped through the
door and noticed the bed, she sensed danger; so instead of sitting on
the edge of the bed, she sat on a chair to sew the bedcover. The man
began to talk to her, slowly at first, each sentence causing her heart to
speed up. But nothing happened, and Golden Bough felt that he must
have taken pity on her. Next she mended the sleeve of his shirt, which
he took off in front of her. When that was finished, he took a dollar
from his money belt, and as he handed it to her, he made a sympa-
thetic gesture with his moustache-topped mouth and commented:

"Poor little widow, who is there to take pity on you?"

As a peasant, Golden Bough was moved by the word "pity," unable
to see that the man's sympathy was not genuine. With emotion welling
up in her heart, she paused at the door to thank him. But not knowing

what to say, she left. The whistle of a teakettle at a roadside stall greeted her. Vehicles parked in front of the bakery were loading bread. An elderly Russian woman's red scarf whizzed past her.

"Hey, come back . . . come back here. I've got something else for you to mend."

His neck flushed and swollen, the man came after her. But when she returned to his room, there was no work for her. Like a gorilla, the man bared his hairy chest and turned to lock the door with his pudgy hands. Next he undid his pants and said to her:

"Come . . . little darling." When he saw the terror in her eyes, he stopped. "I'm asking you to mend my pants. What are you afraid of?"

After she'd finished, he took out a dollar bill. But instead of putting it in her hand, he tossed it under the bed so she'd have to stoop to pick it up. Then when she retrieved it, he snatched it from her so she'd have to pick it up again.

Suddenly, Golden Bough was engulfed in his arms. She implored hoarsely:

"Forgive me, Mother . . . Mother, forgive me!"

In vain she screamed, her round eyes staring at the locked door she could not open. There was no escape, and what followed was inevitable.

After dinner at the shelter, Golden Bough was treading on waves of tears. She was light-headed; her heart seemed to have fallen into the gutter. Her legs turned rubbery and threatened to give way as she crawled up onto the *kang* to get her old shoes and a handkerchief. She wanted to return to the village, to lie down beside her mother and cry her heart out.

A sick woman at the end of the *kang* was being kicked out even though she was on the verge of death, but the women set aside their discussion of her situation, for Golden Bough had attracted their attention.

"What's the matter? Why are you so troubled?" Zhou Daniang was first to ask.

"She must have cashed in!" The second one to speak was the fat, bald woman.

Zhou Daniang too must have sensed that Golden Bough had earned some extra money, since any newcomer who "earned extra money" for the first time felt ashamed. Shame was devouring Golden Bough now. She felt like the victim of a contagious disease.

"You'll get used to it. It's nothing. Money's the only thing that's real. That's how I got these golden earrings."

The fat, bald woman tried to console her by showing off her ears with her hands. But the others were having none of it:

"You slut. You have no shame at all!"

The women around Golden Bough witnessed her distress, for her suffering was their suffering. But gradually they went back to bed, showing no more sign of surprise or interest in the incident.

Courage had taken Golden Bough to the city, but shame drove her back to the village. On the branches of a tree at the entrance to the village she saw some human heads. A feeling coursed through her marrow, chilling and paralyzing her from head to toe. What horrible, bloody heads!

When her mother took the dollar bill, she grinned so broadly her teeth were exposed. As she studied the pattern on the bill, she was beside herself with joy.

"Stay the night. You can go back tomorrow."

Golden Bough sat on the edge of the *kang* massaging her sore legs. Her mother couldn't see why she was so unhappy, for the bill in front of her led her thoughts to the next one. In her mind she wondered if there was anything that could keep her from handling more and more of these bills. She must encourage her daughter.

"Wash your clothes and tidy up a bit. You can take off early tomorrow morning. There's no future in the village."

In her impatience she sounded as if she were scolding her daughter, as if she didn't care for her at all.

The window flew open and the dark-faced armed man jumped in, stepping on Golden Bough's left leg as he did so. He glanced at the rafters, and with practice climbed up. Mother Wang walked over. She hadn't seen Golden Bough for many days, yet she didn't stop to talk; she seemed oblivious to everything around her as she scrambled up into the rafters. Not knowing what was happening, both Golden Bough and her mother followed him up. Not until dusk fell and no bad news had come did they all crawl down like reptiles. Mother Wang said:

"Harbin must be a lot better than here in the countryside. Next time don't come back. The Japs are getting worse and worse. Now they're slitting open the bellies of pregnant women as a response to the volunteer army called the Red Gun Society. The live fetuses slide right out of their bellies. So to avenge them, Li Qingshan chopped off the heads of two Japs and hung them from a tree."

Golden Bough snorted:

patriarchy　　*evil across national boundaries.*

"I used to hate men, and now I hate those Japs." She'd finally reached the nadir of personal grief: "If I hate the Chinese as well, then there's nothing else for me to hate."

Mother Wang's knowledge no longer seemed the equal of Golden Bough's.

15 THE DUD

As the troops moved out and rounded the bend of Southern Hill Road, children in their mothers' arms bade farewell to their fathers. The men marched down the tree-lined road and past the riverbank; their dress and gait did not suggest a troop of soldiers, but their clothing hid fierce and strong hearts. It was these hearts that led them on. And so they set out with hearts solid as bronze. A split second before the last man disappeared over the slope, a baby in his mother's arms cried out: "Daddy." The boy's cry elicited no response; his father didn't so much as wave. The boy's cry seemed to have come up against solid granite.

The women returned to their houses, which now seemed empty. It was as if they were built in the air; sunlight shining in through the window held no meaning. They didn't need for the men to come home; they needed only good news. Five days later the news came. With his pants rolled up to expose a pair of sinewy legs, old Zhao San ran to Second Aunt Li and reported:

"I hear that Qingshan and the rest were beaten back." He was clearly in a state of panic. Even his whiskers seemed startled, ready to jump off his face.

"Are they really coming back?"

Second Aunt Li's throat was like a long, fine tube, and her voice sounded shrill.

"Ping'er is," Zhao San said.

A night of solemnity descended from the sky. Japanese soldiers raided Fishing Village, White Banner Hamlet, Three-Family Village . . .

Ping'er was at Widow Wang's house relaxing on his mistress' lap when the dogs began to bark outside. Then he heard the Japanese talking, and he fled over the wall. As he hid in a patch of mugwort stalks, toads leaped at his feet.

"We have to catch that guy. He might have ties with the volunteer army."

While lying amid the stalks, he heard someone say: "Running dogs!" He recognized the voice.

He then heard the sounds of his mistress being beaten.

"Where did he go? Speak up or you'll be shot."

Over and over they cursed: "You bitches, you're all bred by pigs."

Ping'er was stark naked. After he'd run awhile, he felt for the lapel of his coat to wipe his sweat; there was no lapel. He felt his legs, then realized that his shadow on the ground was naked as a newborn baby.

Two-and-a-Half Li's pockmarked wife was killed. So was Tunnel Legs. With two people slain, the village was left alone for two days. But on the third day it was time to kill again, and Japanese soldiers overran the village. Ping'er went to Golden Bough's house to spend the night in the rafters, but she said:

"No, those devils were just here to search the rafters."

So Ping'er was back in the fields, running, as a spray of bullets followed him. His eyes were frozen in place; he heard them yell:

"Take him alive . . . alive!"

No sound escaped him. He came to a door and burst in; an old man was cooking a meal. Ping'er was close to tears.

"Save me, uncle, hide me. Help me, quick!"

"What's wrong?" the old man asked.

"The Japs are after me."

Ping'er's nose started bleeding as soon as he mentioned the Japs. He looked around the house, but there was no place to hide. So he turned to run back outside, but the old man grabbed him and dragged him out the back door. A manure trough stood beside the door. The old man lifted up the lid and said:

"Crawl in here and control your breathing."

The old man put some sticky rice on two strips of paper and pasted them over the door. Then he returned to his meal. From the manure trough Ping'er heard the old man talking with someone. After that, someone tried the door. "The door's going to open and I'll be caught." He was about to jump out of the trough, but then the men—the devils—left.

Ping'er emerged from his hiding place, manure stuck to his ashen face. What with the streaks of blood and his nose still bleeding, he looked a sorry sight.

Li Qingshan now believed in the effectiveness of the Revolutionary Army. When he made it back to the village, he wasn't as pessimistic as the others. In Mother Wang's house he said:

"What's good about the Revolutionary Army is that they don't do things in a half-assed manner. They've got discipline. They've made a believer out of me. The Red Whiskers are finished. All they do is fight among themselves and make a mess of things."

This time few people listened to him, for they no longer trusted him. All country folk are easily discouraged. Everyone felt that the end was near. Zhao San alone did not lose faith.

"Let's organize and join the Revolutionary Army," he said.

To Mother Wang, Zhao San sounded like a naïve child, but she didn't laugh at him. Sitting next to her and wearing a man's hat was a courageous young woman who had joined the bandits and fought for her country.

"You left the dead behind, but what about the wounded?" Mother Wang asked her.

"Those with light wounds all returned, didn't they? There was nothing we could do for the seriously wounded. They're as good as dead."

Just then an old woman from North Village charged in, weeping hysterically and intent on tearing Li Qingshan to pieces. Holding her head as if it were a rock, she dashed toward the wall, uttering almost incoherently:

"Li Qingshan . . . enemy . . . you led my son to his death!"

They tried to drag her away, but she was stronger than a crazed bull. "I can't go on. You might as well deliver me over to the Japs! I want to die . . . it's time for me to die."

She kept tearing at her hair as she sank slowly to the ground, out of breath. She patted Mother Wang's knees gently.

"Old sister, you know how I feel. Widowed at nineteen, I struggled for decades, struggled for the boy . . . all those days I had to go hungry, I went with my son to the hillside to cut grasses. But the rains came, and we were washed down the hill. My head, I thought it was broken. Who'd have thought . . . but I didn't die . . . I should have died a long time ago."

Her warm tears soaked through and drenched Mother Wang's knees. She began to sob quietly.

"Tell me, what's left for me? I might as well die. With the Japs waiting, the girl Linghua will never live to adulthood. She might as well die too."

And die they did. They were found hanging from a roof beam, the three-year-old Linghua alongside her grandmother. They swung high like a pair of long, thin fish.

The death rate in the village was on the rise again, but the people seemed not to notice. As if caught in the throes of an epidemic, the village struggled in delirium.

The Patriotic Army passed through Three-Family Village flying a yellow flag on which the words "Patriotic Army" were spelled out in red. Some of the men fell in behind it. They did not know how to be patriotic, nor did they know what good would come of their patriotism, but they knew they were hungry.

Li Qingshan did not go with them. He complained that this too was a bandit army. Zhao San had a fight with his son over the Patriotic Army.

"I think you should go. If word leaks out that you're here, someone will come to get you. Go take a look around with them. Even if you end up by killing only one Jap devil, that's still something. It's a chance for revenge. You're young and strong, and revenge is good." *Desire for revenge keeps them living*

Zhao San lacked experience, and this kind of blustering talk could never convert his son. When Ping'er talked with his father, he usually rolled his eyes or shrugged his shoulders. Zhao San resented this kind of treatment.

"Why isn't old Zhao San a young Zhao San?" he sometimes wondered silently.

16 THE NUN

Golden Bough decided to become a nun. *nobody to love / obliterate all hatred*

The red brick nunnery was on the other side of the hill. She tried to open the gate, but it wouldn't budge. Sparrows were pecking in the middle of the courtyard; the stone steps were overgrown with green moss. She questioned a woman next door, who told her:

"After the occupation, the nun disappeared. I heard she ran off with the carpenter who was building the temple."

Golden Bough peered through the gate and could see that the windows hadn't been put up. Pieces of wood of varying lengths lay in the middle of the yard. She could see into the front hall, where a small clay statue of Buddha sat despondently.

Golden Bough observed the woman's swollen belly.

"How can you dare show your face in your condition?" she asked the woman. "Haven't you heard that the Japs use pregnant women to get back at the Red Gun Society? They slit open the women's bellies and take the fetuses with them into battle. They say that the Red Gun Society is afraid of women, and nothing else. The Japs even nicknamed the Red Guns the Iron Children."

The woman began to weep.

"I said I didn't want to get married, but my mother wouldn't listen. She said that the Japs are interested in young maidens. Look at me now. What am I going to do? The baby's father joined the volunteer army and hasn't been back since."

Someone crawled out from the back of the temple. Golden Bough and the woman ran off in terror.

"What's the matter with you? Am I a ghost or something?"

The handsome young man of earlier days had come home crawling like a half-dead snake. When Fifth Sister came out and saw him, she was reminded of a wounded stallion.

"Has the Revolutionary Army been routed?" she asked him

"Yes. All dead. I barely got away." He swung at the grass stalks.

"Well, my unfaithful little wife. Seeing me like this, don't you have some sweet words for me?"

Fifth Sister's head drooped like a sleeping sunflower. The pregnant woman went back into her house. But where could Golden Bough go? The temple on which she had set her heart had long since been abandoned.

17 THE UNSOUND LEG

"Where's the People's Revolutionary Army?" Two-and-a-Half Li blurted out to Zhao San. This set Zhao San to thinking: "Has Two-and-a-Half Li turned traitor?" He wouldn't answer his question, so Two-and-a-Half Li went to ask Qingshan.

"Don't ask questions," Qingshan said. "In a few days you can come with me."

Two-and-a-Half Li acted like a man who couldn't wait to join the Revolutionary Army.

"The Revolutionary Army is at Monument Rock," Qingshan said to him. "Do you think you can you get there alone? You don't have the guts. You can't even kill a goat." Then, as a calculated insult, he added:

"How is your goat faring?"

In his anger, Two-and-a-Half Li rolled his eyes until they showed more white than black. His enthusiasm turned to ice. Li Qingshan said nothing more, and stared at the trees framed against the sky. With a nod of his head, he began to sing a little tune. Two-and-a-Half Li was going out the door when Qingshan's wife, wet with perspiration from her work in the kitchen, said to him:

"Uncle Li, come have a bite with us before you go."

Qingshan, who had begun to feel sorry for him, smiled and said:

"What's the point of going home? You don't have a wife anymore. We'll eat first and talk later."

Having lost his own family, Two-and-a-Half Li felt a longing for the company of other people's families. So he picked up the chopsticks and quickly downed a bowl of wheat porridge. Then he ate two more bowls; before the others had finished, he was puffing on his pipe, passing up the soup.

"Have some soup. Cabbage soup, it's good."

"No. It's been three days since my wife died, and three days since I had a bowl of solid food," he said, shaking his head.

Qingshan cut in: "How about your goat, do you give it real rice?"

With a full stomach, everything looked brighter to Two-and-a-Half Li; so instead of getting angry, he laughed normally. He left Qingshan's house feeling contented, smoking his pipe as he walked along the small path. The boundless sky evoked no sadness in him. Frogs croaked beside the stream; small trees on the bank rustled in the wind. He trod on land that had once been his own vegetable plot, and memories stirred his heart. No vegetables were growing there now.

At dusk, he met an old woman and some children bent low in the field.

"What are you digging for?" he asked. "Buried treasure? If so, I'll get down and help."

"We're scrounging for grains of wheat," one of the children said crisply, apparently enjoying himself.

"Treasure? Good heavens, no," his grandmother sighed. "The children were so hungry I brought them here to glean some grains of wheat to go into the pot at home."

Two-and-a-Half Li passed his pipe over to the old woman, who stuck it into her mouth without wiping it off first. Obviously, she was accustomed to smoking a pipe, and in desperate need of it. She hunched her shoulders and shut her eyes as thick smoke poured from her mouth and issued from her nostrils. She looked as if her nose were on fire. "It's been more than a month since I touched a pipe."

She was reluctant to relinquish the pipe, but Two-and-a-Half Li took it from her and knocked the bowl against the ground.

The world was so lonely: no birds were flying at the crimson edge of the sky, and no dogs were barking beneath the people's fences.

The old woman removed a rolled-up piece of paper from her waistband, which she deliberately smoothed out and then refolded neatly.

"Read this at home," she said. "Your wife and son are both dead. Who can save you? Go home and read this, then you'll understand."

She pointed at the piece of paper as if a spell had been cast on it.

The sky was getting darker, so dark it seemed as if a curtain had been drawn around them. After a few steps, the youngest boy clasped his grandmother's leg and cried:

"Grandma, my basket's full. It's too heavy for me."

She picked up the basket and took his hand. The older children ran on ahead like scouts. When they arrived home, the grandmother lit a lamp and checked to see what they had gotten. The basket was filled with mugwort. It was overflowing with the stuff; there were no grains at all. The grandmother rapped the boy on the head and laughed.

"Is this the wheat you gleaned?" The smile on her face turned into a look of sadness. "The poor child can't even tell what's food and what isn't," she was thinking.

The Summer Festival. Even though it was summer, an autumn wind blew. Two-and-a-Half Li snuffed out the lamp and, with a stern heart, emerged from beneath the eaves, a cleaver in his hand. He looked in the corner of the yard, in the goat's pen, and beneath the poplar tree outside the yard. In order to free himself from all worries and ties, it seemed to him that he must kill the goat without delay.

It was the eve of Two-and-a-Half Li's departure.

The goat returned, bleating, with weeds stuck in its whiskers. It scratched itself noisily on the fence. Two-and-a-Half Li raised the cleaver above his head as he walked toward the fence. The cleaver flew through the air and felled a sapling.

The old animal came up and scratched itself against his legs. For a long time, Two-and-a-Half Li stroked its head. He was overcome with shame, and prayed to the goat like a Christian.

In the morning, he seemed to be talking to the goat again. He muttered for a while in the goat pen, then fastened the gate. The goat went on grazing.

The Summer Festival under sunny blue skies—to Zhao San, it didn't feel like the Summer Festival. The wheat had not sprouted, so he couldn't smell its fragrance, and no paper gourds hung above the doors. Everything had changed, he thought, and so swiftly. He could remember last year's festival, clearly and in great detail, as if it were happening before his eyes. Hadn't the children been catching butter-flies? Hadn't he been drinking? He sat on a fallen tree trunk in front of his house, mourning all that was now lost to him.

Li Qingshan passed by, made up like a laborer, barefoot and with his pant legs rolled up. "I'm leaving," he said to Zhao San. "People are waiting for me in town, so I have to go."

Qingshan made no mention of the Summer Festival.

From a distance Two-and-a-Half Li came limping up. There seemed to be a smile on his dark equine face.

"Look at you sitting here," he said to Zhao San. "I think you're go-ing to rot there on top of that log."

Two-and-a-Half Li turned and saw the goat, which he'd locked up in its pen, following him. Instantly his face grew even longer. "This old goat ... keep it for me, Third Brother Zhao. As long as you're alive, take care of it for me." He buried his hands in the goat's fur to say good-bye. His weeping hands caressed the goat's hair for the last time, then he ran to catch up with Li Qingshan. Behind him, the goat bleated over and over, its whiskers swaying slowly.

Two and a-Half Li hobbled along on his unsound leg. Soon he was a distant blur. Past the hill and the forest. Farther and farther. The goat, bleating in ignorant bliss, kept Zhao San company.

village life - not knowing cruelty of outside world

Value of goat

Realization

Xiao Hong

Tales of Hulan River

Preface to *Tales of Hulan River*

This April, rather sick at heart, I paid my third visit to Hong Kong. When I made up my mind in Chongqing to take this roundabout route back to Shanghai, I did so with mixed feelings and a sinking heart, afraid to travel by the way I myself had chosen, afraid Hong Kong would revive old memories which I wished to forget, yet was eager to recapitulate one last time before they were forgotten.

I stayed first in Canton for one busy, hectic month, so busy I hardly had time to dwell on the past, though I never relinquished hope of reliving it once before forgetting it. I planned to go to Prince Road in Kowloon to see the house where I lived during my first stay in Hong Kong, to see Butterfly Valley where my daughter liked to take her girl friends to play, and to find the American comics my son collected so carefully in those days. I would have a look too at the house on Kennedy Road where I lived during my second stay in Hong Kong, and the Dancing Academy on Tennessee Road where we took refuge after fighting broke out in Hong Kong on December 8. Most of all I was eager to visit Xiao Hong's grave by Repulse Bay.

I kept these fond hopes secret, though they gave me no peace whenever I was free; but I never summoned up the courage to realize them, and throughout my stay in Hong Kong went neither to Kowloon nor to Repulse Bay. As if against my own will, I kept away or found some pretext or other to postpone the visit, not that I had declared my intention to anyone or was being urged to go.

In the last twenty years and more I have had my full share of the joys and sorrows of life. If there is anything which, while not exactly enraging me or making me despair, nevertheless weighs so heavily on my heart that I long to forget it yet cannot easily do so, it is an early death, a lonely death. Somehow a death in battle distresses us less than that of one who has given up childhood's pleasures to search for truth and studied hard to be of use to her country and people, only to die when her student days are over, like a bullet never fired from a gun—this transcends the bounds of simple grief and pity. An untimely death had dealt me a cruel blow, one I longed to forget yet could not easily banish from my mind. So it was futile, during that third visit to Hong Kong, to think of going back to Butterfly Valley. That was not the only place hallowed by memory, and even had I gone I doubt if I could have buried my sorrow there.

Those whose high hopes of life are repeatedly dashed must feel lonely. Even more lonely was she who had confidence in her ability and an ambitious plan of work, yet was so depressed by the cruelty of life that she became unhappy and frustrated. When on top of her spiritual loneliness she suddenly discovered that her days were numbered and there was no remedy for anything, her lonely anguish must have passed all telling. Her lonely death, too, weighed heavily on my heart; I longed to forget it yet could not easily do so. That is why I meant to go to Repulse Bay but against my will put off going time and again.

II

Xiao Hong's grave lies alone by Repulse Bay in Hong Kong.

During the bathing season each year the place is gay with crowds of pleasure-seekers, but Xiao Hong lies lonely there.

In December 1940, a year or so before she died and while her health was still fairly good, Xiao Hong finished her last book, *Tales of Hulan River*. But even then she was lonely.

Moreover, *Tales of Hulan River* shows us what a lonely childhood she had. Read the brief epilogue to the book and you sense Xiao Hong's loneliness as she recalled her lonely childhood days.

In April, the year after she finished this work, Xiao Hong was urged by Agnes Smedley to go to Singapore. (Agnes spent nearly a month in Hong Kong on her way back to the States. When Xiao Hong asked about the situation in the Pacific, she said the Japanese were bound to attack Hong Kong and the South Seas, and Hong Kong could not hold out for more than a month, but Singapore was virtually impregnable, and even if it fell there would be more ways of escape there.) Xiao Hong tried to persuade my wife and me to go too. But I did not want to leave Hong Kong, and had work to keep me there. Imagining Xiao Hong was afraid of being caught in Hong Kong when it fell (if war actually broke out there), I did my best to reassure her. Little did I know that her eagerness to leave arose from her sense of loneliness in Hong Kong, and that she hoped by leaving Hong Kong to escape from that fearful loneliness. This was just after the Southern Anhui Incident, when many writers and artists from the interior had gone to Hong Kong, so that there was more cultural activity there than ever before. Such being the case, it was hard to understand Xiao Hong's sense of isolation. By the time I knew and understood it, she had been buried for nearly a year by Repulse Bay.

In the end, instead of going to Singapore, Xiao Hong fell ill and entered St. Mary's Hospital. In hospital, naturally, she was even more lonely; but her will to live was strong, and hoping to recover she put up with the loneliness of hospital life. Her case was a complicated one, and the attitude of the doctors was outrageous: when finally they diagnosed tuberculosis, they told her they had no drugs to cure her. Still, Xiao Hong was convinced she would recover. Even after fighting broke out in Hong Kong and the shelling seemed just as likely to carry her off as illness, she dreaded the first possibility more; although the greatest threat to her remained her sense of loneliness.

She did not recover from the final operation. Hong Kong had already fallen by then, and most of her friends were away when she breathed her last, so that she departed this life in loneliness.

III

Tales of Hulan River shows us the loneliness of Xiao Hong's childhood.

Life was dull for the precocious little girl. Year after year they planted cucumbers and pumpkins; year after year her playground was the backyard where on fine days there were butterflies, grasshoppers and dragonflies, or the dark, dusty back room piled high with junk. Her only companion was her kindly old grandfather, still a child at heart. In bed in the morning she recited the Tang poems the old man taught her. In the daytime she pestered him to tell the stories she knew only too well, or watched the neighbors, so set in their ways it seemed nothing could change in their lives in a thousand years. If a ripple sometimes disturbed this stagnant pool, it was only when the child bride in the Hu family fell ill, they summoned a soothsayer, and she finally died; or when Harelip Feng suddenly acquired a wife and baby, when later on his wife suddenly died, leaving him with a second child, a new-born baby.

Life in the little town of Hulan River was equally dead and dull.

Life followed a strict pattern the whole year round: dances to exorcise spirits, rice-sprout songs, a lantern festival, operas performed in the open, the big fair at the Immortal Matron's Temple on the eighteenth of the fourth month . . . and the other big, boisterous festivals every year. Yet these festivals were as dull and dead as their ordinary life.

Not that life in the little town lacked sound and color.

From every street, lane and thatched hut, from behind every wicker fence, rose the sound of nagging and quarreling, weeping and laughter, even delirious raving. In every season of the year, the big boisterous festivals which followed each other in due order stood out against the gray background of everyday life like splashes of red and green, bright primitive colors.

Of course, most of them were kindly folk on the banks of the Hulan.

Their thoughts and lives were governed by traditions handed down for thousands of years. They might seem apathetic at times, but in fact they were highly sensitive and particular: they could spend three days and three nights debating and fighting about some trifling matter. They might seem stupid and barbarous, but they did not want to harm others or themselves. They just "did what had to be done" according to their lights.

Of course, we sympathize with the sad fate of the child bride in old Hu's family. We pity her and hate the unfair way she was treated. Yet our hatred is not directed against her mother-in-law because we pity Mrs. Hu, too, regarding her as another victim of the age-old traditions. Her "stand"—which calls more for pity than for hatred—is shown in the way she gladly spends five hundred strings of cash to hire a sooth-sayer to cure the child bride. She made no bones about her attitude, saying:

"I haven't abused her all the time she's been in my house. Where will you find another family that hasn't abused its child bride by giving her beatings and tongue-lashings all day long? Now I may have beaten her a little, but just to get her started off on the right foot, and I only did that for a little over a month. Maybe I beat her pretty severely sometimes, but how was I expected to make a well-mannered girl out of her without being severe once in a while? Believe me, I didn't enjoy beating her so hard, what with all her screaming and carrying on. But I was doing it for her own good, because if I didn't beat her hard, she'd never be good for anything."

Why did Mrs. Hu believe so firmly that she must teach the child bride a good lesson? What displeased her about the girl? The day that the child came to her house, the neighbors' comments were:

"She isn't at all shy around people."

"She isn't a bit shy. Her first day at her mother-in-law's house she ate three bowls of rice!"

"How could a fourteen-year-old be that tall?" (That was unseemly too.)

Because she did not measure up to the neighbors' idea of what a child bride should be, Mrs. Hu had to teach her a lesson; and because the spirited girl would not knuckle under but screamed and shouted and wanted to go home, she had to be beaten hard for a month or more.

The neighbors naturally had no feud with the girl but felt this was for her own good, to make her behave like a normal child bride. So when as a result of this "discipline" she fell ill, Mrs. Hu gladly went to the expense of hiring a soothsayer and trying other means to cure her, while the neighbors eagerly rallied round with advice.

And the result? The result was that a "dark-skinned, laughing" child of twelve, who passed for fourteen and was taller and stronger than most girls of fourteen, was hounded out of this life to her "final home."

The little town of Hulan River was full of sound and color of every kind, yet it was dead and dull.

Life in the little town was lonely.

Xiao Hong passed her childhood in these lonely surroundings. It goes without saying that they left an indelible mark on her mind.

The child bride, who unconsciously defied the age-old traditions, died; and Xiao Hong, who consciously defied these traditions, recollected the lonely little town with a smile but with tears in her eyes. Her heart remained lonely even in the great age of a mighty struggle.

IV

Some readers may not regard *Tales of Hulan River* as a novel.

They may argue: No single thread runs through the whole book, the stories and characters in it are disconnected fragments, the work is not an integrated whole.

Others may look upon *Tales of Hulan River* as an autobiography of an unorthodox sort.

To my mind, the fact that it is not an orthodox autobiography is all to the good and gives it an added interest.

And we may counter: The main point is not that this work is not a novel in the strict sense, but that it has other qualities more "attractive" than those to be found in the average novel. It is a narrative poem, a colorful genre painting, a haunting song.

Satire is here, and humor. At the start you read with a sense of relaxation; then little by little your heart grows heavier. Still there is beauty, slightly morbid perhaps but bound to fascinate you.

You may complain that the work contains not a single positive character. Nothing but poor creatures, full of self-pity, yet choosing to be slaves to tradition. And the author's attitude toward them is perplexing. Flaying them ruthlessly, she nevertheless sympathizes with them. She shows us the stupidity, obstinacy and sometimes the cruelty of these slaves to tradition, yet presents them as by nature good, not given to cheating, hypocrisy, or living in idle comfort, but very easily satisfied. This is true of Second Uncle, the old cook, the whole of old Hu's family, and the men who make bean noodles. Like the lowest forms of plant life, they can live with a minimum of water, soil and sunlight—even with no sunlight at all. Harelip Feng of the mill has the most vitality of them all, so much so that we cannot but admire his spirit. And yet we find nothing outstanding about his character, apart from the tenacity of his will to live, and that is a primitive tenacity.

If we search for a weakness in the author's outlook, we shall probably find it not in the absence of positive characters but in the impression their nightmare existence makes on readers. If not for their own stupidity and conservatism, and the trouble they bring on themselves, their life has its pleasanter side. We are shown no trace of feudal oppression and exploitation, no trace of the savage invasion of Japanese imperialism. But these must surely have weighed more heavily on the people by the Hulan than their own stupidity and conservatism.

V

When Xiao Hong wrote this book, she was lonely.

She was virtually "hibernating" in Hong Kong. It is hard to understand how a woman with her high ideals, who had struggled against reaction, could "hibernate" in such stirring times as the years just before and after 1940. A friend of hers, trying to explain her frustration and apathy, ascribed them to a series of emotional shocks which confined this poet richer in feeling than intellect within the small circle of her private life. (Although she condemned this circle, some inertia kept her from breaking boldly with it.) She was cut off completely from the tremendous life and death struggle being waged outside. As a result, although her high principles made her frown on the activities of the intellectuals of her class and regard them as futile talk, she would not plunge into the laboring masses of workers and peasants or change her life radically. Inevitably then, she was frustrated and lonely. This has cast a shadow over *Tales of Hulan River*, evident not only in the mood of the whole work but in its ideological content as well. This is to be regretted just as we deeply regret Xiao Hong's untimely death.

MAO DUN

After the harsh winter has sealed up the land, the earth's crust begins to crack and split. From south to north, from east to west; from a few feet to several yards in length; anywhere, anytime, the cracks run in every direction. As soon as harsh winter is upon the land, the earth's crust opens up.

The severe winter weather splits the frozen earth.

Old men use whiskbrooms to brush the ice off their beards the moment they enter their homes.

"Oh, it's cold out today!" they say. "The frozen ground has split open."

A carter twirls his long whip as he drives his cart sixty or seventy li under the stars, then at the crack of dawn he strides into an inn, and the first thing he says to the innkeeper is:

"What terrible weather. The cold is like a dagger."

After he has gone into his room at the inn, removed his dog-skin cap with earflaps, and smoked a pipeful of tobacco, he reaches out for a steamed bun. The back of his hand is a mass of cracked, chapped skin.

The freezing cold splits open the skin on people's hands. The man who sells cakes of bean curd is up at dawn to go out among the people's homes and sell his product. If he carelessly sets down his square wooden tray full of bean curd, it sticks to the ground, and he is unable to free it. It will have quickly frozen to the spot.

The old steamed bun peddler lifts his wooden box filled with steaming buns onto his back, and at the first light of day he is out hawking on the street. After emerging from his house, he walks along at a brisk pace shouting at the top of his lungs. But before too long, layers of ice have formed on the bottoms of his shoes, and he walks as though he were treading on rolling and shifting eggs. The snow and ice have encrusted the soles of his shoes. He walks with an unsure step, and if he is not altogether careful he will slip and fall. In fact, he slips and falls despite all his caution. Too bad, for his wooden box crashes to the ground, and the buns come rolling out of the box, one after the other. A witness to the incident takes advantage of the old man's inability to pick himself up and scoops up several of the buns, which he eats as he leaves the scene. By the time the old man has struggled to his feet, gathered up his steamed buns—ice, snow, and all—and put them back in the box, he counts them and discovers that some are missing. He understands at once and shouts to the man who is eating the buns, but hasn't gone too far:

"Hey, the weather's icy cold, the frozen ground's all cracked, and my buns have been swallowed up!"

Passersby laugh when they hear him say this. He then lifts the box up onto his back and walks off again, but the layers of ice on the soles of his shoes seem to have grown even thicker, and the going is more difficult than ever. Drops of sweat begin to form on his back, his eyes become clouded with the frost, icicles gather in even greater quantity on his beard, and the earflaps and front of his tattered cap frost up with the vapor from his breath. The old man walks more and more slowly, his worries and fears causing him to tremble in alarm; he looks like someone on ice skates for the first time who has just been pushed out onto the rink by a friend.

A puppy is so freezing cold it yelps and cries night after night, whimpering as though its claws were being singed by flames.

The days grow even colder.

Water vats freeze and crack.

Wells are frozen solid.

Night snowstorms seal the people's homes; they lie down at night to sleep, and when they get up in the morning, they find they cannot open their doors.

Once the harsh winter season comes to the land, everything undergoes a change: the skies turn ashen gray, as though a strong wind had blown through, leaving in its aftermath a turbid climate accompanied by a constant flurry of snowflakes whirling in the air. People on the road walk at a brisk pace, their breath turning to vapor in the wintry cold. Big carts pulled by teams of seven horses form a caravan in the open country, one following closely upon the other, lanterns flying, whips circling in the air under the starry night. After running two li the horses begin to sweat. They run a bit farther, and in the midst of all that snow and ice, the men and horses are hot and lathered. The horses stop sweating only after the sun emerges and they are finally turned into their stalls. But the moment they stop sweating, a layer of frost forms on their coats.

After the men and horses have eaten their fill they are off and running again. Here in the frigid zones there are few people; unlike the southern regions, where you need not travel far from one village to another, and where each township is near the next, here there is nothing but a blanket of snow as far as the eye can see. There is no neighboring village within the range of sight, and only by relying on the memories of those familiar with the roads can one know the direction to travel. The big carts with their seven-horse teams transport their loads of foodstuffs to one of the neighboring towns. Some have brought in soybeans to sell, others have brought sorghum. Then when they set out on their return trip, they carry back with them oil, salt, and dry goods.

Hulan River is one of these small towns, not a very prosperous place at all. It has only two major streets, one running north and south and one running east and west, but the best-known place in town is The Crossroads, for it is the heart of the town. At The Crossroads there is a jewelry store, a dry goods shop, an oil store, a salt store, a teashop, an herbal pharmacy, and the office of a foreign dentist. Above this dentist's door there hangs a large shingle on which is painted a row of oversized teeth about the size of a rice-measuring basket. The advertisement is hopelessly out of place in this small town, and the people who look at it cannot figure out just what it's supposed to represent. That's because neither the oil store, the dry goods shop, nor the salt store displays any kind of advertisement. Above the door of the salt store, for example, only the word "salt" is written, and hanging above the door of the dry goods shop are two curtains that are as old as the shop. The remainder of the signs are like the one at the pharmacy, which gives nothing more than the name of the bespectacled physician whose job it is to feel women's pulses as they drape their arms across a small pillow. To illustrate: the physician's name is Li Yongchun, and the name of his pharmacy is simply "Li Yongchun." People rely on their memories, and even if Li Yongchun were to take down his sign, the people would still know that he was there. Besides the townsfolk, even people from the countryside are pretty familiar with the streets of the town and what can be found there. No advertisement, no publicity is required. If people are in need of something, like cooking oil, some salt, or a piece of fabric, then they go in and buy it. If they don't need anything, no matter how large a sign may hang outside, they won't buy anything.

That dentist is a case in point. When people from the countryside spot those oversized teeth, they stare at them in bewilderment, and there are often people standing in front of the large sign looking up at it, unable to fathom what it is. Even if one of them were standing there with a toothache, under no circumstances would he let that dentist, with her foreign methods, pull his tooth. Instead he'd go over to the Li Yongchun Pharmacy, buy two ounces of an herb called gold thread, take it home and hold it in his mouth, and let that be the end of that! The teeth on that advertisement are simply too big, too hard to figure out, and just a little frightening.

As a consequence, although that dentist hung her shingle out for two or three years, precious few people ever went to her to have their teeth pulled. Eventually, most likely owing to her inability to make a living, she had no recourse but to engage in midwifery on the side.

In addition to The Crossroads, there are two other streets, one called Road Two East and the other called Road Two West. Both streets run from north to south, probably for five or six li. There's nothing much on these two streets worth noting—a few temples, several stands where flat cakes are sold, and a number of grain storehouses.

On Road Two East there is a fire mill in a spacious courtyard, a large chimney made of fine red brick rising high above it. I've heard that no one is allowed to enter the fire mill, for there are a great many knobs and gadgets inside that must not be touched. If someone did touch them, he might burn himself to death. Otherwise, why would it be called a fire mill? Owing to the flames inside, the mill is reportedly run neither by horses nor donkeys—it's run by fire. Most folks wonder why the mill itself doesn't go up in flames, since only fire is used. They ponder this over and over, but are unable to come up with an answer, and the more they ponder it, the more confused they become, especially since they are not allowed to go inside and check things out for themselves. I've heard they even have a watchman at the door.

There are also two schools on Road Two East, one each at the southern and northern ends. They are both located in temples—one in the Dragon King Temple and one in the Temple of the Patriarch—and both are elementary schools.

The school located in the Dragon King Temple is for the study of raising silkworms, and is called the Agricultural School, while the one in the Temple of the Patriarch is just a regular elementary school with one advanced section added, and is called the Higher Elementary School.

Although the names for these two schools vary, in fact the only real difference between them is that in the one they call the Agricultural School the silkworms are fried in oil in the autumn, and the teachers there enjoy a few sumptuous meals.

There are no edible silkworms in the Higher Elementary School, where the students are clearly taller than those in the Agricultural School. The students in the Agricultural School begin their schoolwork by learning the characters for "man," "hand," "foot," "knife," and "yardstick," and the oldest among them cannot be more than sixteen or seventeen. But not in the Higher Elementary School; there's a twenty-four-year-old student there who is learning to play the foreign bugle and who has already taught in private schools in the countryside for four or five years, but is only now attending the Higher Elementary School. Even the man who has been a grain shop bookkeeper for two years is a student at that school.

When this elementary school student writes a letter to his family he asks questions like: "Has Little Baldy's eye infection gotten better?" Little Baldy is the nickname of his eldest son, who is eight. He doesn't mention his second son or his daughters, because if he were to include them all, the letter would be much too long. Since he's already the father of a whole brood of children—the head of a family—whenever he sends a letter home he is mainly concerned with household matters: "Has tenant Wang sent over his rent yet?" "Have the soybeans been sold?" "How is the market these days?" and the like.

Students like him occupy a favored position in the class; the teacher must treat them with due respect, for if he drops his guard, this kind of student might stand up, classical *Kangxi Dictionary* in hand, and stump the teacher with one of his questions. He will smugly point out that the teacher has used the wrong character in a phrase he has written on the board.

As for Road Two West, not only does it lack a fire mill, it has but one school, a Moslem school situated in the Temple of the City God. With this exception, it is precisely like Road Two East, dusty and barren. When carts and horses pass over these roads, they raise up clouds of dust, and whenever it rains, the roads are covered with mud. There is an added feature on Road Two East: a five- or six-foot-deep quagmire. During dry periods the consistency of the mud inside is about that of gruel, but once it starts to rain, the quagmire turns into a river. The people who live nearby suffer because of it: When their houses are splashed with the water, they wind up covered with mud; and when the waters subside, as the sun reappears in the clearing sky, hordes of mosquitoes emerge to fly around their homes. The longer the sun shines, the more homogenized the quagmire becomes, as if something were being refined in it, as if someone were trying to refine something inside. If more than a month goes by without any rain, the quagmire becomes even more homogenized. All the water having evaporated, the mud has turned black and has become stickier than the gummy residue on a gruel pot, stickier even than paste. It takes on the appearance of a big melting vat, gummy black with an oily glisten, and even swarming flies and mosquitoes stick to it when they land.

Swallows love water, and sometimes they imprudently fly down to skim their wings over the water. It's a dangerous maneuver, as they nearly fall victim to the quagmire, coming perilously close to being mired down in it. Quickly they fly away without a backward glance.

In the case of horses, however, the outcome is different: they invariably bog down in it; even worse, they tumble down into the middle of the quagmire, where they roll about, struggling to free themselves. After a period of floundering they lie down, their energy exhausted, and the moment they do so they are in danger of losing their lives. But this does not happen often, for few people are willing to run the risk of leading their horses or pulling their carts near this dangerous spot.

Most of the accidents occur during drought years, when two or three months pass with no rain, and the big quagmire is at its most dangerous. On the surface it would seem that the more rain there is, the worse the situation, for then a veritable river of water is formed, nearly ten feet in depth. One would think this would make it especially perilous, since anyone who fell in would surely drown. But that is not the case. The people of this small town of Hulan River aren't so stupid that they don't know how brutal this pit can be, and no one would be so foolhardy as to try leading a horse past the quagmire at such times.

But if it hasn't rained for three months the quagmire begins to dry up, until it is no more than two or three feet deep, and there will always be those hardy souls who will attempt to brave the dangers of driving a cart over it or those with somewhat less courage who will watch others make their way past, then follow across themselves. One here, two there, and soon there are deep ruts along both sides of the quagmire formed by the passage of carts. A late arrival spots the signs of previous passings, and this erstwhile coward, feeling bolder than his intrepid predecessors, drives his cart straight ahead.

How could he have known that the ground below is uneven? Others had safely passed by, but his cart flips over.

The carter climbs out of the quagmire, looking like a mud-spattered apparition, then begins digging to free his horse from the mud, quickly making the sad discovery that it is mired down in the middle of the quagmire. Passersby come over to lend a helping hand.

These passersby can be divided into two types. Some are attired in traditional long gowns and short jackets, and are spotlessly clean. Apparently none of them will move a finger to assist in this drama because their hands are so clean. Needless to say, they are members of the gentry class. They stand off to the side and observe the goings-on.

When they see the horse try to stand up, they applaud and shout, "Oh! Oh!" several times. But then they see that the horse is unable to stand and falls back down; again they clap their hands and again they shout several times, "Oh! Oh!" But this time they are registering their displeasure.

The excitement surrounding the horse's attempts to stand and its inability to do so continues for some time, but in the end it cannot get to its feet and just lies there pitifully. By this time those who have only been watching the feverish activity conclude that this is about all that will happen, that nothing new will materialize, and they begin to disperse, each heading off to his home.

But let us return to the plight of the horse. The passersby trying to free it are all common folk, some of the town's green onion peddlers, vegetable sellers, tile masons, carters, and other workers. They roll up their trouser cuffs, remove their shoes, and, seeing no alternative, walk down into the quagmire with the hope that by pooling their strength they will be able to hoist the horse out.

But they fail in their attempts, and by this time the horse's breathing has grown faint. Growing frantic, they hasten to free the horse from its harness, releasing it from the cart on the assumption that it will be able to get up more easily once it is freed from that burden.

But contrary to their expectations, the horse still cannot stand up. Its head sticks up out of the mire, ears twitching, eyes shut, snorts of air emerging from its nostrils.

Seeing this sad state of affairs, people from the neighborhood run home to get ropes and levers. They use the ropes to secure the horse and the levers to pry it free. They bark out orders as if they were building a house or a bridge; finally they manage to lift the animal out.

The horse is still alive, lying at the side of the road. While some people pour water over it and wash the mud off its face, there is a constant flow of people at the scene of the spectacle.

On the following day everyone is saying:

"Another horse has drowned in the quagmire!"

As the story makes its rounds, even though the horse is actually still alive, it is said to have died, for if the people didn't say that, the awe in which they held that big quagmire would suffer.

It's hard to say just how many carts flip over in the quagmire. Throughout the year, with the exception of the winter season, when it is sealed up by the freezing weather, the quagmire looks as if it has acquired a life of its own—it is alive. Its waters rise, then subside; now it has grown larger, in a few days it recedes again. It is an object of enormous concern to all the people.

When the water is high, it is an obstacle not only to horses and carts, but to pedestrians as well. Old men pass along its edge with trembling legs; children cry and wail as they skirt around it.

Once the rain begins to fall, water quickly fills the now glistening quagmire, then overflows and covers the bases of neighboring walls. For people out on the street who approach this place, it is like being dealt a setback on the road of life. They are in for a struggle: sleeves are rolled up, teeth are clenched tightly, all their energy is called forth; hands clutch at a wooden wall, hearts pound; keep your head clear, your eyes in focus . . . face the challenge calmly.

Why is it that this, of all walls, has to be so smooth and neatly built, as if its owners have no intention of coming to anyone's aid in their moment of distress? Regardless of how skillfully pedestrians reach out, the wall offers no succor; clawing here and groping there, they grab nothing but handfuls of air. Where in the world is there a mountain on which wood like this grows, so perfectly smooth and devoid of blemishes or knots?

After five or six minutes of struggling, the quagmire has been crossed. Needless to say, the person is by then covered with sweat and hot all over. Then comes the next individual, who must prepare himself for a dose of the same medicine. There are few choices available to him—about all he can do is grab hold here and clutch there. After five or six minutes he too has crossed. Then, once he's on the other side, he feels revitalized, bursts out laughing, and looks back to the next person to cross, saying to him in the midst of his difficult struggle:

"What's the big deal? You can't call yourself a hero unless you've faced a few dangers in your life."

But that's not how it always goes—not all are revitalized; in fact, most people are so frightened that their faces are drained of color. There are some whose trembling legs are so rubbery after they have crossed the quagmire that they cannot walk right away.

For timid souls like this, even the successful negotiating of this dangerous stretch of road cannot dispel the sorrow that has settled upon them; their fluttering hearts seemingly put into motion by the quagmire, they invariably cast a look behind them and size it up for a moment, looking as if they want to say something. But in the end they say nothing, and simply walk off.

One very rainy day a young child fell into the quagmire and was rescued by a bean curd peddler. Once they got him out, they discovered he was the son of the Agricultural School principal. A lively discussion ensued. Someone said that it happened because the Agricultural School was located in the Dragon King Temple, which angered the venerable Dragon King. The Dragon King had caused the heavy downpour in order to drown the child.

Someone disagreed with him, saying that the cause of the incident rested with the father, for during his highly animated lectures in the classroom he had once said that the venerable Dragon King was not responsible for rainfall, and for that matter, did not even exist. Knowing how furious this would make the venerable Dragon King, you can imagine how he'd find a way to vent his anger! So he grabbed hold of the son as a means of gaining retribution.

Someone else said that the students at the school were so incorrigible that one had even climbed up onto the old Dragon King's head and capped him with a straw hat. What are the times coming to when a child who isn't even dry behind the ears would dare to invite such tremendous calamities down upon himself? How could the old Dragon King not seek retribution? Mark my word, it's not finished yet. Don't get the idea that the Dragon King is a moron! Do you think he'd let you off once you've provoked his anger? It's not like dealing with a rickshaw boy or a vegetable peddler whom you can kick at will, then let him be on his way. This is the Dragon King we're talking about! Do you think that the Dragon King is someone who can easily be pushed around?

Then there was someone who said that the students at that school were truly undisciplined, and that with his own eyes he'd seen some of them in the main hall putting silkworms into the old Dragon King's hands. How do you think the old Dragon King could stand for something like that?

Another person said that the schools were no good at all, and that anyone with children should not allow them to go to school, since they quickly lost respect for everyone and everything.

Someone remarked that he was going to the school to get his son and take him home—there would be no more school for him.

Someone else commented that the more the children study, the worse they become. Take, for example, when their souls are frightened out of their bodies; the minute their mothers call for the souls to return, what do you think they say? They announce that this is nothing but superstition! Now what in the world do you think they'll be saying if they continue going to school?

And so they talked, drifting further and further away from the original topic.

Before many days had passed, the big quagmire receded once again, and pedestrians were soon passing along either side unimpeded. More days passed without any new rainfall, and the quagmire began to dry up, at which time carts and horses recommenced their crossings; then more overturned carts, more horses falling into it and thrashing around; again the ropes and levers appeared, again they were used to lift and drag the horses out. As the righted carts drove off, more followed: into the quagmire, and the lifting began anew.

How many carts and horses are extricated from the quagmire each year may never be known. But does no one ever think of solving the problem by filling it in? No, not a single one.

An elderly member of the gentry once fell into the quagmire at high water. As soon as he crawled out he said:

"This street is too narrow. If you have to pass by this water hazard there isn't even room to walk. Why don't the two families whose yards are on either side take down their walls and open up some paths?"

As he was saying this, an old woman sitting in her yard on the other side of the wall chimed in with the comment that the walls could not be taken down, and that the best course of action would be to plant some trees; if a row of trees were planted alongside the wall, then when it rained, the people could cross over by holding on to the trees.

Some advise taking down walls and some advise planting trees, but as for filling up the quagmire, there isn't a single person who advocates that.

Many pigs meet their end by drowning in this quagmire; dogs are suffocated in the mud, cats too; chickens and ducks often lose their lives there as well. This is because the quagmire is covered with a layer of husks; the animals are unaware that a trap lies below, and once they realize that fact it is already too late. Whether they come on foot or by air, the instant they alight on the husk-covered mire they cannot free themselves. If it happens in the daytime there is still a chance that a passerby by might save them, but once night falls they are doomed. They struggle all alone until they exhaust their strength and begin to sink slowly into the mire. The more they struggle, the faster they sink. Sometimes, they die without sinking below the surface, but that happens when the mud is gummy.

What might happen then is that some cheap pork will suddenly appear in the marketplace, and people's thoughts turn to the quagmire.

"Has another pig drowned in the quagmire?" they ask.

Once the word is out, the fleet-footed lose no time in running to their neighbors with the news:

"Hurry over and get some cheap pork. Hurry, hurry, before it's all gone."

After it's bought and brought home, a closer look reveals that there seems to be something wrong with it. Why is the meat all dark and discolored? Maybe this pork is plague-ridden. But on second thought, how could it be? No, it must have been a pig that drowned in the quagmire. So then family after family sautés, fries, steams, boils, and then eats this cheap pork. But though they eat it, they feel always that it doesn't have a fragrant enough aroma, and fear it might have been plague after all. But then they think: "Plague-ridden pork would be unpalatable, so this must be from a pig that drowned in the quagmire."

Actually, only one or two pigs drown each year in the quagmire, three at the most, and some years not a single one. How the residents manage to eat the meat of a drowned pig so often is hard to imagine. I'm afraid only the Dragon King knows the answer.

Though the people who eat the meat say it is from a pig drowned in the quagmire, there are still some who get sick from it, and those unfortunates are ready with their opinions:

"Even if the pork was from a drowned pig, it shouldn't have been sold in the marketplace; meat from animals that have died isn't fresh, and the revenue office isn't doing its job if it allows meat like that to be sold on the street in broad daylight!"

Those who do not become ill are of a different opinion:

"You can't say that. You're letting your suspicions get the best of you. If you'd just eat it and not give it another thought, everything would be fine. Look at the rest of us. We ate it too, so how come we're not sick?"

Now and then a child lacking common sense will tell people that his mother wouldn't allow him to eat the pork since it was plague-ridden. No one likes this kind of child. Everyone gives him hard looks and accuses him of speaking nonsense.

For example, a child says that it's definitely plague pork—this he tells a neighbor right in front of his mother. There is little reaction from the neighbor, but the mother's face turns beet red. She smacks him.

But he's a stubborn child, and he keeps saying:

"It's plague pork! It's plague pork!"

His embarrassed mother picks up a poker lying by the door and hits him on the shoulder, sending him crying into the house. As he enters the room he sees his maternal grandmother sitting on the edge of the *kang*, so he runs into her arms.

"Granny," he sobs, "wasn't that plague pork you ate? Mama just hit me."

Now this maternal grandmother wants to comfort the poor abused child, but then she looks up to see the wet nurse of the Li family who shares the compound standing in the doorway looking at her. So she lifts up the back of the child's shirttail and spanks him loudly.

"Whoever saw a child as small as you speaking such nonsense?" she exclaims. She keeps spanking him until the wet nurse walks off with the Li child in her arms. By then, the spanked child is screaming and crying uncontrollably, so hard that no one can make heads or tails of his shouts of "plague pork this" and "plague pork that."

In all, the quagmire brings two benefits to local residents: The first is that the overturned carts and horses and the drowned chickens and ducks always produce a lot of excitement, which keeps the inhabitants buzzing for some time and gives them something to while away the hours.

The second is in relation to the matter of pork. Were there no quagmire, how could they have their plague pork? Naturally, they might still eat it, but how do they explain it away? If they simply admit they are eating plague pork, it would be too unsanitary for words. But the quagmire solves their problem: plague pork becomes the meat of drowned pigs, which means that when they buy the meat, not only is it economical, but there are no sanitation problems either.

II

Besides the special attraction of the quagmire, there is little else to be seen on Road Two East: one or two grain mills, a few bean curd shops, a weaving mill or two, and perhaps one or two dyeing establishments. These are all operated by people who quietly do their work, bringing no entertainment to the local inhabitants, and are thus unworthy of any discussion. When the sun sets, these people go to bed, and when the sun rises, they get up and begin their day. Throughout the year—warm spring with its blooming flowers, autumn with its rains, and winter with its snows—they simply feel the seasonal changes as they go from padded coats to unlined jackets. The cycle of birth, old age, sickness, and death is managed in complete silence.

Take, for example, Widow Wang, who sells bean sprouts at the southern end of Road Two East. She erected a long pole above her house, on top of which she hung a battered old basket. The pole is nearly on a level with the wind chimes atop the Dragon King Temple. On windy days the chimes clang, and although Widow Wang's battered basket doesn't, it makes its presence known by waving back and forth.

Year in and year out that's how it goes, and year in and year out Widow Wang sells her bean sprouts, passing her days tranquilly and uneventfully at an unhurried pace.

But one summer day her only son went down to the river to bathe, where he fell in and drowned. The incident caused a sensation and was the talk of the town for a while, but before many days had passed, the talk died away. Not only Widow Wang's neighbors and others who lived nearby, but her friends and relatives also soon forgot all about it.

As for Widow Wang, though this caused her to lose her mind, she retained her ability to sell bean sprouts and continued as before to live an uneventful, quiet life. Occasionally, someone would steal her bean sprouts, and she would be overcome by a fit of wailing on the street or on the steps of the temple; but it soon passed, and she returned to her uneventful existence.

Whenever neighbors or other passersby witnessed the scene of her crying on the temple steps, their hearts were momentarily touched by compassion, but only for a moment.

Some people are given to lumping together misfits of all kinds, such as the insane and the slow-witted, and treating them identically.

There are unfortunates in every district, every county, and every village: the tumorous, the blind, the insane, the slow-witted. There are many such people in our little town of Hulan River, but the local inhabitants have apparently heard and seen so much of them that their presence does not seem unusual. If, unhappily, they encounter one of them on the temple steps or inside a gateway alcove, they feel a momentary pang of compassion for that particular individual, but that is quickly supplanted by the rationalization that the world has untold numbers of such people. They then turn their glances away and walk rapidly past the person. Once in a while someone stops there, but he is just one of those who, like children with short memories, might throw stones at the insane or willfully lead the blind into a nearby water-filled ditch.

The unfortunates are beggars, one and all. At least that's the way it is in the town of Hulan River. The people there treat beggars in a most ordinary fashion. A pack of dogs bark at something outside the door, and the master of the house shouts out: "What are those animals barking at?"

"A beggar," the servant answers.

That ends the affair. Obviously, the life of a beggar is not worth a second thought.

The madwoman who sells bean sprouts cannot forget her grief even in her madness, and every few days she goes to wail at the steps of the temple; but once her crying has ended, she returns home to eat, to sleep, and to sell her bean sprouts. As ever, she returns to her quiet existence.

III

A calamity struck the dyer's shop: Two young apprentices were fighting over a woman on the street, when one of them pushed the other into the dyeing vat and drowned him. We need not concern ourselves here with the one who died, but the survivor was sent to prison for life.

Yet this affair too was disposed of silently and without a ripple. Two or three years later, whenever people mentioned the incident, they discussed it as they would the famous confrontation between the heroic general Yue Fei and the evil prime minister Qin Kuai, something that occurred in the long distant past.

Meanwhile the dyer's shop remains at its original location, and even the vat in which the young man drowned is quite possibly still in use to this day. The bolts of cloth that come from that dye shop still turn up in villages and towns far and near. The blue cloth is used to make padded cotton pants and jackets, which men wear in the winter to ward off the severe cold, while the red cloth is used to make gowns for eighteen- and nineteen-year-old girls for their wedding days.

In short, though someone had drowned in the dyer's shop on such and such a day during such and such a month and year, the rest of the world goes on as before without change.

Then there was the calamity that struck the bean curd shop: During a fight between two of the employees, the donkey that turned the mill suffered a broken leg. Since it was only a donkey, there wasn't much to be said on that score. But a woman lost her sight as a result of crying over the donkey (she was the mother of the employee who had hit the donkey), so the episode could not simply be overlooked.

Then there was the paper mill in which a bastard child was starved to death. But since it was a newborn baby, the incident didn't amount to much, and nothing more need be said about it.

IV

Then, too, on Road Two East there are a few ornament shops, which are there to serve the dead.

After a person dies, his soul goes down to the nether world, and the living, fearing that in that other world the dear departed will have no domicile, no clothes to wear, and no horse to ride, have these things made of papier-mâché, then burn them for his benefit. The townspeople believe that this is how they can ensure that the dead will have everything he needs in the nether world.

On display are grand objects like money-spewing animals, treasure-gathering basins, and great gold and silver mountains; smaller things like slave girls, maidservants, cooks in the kitchen, and attendants who care for the pigs; and even smaller things like flower vases, tea services, chickens, ducks, geese, and dogs. There are even parrots on the window ledges.

These papier-mâché objects are enormously eye-catching. There's a courtyard surrounded by a garden wall, the top of which is covered with gold-colored glazed tiles. Just inside the courtyard is the principal house, with five main rooms and three side rooms, all topped with green- and red-brick tiles; the windows are clean, the furniture spotless, and the air fresh as can be. Flowerpots are arranged on the flower racks; there are cassias, pure-white lilies, purslanes, September mums, and all are in bloom. No one can tell what season it is—is it summer or is it autumn?—since inexplicably, the flowers of the purslanes and the mums stand side by side; maybe there's no division of spring, summer, autumn, and winter in the nether world. But this need not concern us.

Then there is the cook in his kitchen, vivid and lifelike; he is a thousand times cleaner than a true-to-life cook. He has a white cap on his head and a white apron girding his body as he stands there preparing noodles. It seems that no sooner has lunchtime arrived than the noodles have been cooked and are ready to be served.

In the courtyard a groom stands beside a big white horse, which is so large and so tall that it looks to be an Arabian; it stands erect and majestic, and if there were a rider in the saddle, there's every reason to believe it could outrun a train. I'm sure that not even the general here in the town of Hulan River has ever ridden such a steed.

Off to one side stand a carriage and a mule. The mule is black and shiny, and its eyes, made of eggshells, are stationary. A fetching little mule with eyes as large as the big mule's stands beside it.

The carriage, with silvery wheels, is decorated in especially beautiful colors. The curtain across the front is rolled halfway up so people can see the interior of the carriage, which is all red and sports a bright red cushion. The driver perched on the running board, his face beaming proudly, is dressed magnificently, with a purple sash girding his waist over a fancy blue silk, embroidered gown, and black satin shoes with snow-white soles on his feet. (After putting on these shoes he probably drove the carriage over without taking a single step on the ground.) His cap is red with a black brim. His head is raised as if he disdained everything, and the more the people look at him, the less he resembles a carriage driver—he looks more like a bridegroom.

Two or three roosters and seven or eight hens are in the courtyard peacefully eating grain without making a sound, and even the ducks are not making those quacking noises that so annoy people. A dog crouching beside the door of the master's quarters maintains a motionless vigil.

All the bystanders comment favorably, each voicing his praise. The poor look at it and experience a feeling that it must be better to be dead than alive.

The main room is furnished with window curtains, beds, tables, chairs, and benches. Everything is complete to the last detail.

There is also a steward figuring accounts on an abacus; beside him is an open ledger in which is written:

"Twenty-two catties of wine are owed to the northern distillery.

"Wang Family of East Village yesterday borrowed 2,000 piculs of rice."

"Niren Hamlet of White Flag Village yesterday sent land rent of 430 strings of cash."

"Together the two hamlets of White Flag Village still owe land rent of 2,000 strings of cash."

Below these lines is written the date: "April twenty-eighth."

This page constitutes the running account for the twenty-seventh of April; the accounts for the twenty-eighth have evidently not yet been entered. A look at this ledger shows that there is no haphazard accounting of debts in the nether world, and a special type of individual whose job it is to manage these accounts. It also goes without saying that the master of this grand house is a landlord.

Everything in the compound is complete to the last detail and very fine. The only thing missing is the master of the compound, a discovery that seems puzzling: could there be no master of such a fine compound? This is bewildering and uncertain.

When they have looked more closely, the people sense something else unusual about the compound: how is it that the slave girls and maidservants, the carriage drivers and the groom all have a piece of white paper on their chests on which their names are written?

The name of the carriage driver, whose good looks give the appearance of a bridegroom, is:

"Long Whip."

The groom's name is:

"Fleet of Foot."

The name of the slave girl holding a water pipe in her left hand and an embroidered handkerchief in her right is:

"Virtuous Obedience."

The other's name is:

"Fortuitous Peace."

The man figuring accounts is named:

"Wizard of Calculations."

The name of the maid spraying the flowers with water is:

"Flower Sister."

A closer look reveals that even the big white horse has a name; the tag on its rump shows that it is called:

"Thousand-Li Steed."

As for the others—the mules, the dogs, the chickens, and the ducks—they are nameless.

The cook making noodles in the kitchen is called "Old Wang," and the strip of paper on which his name is written flaps with each gust of wind.

This is all quite strange: the master of the compound doesn't even recognize his own servants, and has to hang nametags around their necks! This cannot but confuse and bewilder people who think that perhaps this world of ours is better than the nether world after all!

But though that is the opinion of some, there are still many who are envious of this grand house, which is so indisputably elegant, peaceful, and quiet (silence reigns), neat and tidy, with no trace of disorder. The slave girls and maidservants are fashioned exactly like those in this world; the chickens, dogs, pigs, and horses are also just like those in this world. Everything in the world can be found in the nether world: people eat noodles in this world, and in the nether world they eat them too; people have carriages to ride in this world, and in the nether world they also ride them; the nether world is just like this world—the two are exactly alike.

That is, of course, except for the quagmire on Road Two East. Everything desirable is there; undesirable things need not be there.

V

These are the objects the ornament shops on Road Two East produce. The displayed handiwork is both awesome and eye-catching, but the inside of the shop is a mass of confusion. Shredded paper lies everywhere; there are rods and sticks all in a heap; crushed boxes and a welter of cans, paint jars, paste dishes, thin string, and heavy cord abound. A person could easily trip just walking through the shop, with its constant activity of chopping and tying, as flies dart through the air.

When making paper human figures, the first to be fashioned is the head; once it has been pasted together it is hung on a wall along with other heads—men's and women's—until it is taken down to be used. All that's needed then is to put it atop a torso made of rods and sticks on which some clothes have been added, and you have a human figure. By cutting up white paper hair and pasting it all over a stick-like papier-mâché horse, you have a handsome steed.

The people who make their living this way are extremely coarse, ugly men. They may know how to fashion a groom or a carriage driver, and how to make up women and young girls, but they pay not the slightest attention to their own appearance. Long scraggly hair, short bristly hair, twisted mouths, crooked eyes, bare feet and legs; it's hard to believe that such splendid and dazzlingly beautiful lifelike human figures could have been created by those hands.

Their daily fare is coarse vegetables and coarse rice; they are dressed in tattered clothes; and they make their beds among piles of carriages, horses, human figures, and heads. Their lives are bitter, though they actually just muddle their way through, day by day, the year round, exchanging their unlined jackets for padded coats with each seasonal change.

Birth, old age, sickness, death—each is met with a stoic absence of expression. They are born and grow in accordance with nature's dictates. If they are meant not to grow old, then so be it.

Old age—getting old has no effect on them at all: when their eyesight fails, they stop looking at things; when their hearing fades, they stop listening; when their teeth fall out, they swallow things whole; and when they can no longer move about, they lie flat on their backs. What else can they do? Anyone who grows old deserves exactly what he gets!

Sickness—among people whose diet consists of an assortment of grains, who is there who does not fall prey to illness?

Death—this, on the other hand, is a sad and mournful affair. When a father dies, his sons weep; when a son dies, his mother weeps; when a brother dies, the whole family weeps; and when a son's wife dies, her family comes to weep.

After crying for one, or as many as three, days, they must go to the outskirts of town, dig a hole, and bury the person. After the burial, the surviving family members still have to go back home and carry on their daily routine. When it's time to eat, they eat; when it's time to sleep, they sleep. Outsiders are unable tell that this family is now bereft of a father or has just lost an old brother. The members of the family don't even lock themselves in their home each day and wail. The only expression of the grief they feel in their hearts is to join the stream of people who go to visit the graves on the various festivals each year, as prescribed by local custom. During the Qingming Festival—a time for visiting ancestral graves—each family prepares incense and candles and sets out for the family gravesite. At the heads of some of the graves the earth has settled and formed a small pit, while others have several small holes in them. The people glance at one another, are moved to sighing, then light the incense and pour the wine. If the survivor is a close relative, such as a son, a daughter, or a parent, then they will let forth a fit of wailing, the broken rhythm of which makes it sound as if they were reading a composition or chanting a poem. When their incantation is finished, they rise to their feet, brush the dirt from their behinds, and join the procession of people leaving the gravesites to return to town.

Back home they must carry on as before. All year round there's firewood, rice, oil, and salt to worry about, and there's clothing to starch and mend. From morning till evening they're busy without respite. Nighttime finds them exhausted, and they're asleep as soon as they lie down on the *kang*. They dream neither of mournful nor happy events, but merely grind their teeth and snore, passing the night like every other night.

If someone were to ask them what man lives for, they would not be confounded by the question, but would state unhesitatingly, directly, and unequivocally:

"Man lives to eat food and wear clothes."

If they were then asked about death, they'd say: "When a man dies, that's the end of it."

Consequently, no one has ever seen one of those ornament craftsmen fashion an underworld home for himself; more than likely he doesn't much believe in the nether world. And even if there were such a place, he would probably open an ornament shop when he got there; worse luck, he'd doubtless have to rent a place to open the shop too.

VI

In the town of Hulan River, besides Road Two East, Road Two West, and The Crossroads, there remain only a number of small lanes.

There is even less worth noting on these small byways. One of the few little stalls where flat cakes and fried sesame twists are made and sold, and the tiny stands that sell red and green candy balls are mainly located where the lanes give out onto the road—few find their way into the lanes themselves. People who live in these lanes seldom see a casual stroller. They hear and see less than other people, and as a result pass their lonely days behind closed doors. They live in broken-down huts, buy two pecks of beans, which they salt and cook to go with their rice, and there goes another year. These people are isolated and lonely.

A peddler hawking a basket of flat cakes at the eastern end of the lane can be heard at the western end. Although the people inside the houses don't normally buy any, whenever he stops at their doors, they poke their heads out to take a look, and may on occasion even ask a price or ask whether or not the glazed or fried sesame twists still sell for the same price as before.

Every once in a while someone will walk over and lift up the piece of cloth that covers the basket, as if she were a potential customer, then pick one out and feel to see if it's still hot. After she has felt it, she puts it right back, and the peddler is not the least bit angry. He simply picks up his basket and carries it to the next house.

The lady of this second house has nothing in particular to do either, so she too opens up the basket and feels around for a while. But she also touches one without buying.

When the peddler reaches the third house, a potential custom is waiting for him. Out from the house comes a woman in her thirties who has just gotten up from a nap. Her hair is done up in a bun, and probably because it isn't very neat, she has covered it with a black hairnet and fastened it with hairpins. But since she's just slept on it, not only is her hair a mess, even the hairpins have worked their way out, so that the bun atop her head looks as if it has been shot full of darts.

She walks out of her house in high spirits, throwing the door open and virtually bursting through the doorway. Five children follow in her wake, each in high spirits; as they emerge they look like a platoon marching in a column.

The first one, a girl of twelve or thirteen, reaches in and picks out one of the sesame twists. It's about the length of a bamboo chopstick, and sells for fifty strings of cash. Having the quickest eye among them, she has chosen not only the biggest one in the basket, but the only one in that size category.

The second child, a boy, chooses one that sells for twenty strings of cash.

The third child also chooses one that sells for twenty strings of cash; he, too, is a boy.

After looking them all over, the fourth child has no alternative but to choose one that sells for twenty strings of cash; and he, too, is a boy

Then it's the fifth child's turn. There's no way of telling if this one is a boy or a girl—no hair on the head, a clip hanging from one ear, skinny as a dry willow branch, but with a protruding belly, it looks to be about five years old. The child sticks out its hands, which are far blacker than any of the other four children's—the hands of the other four are filthy black, all right, but at least they still look like human hands and not some other strange objects. Only this child's hands are nondescript. Shall we call them hands? Or what shall we call them? I guess we can call them anything we like. They are a mottled mixture of blacks and grays, darks and lights, so that looking at them, like viewing layers of floating clouds, can be a most interesting pastime.

The child sticks its hands into the basket to choose one of the sesame twists, nearly each of which is touched and felt in the process, until the entire basket is a jumble. Although the basket is fairly large, not many twists had been inside to begin with: besides the single big one, there were only ten or so of the smaller ones. After this child has turned them all over, the ones that remain are strewn throughout the basket, while the child's black hands are now covered with oil as well as being filthy, and virtually glisten like ebony.

Finally the child cries out:

"I want a big one."

A fight erupts by the front door.

The child, a fast runner, takes out after its elder sister. Its two elder brothers also take off running, both easily outdistancing this smallest child. The elder sister, holding the largest twist in her hand, is unimaginably faster on her feet than the small child, and in an instant she has found a break in the wall and has jumped through. The others follow and disappear on the other side. By the time all the others have made it through the wall, she has jumped back across and is running around the yard like a whirlwind.

The smallest child—the one of indeterminate sex—cannot catch up and has long since fallen behind, screaming and crying. Now and then, while the elder sister is being held fast by her two brothers, the child runs over and tries to snatch the sesame twist out of her hand, but after several misses, falls behind again, screaming and crying.

As for their mother, although she looks imposing, actually she cannot control the children without using her hands, and so, seeing how things are going, with no end in sight, she goes into the house, picks up a steel poker, and chases after her children. But unhappily for her, there is a small mud puddle in the yard where the pigs wallow, and she falls smack into the middle, the poker flying from her hand and sailing five feet or so away.

With that this little drama reaches its climax, and every person watching the commotion is in stitches, delighted with the whole affair. Even the peddler is engrossed in what is happening, and when the woman plops down into the mud puddle and splashes muck all over, he nearly lets his basket fall to the ground. He is so tickled he has forgotten all about it.

The children, naturally, have long since disappeared from sight. By the time the mother gets them all rounded up she has regained her imposing parental airs. She has each of them kneel on the ground facing the sun to form a line, then has them surrender up their twists.

Little remains of the eldest child's twist—it was broken up in the commotion.

The third child has eaten all of his.

The second one has a tiny bit left.

Only the fourth one is still clenching his.

As for the fifth child, well, it never had one to begin with.

The whole chaotic episode ends with a shouting match between the peddler and the woman, after which he picks up his basket and walks over to the next house to try to make another sale. The argument between the two of them is over the woman's wanting to return the sesame twist that the fourth child had been holding onto all that time. The peddler flatly refuses to take it back, and the woman is just as determined to return it. The end result is that she pays for three twists and drives the peddler with his basket out of her yard.

Nothing more need be said about the five children who were forced to kneel on the ground because of those twists; as for the remainder of twists that had been taken into the lane to be handled and felt by nearly everyone, they are then carried over into the next lane and eventually sold.

A toothless old woman buys one of them and carries it back wrapped in a piece of paper, saying:

"This sesame twist is certainly clean, all nice and oily."

Then she calls out to her grandchild to hurry on over.

The peddler, seeing how pleased the old woman is, says to her:

"It's just come from the pan, still nice and warm!"

VII

In the afternoon, after the sesame twist peddler has passed by, a seller of bean jelly may come by; like the other peddlers, his shouts from one end of the lane can be heard at the other end. People who want to buy his product bring along a small ceramic bowl, while others who are not interested in buying just sit inside their homes; as soon as they hear his shouts, they know it's time to start dinner, since throughout the summer this peddler comes when the sun is setting in the west. He comes at the same time every day, like clockwork, between the hours of four and five. One would think that his sole occupation is bringing bean jelly to sell in this particular lane, and that he isn't about to jeopardize his punctual appearance in order to sell to one or two additional homes in another lane. By the time the bean jelly peddler has gone, the sky is nearly dark.

Once the sun begins to set in the west, the peddler of odds and ends, who announces his presence with a wooden rattle, no longer enters the lanes to peddle his wares. In fact, he does no more business on the quieter roadways either, but merely shoulders his load and makes his way home along the main streets.

The pottery seller has by then closed shop for the day.

The scavengers and rag collectors also head for home.

The only one to come out at this time is the bean curd peddler.

At dinnertime some scallions and bean paste make for a tasty meal, but a piece of bean curd to go along with it adds a pleasant finishing touch, requiring at least two additional bowlfuls of corn-and-bean gruel. So the people eat more at each sitting, which is only natural; add a little hot-pepper oil and a touch of bean sauce to the bean curd, and the meal is greatly enhanced. Just a little piece of bean curd on the tips of chopsticks can last a half bowlful of gruel, and soon after the chopsticks have broken off another chunk of bean curd, a full bowlful of gruel has disappeared. Two extra bowlfuls are consumed because of the addition of the bean curd, but that doesn't mean that the person has overeaten; anyone who's never tasted bean curd cannot imagine its delightful flavor.

It is for this reason that the arrival of the bean curd peddler is so warmly welcomed by everyone—men, women, young, and old alike. When they open their doors, there are smiles everywhere, and though nothing is said, a sort of mutual affinity quietly develops between buyer and seller. It is as if the bean curd peddler were saying:

"I have some fine bean curd here."

And it is as if the customer were answering:

"Your bean curd is very good indeed."

Those who cannot afford to buy the bean curd are especially envious of the bean curd peddler. The moment they hear the sound of his shouts down the lane draw near, they are sorely tempted: Wouldn't it be nice to have a piece of bean curd with some green chili peppers and scallions.

But though they think the same thought day in and day out, they never quite manage to buy a piece, and each time the bean curd peddler comes, all his presence does for these people is confront them with an unrealizable temptation. These people, for whom temptation calls, just cannot make the decision to buy, so they merely eat a few extra mouthfuls of chili peppers, after which their foreheads are bathed in perspiration. Wouldn't it be wonderful, they dream, if a person could just open his own bean curd shop? Then he could eat bean curd anytime he felt like it!

And sure enough, when one of their sons gets to be about five years of age, if he is asked:

"What do you want to do when you grow up?"

He will answer:

"I want to open a bean curd shop." Obviously, he has hopes of realizing his father's unfulfilled ambition.

The fondness these people have for this marvelous dish called bean curd sometimes goes even beyond this; some people would even lead their families into bankruptcy over it. There's a story about the head of a household who came to just such a decision, saying:

"I'm going for broke. I'll buy myself a piece of bean curd!" In the classical language, the words "going for broke" would be the equivalent of giving up everything to get out of a difficult situation, but in modern speech most people would just say: "I'm wiped out!"

VIII

Once the bean curd peddler packs up and heads for home, the affairs of another day have come to an end.

Every family sits down to its evening meal; then, after they've finished, some stay up to watch the sunset, while others simply lie down on their *kangs* and go to sleep.

The sunsets in this place are beautiful to behold. There's a local expression here: "fire clouds" If you say "sunset," no one will understand you, but if you say "fire clouds," even a three-year-old child will point up to the western sky with a shout of delight.

Right after the evening meal the "fire clouds" come. The children's faces all reflect a red glow, while the big white dog turns red, red roosters become golden ones, and black hens become a dark purple. An old man feeding his pigs leans against the base of a wall and chuckles as he sees his two white pigs turn into little golden ones. He's about to say, "I'll be damned, even you've changed," when a man out for a refreshing evening stroll walks by and comments: "Old man, you're sure to live to a ripe old age, with that golden beard!"

The clouds burn their way in the sky from the west to the east, a glowing red, as if the sky had caught fire.

The variations of the "fire clouds" here are many: one moment they are a glowing red, a moment later they become a clear gold, then half purple-half yellow, and then a blend of gray and white. Grape gray, pear yellow, eggplant purple—all these colors appear in the sky. Every imaginable color is there, some that words cannot describe and others you would swear you've never seen before.

Within the space of five seconds a horse is formed in the sky, with its head facing south and its tail pointing west. The horse is kneeling, looking as if it were waiting for someone to climb up onto its back before it will stand up. Nothing much changes within the next second, but two or three seconds later the horse has gotten bigger, its legs have spread out, and its neck has elongated; but there is no longer any tail to be seen. And then, just when the people watching from below are trying to locate the tail, the horse vanishes.

Suddenly a big dog appears, a ferocious animal running ahead of what looks like several puppies. They run and they run, and before long the puppies have run from sight; then the big dog disappears.

A great lion is then formed, looking exactly like one of the stone lions in front of the Temple of the Immortal Matron. It's about the same size, and it, too, is crouching, looking powerful and dominant as it calmly crouches there. It appears contemptuous of all around it, not deigning to look at anything. The people search the sky, and before they know it, something else has caught their eye. Now they're in a predicament—since they can't be looking at something to the east and something to the west at the same time—and the lion is spoiled. A shift of the eyes, a lowering of the head, and the objects in the sky undergo a transformation. But now as you search for yet something else, you could look until you go blind before finding a single thing. The great lion can no longer be seen, nor is there anything else to be found—not even, for example, a monkey, which is certainly no match for a great lion.

For a brief moment the sky gives the illusion of forming this object or that, but in fact, there are no distinguishable shapes; there is nothing anymore. It is then that the people lower their heads and rub their eyes, or perhaps just rest them for a moment before taking another look. But the "fire clouds" do not often wait around to satisfy the children below who are so fond of them, and in this short space of time they are gone.

The town's children return to their rooms and go to sleep. Some are so tired they cannot make it to their beds, but fall asleep lying across their elder sister's legs or in the arms of their grandmother. The grandmother has a horsehair fly swatter, which she flicks in the air to keep the bugs and mosquitoes away. She does not know that her grandchild has fallen asleep, but thinks he's still awake.

"You get down and play; Grandma's legs are falling asleep." She gives the child a push, but he is fast asleep.

By this time the "fire clouds" have disappeared without a trace. The people in every family get up and go to their rooms to sleep for the night after closing the windows and doors.

Even in July it's not terribly hot in Hulan River, and at night the people cover themselves with thin quilts as they sleep.

As night falls and crows fly by, the voices of the few children who are not yet asleep can be heard through the windows as they call out:

> Raven, raven, work the grain-threshing floor;
> Two pecks for you, not a tiny bit more.

The flocks of crows that cover the sky with their shouts of *caw caw* fly over this town from one end to the other. It is said that after they have flown over the southern bank of the Hulan River, they roost in a large wooded area. The following morning they are up in the air flying again. As summer leads into autumn the crows fly by every evening, but just where these large flocks of birds fly to, the children don't really know, and the adults have little to say on the subject. All the children know about them is embodied in their little ditty:

> Raven, raven, work the grain-threshing floor;
> Two pecks for you, not a tiny bit more.

Just why they want to give the crows two pecks of grain doesn't seem to make much sense.

IX

After the crows have flown over, the day has truly come to an end.

The evening star climbs in the sky, shining brightly like a little brass ball.

The Milky Way and the moon also make an appearance.

Bats fly into the night.

All things that come out with the sun have now turned in for the night. The people are all asleep, as are the pigs, horses, cows, and sheep; swallows and butterflies no longer fly. Not a single blossom on the morning glories at the bases of houses remains open—there are the closed buds of new blossoms and the curled petals of the old. The closed buds are preparing to greet the morning sun of the following day, while the curled petals that have already greeted yesterday's sun are about to fall.

Most stars follow the moon's ascent in the sky, while the evening star is like her advance foot soldier, preceding her by a few steps.

As night falls, the croaking of frogs begins to emerge from rivers, streams, and marshes. The chirps of insects issue from foliage in the courtyards, from the large fields outside the city, from potted flowers, and from the graveyard.

This is what the summer nights are like when there is no rain or wind, night after night.

Summer passes quickly, and autumn has arrived. There are few changes as summer leads into autumn, except that the nights turn cooler and everyone must sleep under a quilt. Farmers are busy during the day with the harvest, and at night they dream about harvesting sorghum.

During the month of September the women are kept busy starching clothes and removing the covers to thump the matted cotton of their quilts. From morning till night every street and lane resounds with the hollow twang of their mallets. When their fluffing work is finished, the quilts are re-covered, just in time for the arrival of winter.

Winter brings the snows.

Throughout the seasons the people must put up with wind, frost, rain, and snow; they are beset by the frost and soaked by the rain. When the big winds come, they fill the air with swirling sand and pebbles, almost arrogantly. In winter the ground freezes and cracks, rivers are frozen over, and as the weather turns even colder, the ice on the river splits with resounding cracks. The winter cold freezes off people's ears, splits open their noses, chaps their hands and feet. But this is just nature's way of putting on airs of importance, and the common folk can't do a thing about it.

This is how the people of Hulan River are: when winter comes, they put on their padded clothes, and when summer arrives, they change into their unlined jackets, as mechanically as getting up when the sun rises and going to bed when it sets.

Their fingers, which are chapped and cracked in the winter, heal naturally by the time summer arrives. For those that don't heal by themselves, there is always the Li Yongchun Pharmacy, where the people can buy two ounces of saffron, steep it, and rub the solution on their hands. Sometimes they rub it on until their fingers turn blood red without any sign of healing, or the swelling may even get progressively worse. In such cases they go back to the Li Yongchun Pharmacy, though this time, rather than purchasing saffron, they buy a plaster instead. They take it home, heat it over a fire until it becomes gummy, then stick it on the frostbite sore. This plaster is wonderful, since it doesn't cause any inconvenience when it's stuck on. Carters can still drive their carts, and housewives can still prepare food.

It's truly terrific that the plaster is sticky and gummy; it won't wash off in water, thereby allowing women to wash clothes with it on if they need to. And even if it does rub off, they can always reheat it over a fire and stick it back on. Once applied it stays on for half a month.

The people of Hulan River value things in terms of durability, so something as durable as this plaster is perfectly suited to their nature. Even if it's applied for two weeks, and the hand remains unhealed, the plaster is, after all, durable, and money paid for it has not been spent in vain.

They go back and buy another, and another, and yet another; the swelling on the hand grows worse and worse. For people who cannot afford the plasters, they can pick up the ones others have discarded and stick them on their own sores. Since the final outcome is always unpredictable, why not just muddle through the best one can?

Spring, summer, autumn, winter—the seasonal cycle continues inexorably, and always has since the beginning of time. Wind, frost, rain, snow; those who can bear up under these forces manage to get by; those who cannot must seek a natural solution. This natural solution is not so very good, for these people are quietly and wordlessly taken from this life and this world.

Those who have not yet been taken away are left at the mercy of the wind, the frost, the rain, and the snow . . . as always.

CHAPTER TWO   *I*

In Hulan River, besides these inconsequential and common realities of daily life, there are special events not immediately related to the villagers' hand-to-mouth existence, such as:

The dance of the sorceress;

The harvest dances;

Releasing river lanterns;

Outdoor opera performances; and

The festival at the Temple of the Immortal Matron on the eighteenth day of the fourth lunar month.

We'll begin with the sorceress. The sorceress can cure diseases, and she dresses herself in peculiar clothing of a type that ordinary people do not wear. She is all in red—a red skirt—and the moment she puts this skirt around her waist she undergoes a transformation. Rather than starting by beating her drum, she wraps her embroidered red skirt around herself and begins to tremble. Every part of her body, from her head to her toes, trembles at once, then begins to quake violently. With her eyes closed, she mumbles constantly. Whenever her body begins to quake, she looks as if she is about to collapse, throwing a scare into the people watching; but somehow she always manages to sit down properly.

The sorceress seats herself on a stool directly opposite a spirit tablet on which black letters are written on a piece of red paper. The older the spirit tablet, the better, for it gives evidence of the many occasions she has had during the course of a year to perform her dance; and the more dances she performs, the further her reputation will spread, causing her business to prosper. Lighted incense is placed in front of the spirit tablet, from which smoke curls slowly upward.

Usually the spirit enters the sorceress' body when the incense has burned halfway down. As soon as she is possessed by the spirit, she becomes an imposing figure, as if she were in command of an army of soldiers and horses; invigorated, she rises to her feet and begins to cavort and jump around.

A spirit attendant—a man—stands off to the sorceress' side. Unlike the woman, he presents a picture of orderliness, and is as composed as the next man. He quickly places a round drum in the sorceress' hand, which she holds as she cavorts and begins to narrate the descent from the mountain of the spirit that has possessed her—how it has ridden on the clouds, flown with the winds, or been carried by the mist on its journey. It is a most impressive story. Whatever the sorceress asks the attendant standing beside her, he answers. Appropriate answers will flow from the mouth of a good attendant, while the occasional careless response from a less competent one will throw the sorceress into a fit. She is then driven to beating on her drum and letting loose a volley of epithets. She will curse the afflicted person, saying he will die before the night is out, that his ghost will not depart, but will linger endlessly, and that his immediate family, relatives, and neighbors will all be visited by fiery calamities. Members of the terror-stricken family that has requested the services of the sorceress frantically light incense and offer libations. But if these offerings fail to placate her, they must hurriedly make a presentation of red cloth, which they drape over the spirit tablet. If this too fails, they must then sacrifice a chicken. Once the tumult has reached the stage of sacrificing a chicken, it seldom goes further, for there would be nothing more to be gained from continuing along this course.

The chicken and the cloth become the sorceress' property: after she has finished her dance, she takes the chicken home to cook and eat; the red cloth she dyes a dark blue and makes into a pair of pants for her own use.

But no matter what some sorceresses do, the spirits fail to make an appearance. The family that has requested her services must then quickly sacrifice another chicken; if they are even a little slow in doing so, the sorceress will stop in mid-dance and begin haranguing them. Now since the sorceress has been invited to cure an illness, shouted curses are an unlucky omen. As a result, she is greatly respected and greatly feared.

The dance of the sorceress normally commences at dusk. At the sound of her drum, men, women, and children dash over to the house where she is engaged; on summer evenings, crowds of people fill the rooms and the yard outside. Excited, shouting women drag or carry their children along as they clamber over walls to watch the dance of the sorceress, which continues late into the night, until at last the spirit is sent back up the mountain. That moment is signaled by resounding drumbeats and the sorceress' enthralling chants, sounds that reach all the neighboring homes and produce in everyone within earshot a sense of desolation. The attendant begins to chant:

"Return to your mountain, Great Fairy; proceed with care and deliberation."

The sorceress responds:

"Spirit attendant of mine . . . Green Dragon Mountain, White Tiger Peak . . . three thousand li in a single night is an easy task when riding on the wind."

The lyrics and melody of her incantation merge with the beat of the drum and carry a great distance; it is an eerie, depressing sound, which adds to the desolation of those who hear it. Often there are people who cannot sleep at night after hearing these pulsating sounds.

The sorceress has been requested by a family to drive away an illness, but has the patient been cured? This question produces anguished sighs throughout the neighborhood, and there are often those who lie awake all night troubled by this thought.

A star-filled sky, moonlight floods the rooms; what is human existence and why must it be so desolate?

Ten days or two weeks later, the thudding drumbeat of the sorceress' dance is heard again, and once more the people are aroused. They climb over walls and pour through the gate to take a look at the sorceress who has been summoned: What are her special talents? What is she wearing? Listen to hear what chants she sings; look to see how beautiful her clothing is.

She dances into the still of the night, then the spirit is sent back up the mountain, escorted by a tantalizing cadence on the decorative drum.

The feelings of desolation are particularly strong on rainy nights: widows are moved to tears, widowers wander aimlessly about. The drumbeat seems designed to torment the unfortunates. Alternating between a rapid and a languid cadence, it calls forth the image of a lost traveler giving voice to his confusion, or of an unfortunate old man recalling the happier days of his all-too-short childhood. It is also reminiscent of a loving mother sending her son off on a long journey, or of someone at the point of death who isn't willing to part with this world.

What is human existence all about? Why must there be nights of such desolation?

Seemingly, the next time the sound of drums is heard, no one would willingly listen; but such is not the case. At the first beat of the drum, people again clamber over the walls, straining their ears to the sound with more enthusiasm than Westerners going to a concert.

II

On the fifteenth day of the seventh month—during the Festival of the Hungry Ghosts—river lanterns are set adrift on the Hulan River. There are lanterns shaped like cabbages, watermelon and lotuses.

Buddhist monks and Taoist priests, dressed in bright red satin robes with gold designs, play their reed organs, flutes, and panpipes along the riverbank, calling the people together to an open-air ritual. The music from their instruments can be heard at a distance of two li from the river. At dusk, before the sky has turned completely dark, a continuous stream of people rushes to watch the river lanterns. Even people who never leave their homes at any other time fill streets and lanes as they join the procession to the riverbank. First arrivals squat at the edge of the river, until both banks are crowded with people resting on their haunches, while an unbroken line of people continues to emerge. Even the blind and the crippled come to *see* the river lanterns (no, I'm wrong; the blind, of course, do not come to see the river lanterns), raising a cloud of dust over the roadway. There is no need to ask the maidens and the young married women who emerge from their gates in groups of twos and threes where they are headed. For they are all going to see the river lanterns.

By dusk during the seventh lunar month the "fire clouds" have just disappeared and a pale glow illuminates the streets; the noise of activity disturbs the silence of the preceding days, as each roadway comes alive. It is as if a huge fire had broken out in town and everyone was rushing to put it out. There is a sense of great urgency among the people surging forward on flying feet. The first to arrive at the river's edge squat down, and those who follow wedge themselves in and squat down on their haunches beside the others. Everyone waits; they are waiting for the moon to climb into the sky, at which time the river lanterns will be set adrift on the water.

The fifteenth day of the seventh lunar month, which is a festival devoted to spirits, is for the ghosts of the wronged who are denied transmigration and cannot extricate themselves from their bitter existence in the nether world; they are unable to find the road that will release them. On this night each of them who is able to hold a river lantern can gain release—apparently the road leading from the nether world to this world is so dark that it cannot be seen without the aid of a lantern. Therefore the releasing of river lanterns is a charitable act. It is to show that the living—shall we call them the gentlefolk?—have not forgotten the ghosts of those who have been wronged.

But the day is not without its contradictions, for a child born on the fifteenth day of the seventh lunar month is held in low esteem, since it is thought that his soul is a wild ghost that has come to him on a lotus lantern. These children will grow up without the love of their parents. Now when boys and girls reach marrying age, their families must exchange and compare the children's horoscopes to determine their suitability before the nuptials can take place. If it is a girl who was born on the fifteenth day of the seventh lunar month, it will be difficult to arrange a marriage for her, and she must deceive the boy's family by altering her birth date. If it is a boy who was born on this day, the outlook is not much better; but if his family is a wealthy one, this shortcoming can be overlooked and he is still considered marriageable. Possessed though he may be by an evil spirit, the fact that he is wealthy proves that it cannot be all that evil. But if it is the girl in this position, the situation is hopeless. That is, unless she is the only child of a wealthy widow; that is another matter altogether, for marrying one of those girls means that her wealth dangles before one's eyes. Even if she does not bring her entire fortune with her in the marriage, the dowry alone will be of considerable size, and the fact that she is the reincarnation of an evil spirit will lose its importance. The people have a saying: "Money can make even a ghost put his shoulder to the grindstone." It would seem that they don't really believe in ghosts and that reports of their existence are not altogether true.

And yet the monks beat their drums resoundingly as the river lanterns are released, urgently reciting their charm-like sutras in celebration of the ghosts' transmigration. They therefore give witness to the belief of the critical nature of this fleeting moment; it is an opportunity that cannot be missed, one in which each ghost—male or female—must quickly raise a river lantern on the palm of its hand in order to achieve reincarnation. After they have finished reciting the sutras, the monks begin to play their reed organs, flutes, and panpipes again, producing beautiful sounds that are heard far and wide.

It is at this time that the river lanterns begin floating downstream in bunches. They drift slowly, calmly, and steadily, and there are no visible signs that ghosts in the river are waiting to snatch them away. As the lanterns drift downstream they give off golden flashes of light that combine with the masses of spectators to give a sense of real activity. There are more river lanterns than can be counted, perhaps hundreds or even thousands. The children on the riverbank clap their hands, jump up and down, and shout continuously in appreciative delight. The adults, on the other hand, are so completely absorbed in the sight that they utter not a sound and act as if they were mesmerized by the lights glistening on the river. The water glimmers under the rays of the lanterns, and moonlight dances on the surface. When in the history of man has there ever been such a magnificent spectacle?

The clamor continues until the moon is directly overhead and the evening star and its followers fill the sky, at which time the grand spectacle gradually begins to abate.

The river lanterns have begun their voyage several li upstream, and after a long, long while, start passing in front of the people. They continue to drift for a long, long while before they have all passed by. During this process some are extinguished in the middle of their voyage, others are dashed against the riverbank, where they are snagged in the wild grass growing there. Then, too, when the river lanterns get to the lower reaches, children use poles to snatch them out of the water and fishermen lift out a couple that drift near their boats, so that as time goes by the number of lanterns diminishes.

As they approach the lower reaches, they have thinned out to the point that they present a desolate and lonely sight. They drift to the farthest part of the river, which appears pitch black, and one after another they disappear.

As the river lanterns pass by, though many fall behind and many others sink below the surface, nonetheless one still does not have the feeling that they are disappearing on the palms of ghosts. As the river lanterns begin their voyage far upstream, the people's hearts are light and gay, and they experience little emotional change as the lanterns pass in front of them; it is only at the end, when they have drifted to the farthest point of the lower reaches, that an involuntary emptiness grips the hearts of the lantern watchers.

"Where do those lanterns float to, after all?"

When things have reached this point, most people pick themselves up and leave the riverbank to return to their homes. By then, not only have the waters grown desolate, but the riverbank, too, is deserted and quiet. If you should gaze far downstream, with each successive glance still another river lantern is extinguished, or perhaps two die out simultaneously, and at this time it truly looks as if they were being carried away on the palms of ghosts.

By the third watch the banks are completely deserted and the river is devoid of lanterns. The river waters are calm as ever, though breezes now and then raise ripples on the surface. The moon's rays do not strike the river as they do the ocean, where splinters of gold flash about on the surface; here the reflection of the moon sinks to the bottom of the river, making it seem as if a fisherman could simply reach out and lift it into his boat.

The southern bank of the river is lined with willow groves; the northern bank of the river is the site of Hulan River. The people who have returned home after watching the river lanterns are probably all fast asleep, but the moon continues to cast its rays down onto the river.

III

The open-air opera is also performed on the bank of the river, and also in the autumn. If, for example, the autumn harvest is good, there will be an opera performance to thank the gods. If there is a summer drought, people will put on willow headdresses to call for rain; dozens of them will dash back and forth in the streets for days, singing and beating drums. These rain dancers are not permitted to wear shoes, so that the venerable Dragon King will take pity on them, as their feet are scalded on the sun-drenched ground, and reward them with rain.

Then if the rains do in fact come, there will be an opera performance in the autumn as fulfillment of a vow taken during the rain dance. All vows must be fulfilled, and since the vow was the offering of an opera, then that opera must be performed.

A performance lasts for three days.

A stage is put up on a sandbar alongside the river. It is erected on poles that are tied together and covered with an awning, so it won't matter if it drizzles, and the stage will be protected from the sun's rays.

After the stage has been finished, bleachers are erected on both sides, which include gallery seats. Sitting in the gallery seats is preferred; not only is it cooler there, it also affords one the opportunity to look around the area. But gallery seats are not easy to come by, as they are reserved for local officials and members of the gentry; most people seldom get the chance to use them, and since tickets aren't sold, even money won't won't gain a person entrance.

The construction of the stage alone takes nearly a week. When the stage framework has been put in place, the townspeople say:

"The stage framework is up."

Then, when the awning is in place, they say:

"The stage awning is in place."

Once the stage is completed, a row of bleacher seats is placed to the left and to the right of it, parallel and facing each other. They extend for a distance of perhaps fifty yards.

Seeing that the structure is nearly completed, the people go to fetch their kinfolk and call their friends. For example, when a young married woman visiting her parents is about to return to her husband's home, her mother will see her just beyond the front gate, wave to her, and say:

"When the opera is performed in the autumn I'll come fetch you."

Then as the cart bearing her daughter moves off into the distance, the mother says again, with tears in her eyes:

"I'll come fetch you when it's time to watch the opera."

And so the opera entails more than just the simple entertainment of watching a performance; it is an occasion to summon daughters and sons-in-law, a time of great festivity.

The daughter of a family to the east has grown up, and it is time for the son of a family to the west to take a wife; whereupon the matchmaker begins to make her calls on the two families. Arrangements are made for the parents of both children to look them over at the foot of the opera stage on the first or second day of the performance Sometimes these arrangements are made only with the boy's family, without telling the girl's, something known as "stealing a look." This way it matters not whether the match is made, and it offers more freedom; for, after all, the girl is unaware of what is going on.

With this in mind, all the young maidens who go to watch the opera make themselves up as nicely as they can; they wear new clothes, apply rouge and powder to their faces, trim their bangs neatly, and comb their braids so that not a hair is out of place. Then they tie their braids with red bands at the top and green at the bottom, or perhaps with bands of pink or lavender. They carry themselves with the airs of honored guests, and as they nibble on melon seeds, they hold their heads high and keep their eyes fixed straight ahead in a cultured and refined manner, as if they had become the daughters of highly respected families. Some are dressed in long robin's-egg-blue cotton, some in lavender, and others in silvery gray. Some have added borders to their gowns: there are robin's-egg-blue gowns with black borders, and there are pink gowns made of muslin adorned with lavender borders. On their feet they wear shoes of blue satin or black satin. The shoes are embroidered with all manner of designs: butterflies, dragonflies, lotus flowers, and peonies.

The girls carry embroidered hankies and wear long earrings, which the locals call "grain-tassel earrings." These earrings come in two types: one is made of gold and jadeite, the other of copper and glass. Girls from wealthy families wear gold ones, those from less-well-off families wear glass ones. At any rate, they are all attractive as they dangle beneath the girls' ears. Dazzling yellows and deep greens, set off by correct smiles. Who can all these respectable young ladies be?

Young married women also make themselves up and gather to meet their sisters of the neighborhood at the foot of the stage, where they examine and compare each other. So-and-so looks very comely, the curls of temple hair on so-and-so are shiny black; so-and-so's bracelet is the newest thing at the Futai Jewelry Shop, so-and-so's hair ornaments are dainty and lovely; the embroidery on so-and-so's dark purple satin shoes is exquisitely done.

Older women shy away from colorful clothes, although every one of them is neat as a pin. They carry long pipes and arrange their hair in buns atop their heads, looking very kindly and sweet.

Before the opera performances have even begun, the town of Hulan River is all a-bustle, as the people scurry about fetching the young married daughters and summoning sons-in-law; there is a delightful little ditty that goes:

> Pull the long saw,
> Drag the long saw;
> By Grandpa's gate they sing an opera song.
> The daughters are brought,
> The sons-in-law too;
> Even the grandchildren all go along.

By then young nephews, third aunts, second aunts by marriage—the reunions all start taking place.

Every family performs the same tasks: they kill chickens, buy wine, greet visitors with smiles, and talk among themselves of family affairs. They share funny stories deep into the night, wasting more lamp oil than anyone knows.

An old woman in such-and-such village is mistreating her daughter-in-law. The old grandfather of such-and-such family makes a scene whenever he drinks. And how about the girl who married into such-and-such family just barely a year before giving birth to twins! Did you hear about so-and-so's thirteen-year-old son who's been betrothed to an eighteen-year-old girl? The people nearly talk the night away under the light of candles and lamps amid a warm and cheery atmosphere of intimacy.

In families where there are many daughters who have already married it sometimes happens that as many as two or three years pass without an opportunity for the sisters to be reunited, since they usually live far apart. Separated by rivers or mountains and encumbered with many children and household duties, it is fruitless to even think of calling on one another.

And so, when their mother summons them all home at the same time, their meeting truly seems as if it follows a separation of decades. At their family reunion they are at a loss for words and terribly shy; wanting desperately to say something, they hold back, overcome by embarrassment the moment they begin to speak. Before long their faces are flushed. They greet each other with silence, their hearts torn between happiness and sadness. But after the time it takes to smoke a pipeful, when the blood that had rushed to their faces has receded and the dizzying effects of their meeting have abated, they finally manage a few short comments of little relevance, such as:

"When did you arrive?"

or:

"Did you bring the children?" They dare not utter a single word regarding their long separation of several years.

On the surface they don't seem the least bit like sisters, since there isn't the slightest trace of an expression of affection; as they face each other, it's impossible to determine their relationship. Coolly formal, they look like total strangers, as if they had never met before and are seeing each other for the first time today. But this is only the surface; a mutual understanding has long filled their hearts. For that matter, as many as ten days or two weeks earlier, their hearts had already begun to stir, starting from the moment they received heir mother's letters. The letters had said that she was summoning the sisters home to watch the opera, and from that moment on, each of them began deciding upon the gifts she was going to take home to give her sisters.

It might be a pair of black velvet cloud-slippers that she made with her own hands. Or perhaps in the town or village where one of them is living there is a famous dyer's shop that produces beautiful floral linen, so she will supply the shop with a couple of bolts of white cotton fabric and instructions to dye them as delicately as possible. One bolt is to have blue designs over a white background, the other white designs on a blue background. The design on the blue material is to be a little boy with bangs playing with a gold coin; that on the white material is to be butterflies frolicking among lotus flowers. One bolt will be given to elder sister, the other to younger sister.

All these things are packed in a suitcase and brought along. Then, after a day or two, during a quiet evening, she will gently remove them from her suitcase and place her elder sister's gift in front of her, saying:

"Why don't you take this dyed cotton quilt cover back home with you?"

That is all she says, not the sort of thing one would expect from someone giving a gift. Her way is quite different from that of modern times, where a person gives some little present and, afraid that the neighbors might miss the event, shouts and carries on, boasting that it comes from a certain mountain somewhere, or that it was taken from some ocean. Even if it has only been gotten from a little stream somewhere, the glories of that particular stream have to be sung—how uncommon and unique it is, not at all your average stream.

These country folk with their muddling ways don't know how to express what they feel, and so they say nothing; they simply hand the thing over and are done with it.

The recipient of the gift says nothing either—not a single word of thanks—and merely takes it from her. Some will briefly decline to accept the gift, saying:

"Why don't you just keep it for your own use?" Naturally the giver refuses to do so, at which time the gift is accepted.

Every young woman who returns to her mother's home to watch the opera brings a great many items along with her—gifts for her parents, her brothers and their wives, nieces, nephews, and other members of the family. Whoever brings the most and can produce a little something for each of her elders and all the young children is the one judged to be the warmest and most affectionate.

Talk of these things, however, must await the completion of the opera performances and the dismantling of the stage; then they gradually work their way into each family's conversations.

Every young woman who then returns to her husband from the home of her parents takes with her a wealth of objects that have been given to her as gifts. There is an abundance of things to use and things to eat: salted meat that her mother had prepared herself, fish that her elder sister had personally dried and cured, and the pickled drumstick of a wild goose that her brother had shot on a hunting trip in the mountains (this has been given to the young woman who had come home for the opera to take for her father-in-law to enjoy with his wine). With one thing and another to keep them busy on the night before their departure, the sisters don't even have a free moment to talk, and when they finish, there is a pile of packages of all sizes.

During the period of the opera performances, besides family reunions and gatherings of friends, many other happy events take place, specifically the engagements of young couples and the announcements of their forthcoming weddings in March or April of the following year. After the drinking of the betrothal wine comes the exchanging of the "engagement gifts," constituting a legal commitment; once it has been completed, the girl is considered a daughter-in-law in the boy's family.

Families with marriageable children from neighboring villages also come to town for the opera, leaving the young boys and girls at home, and make arrangements for the nuptials through a matchmaker. Sometimes during the drinking and festivities families will casually promise a daughter to someone, and there are even those who betroth their unborn sons and daughters. This is called a "womb marriage," and it generally only occurs between families of substantial means.

There are two wealthy families: one operates the local distillery, the other is a big landowner from White Flag Village. One of the two families plants sorghum, the other distills liquor. The distiller needs sorghum, and the sorghum farmer needs a distiller to buy his harvest; a distillery cannot get by without sorghum, and sorghum must have its distillery. By a happy coincidence, the wives of both families are pregnant, and so they arrange a "womb marriage." It makes no difference who has a boy and who has a girl, for as long as there is one of each, they are proclaimed husband and wife. Now if both give birth to boys, there is no need to force the issue of their marriage, and the same holds true if both give birth to girls.

The drawbacks of these "womb marriages," however, greatly outnumber the advantages. If along the way the fortunes of one of the families should decline—if the distillery should go out of business or the landowner lose his land—then the remaining family would be unwilling to gain a poverty-stricken daughter-in-law or lose its daughter to a family of no means. If it is the girl's family that has suffered reverses, then the matter is easily disposed of, for if the marriage agreement is not honored, there is nothing they can do about it. But in cases where the boy's family has fallen on bad times, it will insist on the marriage; if it is then canceled, the girl's reputation is ruined. People will say that she "brought injury" to so-and-so's family and then would not marry into it. The superstition surrounding the words "brought injury" is that a certain family has been reduced to poverty owing to the harshness of the girl's horoscope. From that time on it will be extremely difficult to find a family that will accept her as a daughter-in-law, and she will be labeled an "undesirable spinster." With this unhappy prospect before it, her family will reluctantly allow the marriage to take place. But as time goes on, her sisters-in-law will accuse her of being a woman who cares only for luxury, and they will insult her in every conceivable manner. Eventually, even her husband will come to dislike her, and her in-laws will mistreat her; unable to withstand so much abuse, this unworldly young woman returns to her parents' home, but there is nothing that can be done there either. The mother who years before had been a party to the "womb marriage" will say to her:

"This is all part of your 'fate,' and you must accept it as best you can."

The young women, bewildered, cannot understand why they must suffer such a fate, and so tragedy is often the result; some jump down wells, others hang themselves.

An old saying goes: "A battlefield is no place for a woman."

Actually, that's not a fair statement; those wells are terribly deep, and if you were to casually ask a man whether or not he would dare to jump down one, I'm afraid the answer would be 'no.' A young woman, on the other hand, would certainly do so. Now while an appearance on a battlefield doesn't necessarily lead to death, and in fact might even result in an official position, there's not much chance of someone emerging alive after jumping down a well—most never do.

Then why is it that no words of praise for the courage of these women who jump down wells are included in the memorial arches for chaste women? That is because they have all been intentionally omitted by the compilers of such memorials, nearly all of whom are men, each with a wife at home. They are afraid that if they write such things, one day, when they beat their own wife, she too may jump down a well; if she did she would leave behind a brood of children, and what would these men do then? So with unanimity they avoid writing such things, and concern themselves only with "the refined, the cultured, and the filial . . ."

These are some of the things that happen before the staging of the first opera. Once the performances actually begin, throngs of people swarm around the foot of the stage, pushing and shoving insufferably. The people who erect the stage know their business: they select a big, level sandbar beside the river that is both smooth and clean, so even if someone were to fall down, his clothing wouldn't be soiled. The sandbar is about a half li in length.

The people are laughing and carrying on, they don't appear to be watching the opera at all. The commotion they make drowns out the chorus of gongs and drums. On the stage someone dressed in red walks on as someone in green walks off, and this parade of people walking on and off is about all the spectators notice; naturally they cannot tell you if the singing is good or not, since they cannot hear it. Those closer to the stage can see that the beardless actor's mouth is open; those farther away can't even tell whether the performer in red is male or female. One might think it would be better to watch a puppet show.

But supposing a puppeteer were to come around then and begin singing; if you asked these people if they'd rather watch him, their answer would be emphatically negative, and even those who are so far away they cannot even make out the edge of the stage, or, for that matter, those as much as two li distant, would not choose to watch the puppet show. For even if all they do is take a little snooze beneath the big stage and then go home, what counts is that they have returned from a spot beneath the big opera stage, and not from some other place. Since there isn't much of anything else to see during the year, how could they lightly let this opera performance pass them by? And so, whether they watch it or not, they must at least put in an appearance at the foot of the opera stage.

So the country folk come in great wagons with teams of horses, in carts pulled by old oxen, in fancily decorated carriages, and in small drays pulled by big mules. In a word, they arrive in whatever vehicle they happen to own, and those who don't raise horses or other beasts of burden hook up a young donkey to a carriage they've decorated and come in it.

After they arrive, they leave their vehicles and animals on the sandbar, where the horses feed on the grass and the mules go down to the river to drink. Awnings are put up over their carts, which then become little bleachers standing in a line some distance from the stage. The carts and wagons have brought entire families, from grandmothers to the wives of their grandsons—three generations of family—and have deposited them a considerable distance from the stage. They can hear nothing and can see only figures in red and green wearing strange hats and clothing run around in circles on the stage. Who can tell what they're doing up there on the stage? Some people attend all three days of the performances, yet cannot tell you the name of a single opera performed. They return to their villages and relate to others their experiences, and if by chance someone should ask them what opera they're talking about, their sole answer is a long, hard stare.

The children at the foot of the stage are even less aware of what is going on. About all they know is that there is someone with a beard and someone else with a painted face up there, but they haven't the slightest idea what they're doing; just a confusion of movements and a flurry of swords, spears, clubs, and staffs. At any rate, there are peddlers of rice pudding and candy balls beneath the stage, so the children can always go and eat what they like. There are all kinds of things, like rice cakes, pan-fried buns, and fermented bean curd; and since these things are not filling, they can always sample a little of everything. Watermelons are sold there, and muskmelons, around which swarms of flies buzz to and fro.

The heavens reverberate with the clanging of gongs and the beating of drums at the foot of the stage. Apparently concerned that the people in the rear cannot hear them, the actors shout their songs for all they're worth; but they could never drown out the chorus of gongs and drums, even if they destroyed their vocal cords in the process. People beneath the stage have long since forgotten that they are there to watch the opera, as they talk interminably about this or that. Men and women alike spend their time discussing domestic affairs. Then there are the distant relatives who never see each other throughout the year; meeting here today—how could they not greet one another? So maternal and paternal aunties shout to each other amid the crowds of people. Suddenly an old woman sitting in the bleachers beneath one of the awnings jumps to her feet and shouts out:

"Second Maternal Auntie, when did you get here?"

The person called to answers her. Now the people in the gallery seats are relatively near the stage, close enough to actually hear the singing, so it's generally less noisy there. Young women—married and unmarried—sit there nibbling melon seeds and sipping tea. People are naturally annoyed by the shouts of this old woman, but they dare not try to stop her, for the minute they asked her to speak a little more softly, she would bark at them:

"This opera isn't being performed just for your family, you know! If you want to hear some opera, then invite the troupe of actors to come to your house to sing it!"

Then the other woman would chime in with:

"Well, I'll be! I've never seen anything like it. Once they start watching the opera, they don't give a damn about their own kin. Why, a person can't even talk . . ."

These are some of the nicer things; there are worse. Out of their mouths might come such comments as:

"You husband-stealing slut . . . screw your grandmother! Never in my life have I heard a harsh or angry word from anyone, and now you expect me to let you tell me what to do . . . up your mother's . . ."

If the abused party lets this pass without notice, the incident is soon forgotten, but if there's a reply, naturally, it will not be pleasing to the ear. What ensues is a brawl between the two parties, with watermelon rinds and other objects flying back and forth.

Here we have people who have come to watch an opera performance, but who have unexpectedly begun putting on their own show beneath the stage. Like a swarm of bees, people rush over to watch this real-life, knock-down-drag-out performance. Several ruffians and good-for-nothings in the crowd shout their approval, causing all present to roar with laughter. If one of the combatants is a young woman, then those irksome ruffians, with their lewd comments, provoke her into more volatile and viciously abusive language.

Naturally, the old woman has been guilty of shouting abuses at the other without regard for propriety or reason. But after a while it's impossible to tell who's in the right and who isn't.

Fortunately, the actors on the stage remain cool and collected, not wavering from their singing in the face of this disruption, so that in the end the slugfest and all its attendant commotion gradually dies down.

Another activity at the foot of the stage is the flirting that goes on, primarily by people like the married woman from the bean curd shop on Avenue South, or the wife of the miller who runs the grain mill. The miller's wife has her eye on one of the carters, or a bean curd maker casts amorous looks at the daughter of a grain shop proprietor. With some, furtive glances pass back and forth between both of them, but on other occasions, one of the parties is eagerly attentive, while the other demonstrates total indifference. The latter situation usually involves a member of the upper class and one from a lower class, two people with a great disparity in family wealth.

Members of the gentry also have their flirtations as they sit in the gallery seats casting glances here and there. They cannot help but eye members of their own families—in-laws, cousins, and the rest—especially since every one of them is made up so beautifully and is so eye-catching.

Normally, when members of the gentry call upon one another in the guest halls of their homes, they will not allow themselves to ogle their host's daughter; this would be terribly ungentry-like behavior, not to mention immoral. And if one of these young girls were to tell her parents, they would immediately sever their relationship with the friend in question. Actually, a severed relationship isn't all that serious; more important is that once this information has leaked out, the person's reputation is ruined, and since the gentry are supposed to be noble, how could they let their names be besmirched? How could they permit themselves to desire the daughter of a friend without respect to the difference in ages, as the lower classes do?

When members of the gentry come calling, they are ushered into the guest hall, where they seat themselves properly, drink a little tea, and smoke a pipe. Well mannered and ceremoniously courteous, they give one another the respect due a peer. The wife and children come out to pay their respects, treating the guest as their elder, and in such a situation the guest can inquire only about how many books the young master has read and how many more characters he has learned to write. He cannot speak more than a few words ever to his friend's wife, to say nothing of the daughter; he cannot even raise his head to face her, let alone give her the once-over.

But here in the gallery seats it makes no difference, for if someone asks what he's doing, he can say he's just looking around to see if some of his friends are in any of the other rows. Besides, with all those people casting glances here and there, most likely no one is even paying attention. A look here and a glance there, and even though he doesn't fall for any of his friends' daughters, he has an infatuation for a woman he's seen somewhere before. She is holding a small goose-feather fan, over which she looks his way. She might be a married woman, but she is certainly young and pretty.

Logically, this particular member of the gentry ought to stand up right then and whistle to show how pleased he is, but older Chinese gentry don't operate that way. They have a different way of acting; he gazes straight ahead, his eyes half-open in that style of his that shows the limitless affection he feels for the woman. But unhappily, she is so far away she probably can't see him clearly, and his efforts may be in vain.

Some of the young people beneath the stage refuse to follow the orders of their parents and the counsel of matchmakers, and pledge their lives to one another on their own, although these activities are generally restricted to cousins who are boys and girls from fairly respectable families. They vow on the spot to share their lives forever. For some of these young couples their parents' obstruction will produce a great many frustrations. But these frustrations will be beautiful ones, as talk of them will engender more interest than a reading of the romance *Dream of the Red Chamber*, and during the opera performances of years to come, the young girls' reminiscences will be greatly enhanced by talk of such delightful things.

The country folk who have come to town in carts for the opera pitch camp on the sandbar beside the river. In the evening, after the day's performance has ended, the townspeople return to their homes, leaving only those with their carts and horses to spend the night on the sandbar. The scene is reminiscent of a military bivouac, with the ground beneath and the sky above. Some just stay for one night and return home the next day, while others stay for all three nights, until the performances are concluded, before they drive their carts back to the country. Needless to say, the sandbar presents a fairly impressive sight at nighttime, as each family sits and drinks tea or chats among itself around a campfire, although, in point of fact, their number is rather small—no more than twenty or thirty carts. Since their camp-fires aren't numerous enough to really light up the sky, there is a certain air of forlornness. In the deep of night the river water turns especially cold, chilling the people sleeping on the riverbank. It's even worse for carters and others who tend the animals, as they cannot sleep for fear that bandits might come and steal their horses, and must be there waiting for the coming day.

Sitting beneath paper lanterns in groups of twos and threes, they gamble until the first light of day, at which time they lead their horses down to the river to drink. There they meet an old fisherman in a crab boat, who says to them:

"Yesterday's performance of *A Fisherman's Revenge* wasn't bad. I hear they're going to do *Fenhe Bay* today."

The fellow who has led his animal to the water knows nothing at all about opera. He listens only to the lapping noises of the drinking animals, having no response for any comments made to him.

IV

The festival at the Temple of the Immortal Matron, which falls on the eighteenth day of the fourth lunar month, is for spirits and ghosts, not people. This festival, which the local people call a "temple stroll," is attended by men and women of all ages, although most are young women.

The young women get up in the morning and begin combing their hair, bathing, and preparing themselves as soon as breakfast is over. Then, after they've finished getting themselves ready, they arrange with neighbor girls to go join the temple stroll. Some begin making themselves up the moment they get out of bed, even before breakfast, then leave the house as soon as they've eaten. In any event, on the day of the temple stroll there is a mad rush to get there early, so that before noon the temple grounds are already so crowded there's barely room to breathe.

Women who have lost their children in the crush stand there shouting, while the children who cannot find their mothers cry in the midst of all those people. Three-year-olds, five-year-olds, and even some two-year-olds who have just learned to walk are separated from their mothers in the crowds.

Consequently, there are policemen at the festival each year whose job it is to collect such children and stand on the temple steps until their parents come to claim them. Since these children are always the more timorous ones, they wail loudly and pitifully until their faces are bathed in tears and sweat. Even twelve- and thirteen-year-olds get lost, and when one of them is asked where he lives, he is invariably stumped for an answer. Pointing first to the east, then to the west, he says that there's a small stream running past his gate, which is called Shrimp Ditch because it's full of tiny shrimp. It's possible that the place where the child lives is itself called Shrimp Ditch, a name that means nothing to the people who hear it. When asked how far from town this Shrimp Ditch is, the child answers that it's about a meal's ride on horseback or three meals' ride in a cart. But this doesn't tell you how far from town the place is. Asked his family name, he answers that his grandfather is called Shi Er and his father, Shi Cheng, and no one dares pursue the matter any further. If he's asked whether or not he's eaten, he answers: "I've already had a nap." There's nothing anyone can do at this point, and it's best to just let him go; and so children of all ages gather at the temple gate under the watchful eyes of policemen, crying and shouting, and sounding like a pack of small animals.

The Temple of the Immortal Matron is on Avenue North, not far from the Temple of the Patriarch.

Even though the people who go to light incense at the temple are doing so to ask for sons and grandsons, and by rights should first light their incense in front of the Immortal Matron, still they believe that men are considered superior to women in the nether world, just as they are here, and they dare not upset the cosmic order. Consequently they always go first to the Temple of the Patriarch, where they strike the gong and kowtow to the deity, as though they were kneeling there to report for duty; then and only then do they proceed to the Temple of the Immortal Matron.

In the Temple of the Patriarch there are more than ten clay images, and it's hard to tell just which one is the Patriarch, as they are all so imposing and stern, truly of surpassing majesty. The fingertips of some of the clay idols have broken off, and they stand there with their fingerless hands raised in the air; some have had their eyes gouged out and look like blind people; some even have written characters scribbled all over their toes, characters with rather inelegant meanings that are not at all suited to deities. There are comments that say that the clay idol should take a wife or else it will be jealous when it sees the monks chasing after the little nuns. Actually, the characters themselves no longer remain, but this is what people say used to be written there.

Because of this the County Magistrate once sent down an order that the doors of all temples were to be closed and locked on days other than the first and fifteenth of each month, and no loiterers were to be allowed entrance.

This magistrate is a man particularly concerned with the Confucian concepts of humanity, justice, and morality. The story has it that his fifth concubine was taken from the nunnery, so he has always been convinced that no nun would ever try to tempt a monk. From earliest times, nuns have been linked with monks, and inasmuch as the common people do not personally investigate the situation, they simply parrot what others before them have said. Take the Magistrate's number five concubine, for example: she herself was a nun, and how could she have been sought out by some monk? There isn't the slightest chance of that. And so the order was sent to close all temple doors.

The Temple of the Immortal Matron is generally more serene than the others. There are clay idols there too, mostly female, and they are for the most part devoid of harsh, malignant stares. People are simply not frightened by them when they enter the main hall, since the idols look pretty much like common people. Obviously, these are the Matrons, and of course they are good and obedient females. Why, even the female demons aren't particularly malevolent; their hair is a little mussed up and that's about all. There isn't a single one that resembles the clay idols in the Temple of the Patriarch, with their flaming eyes or tiger-like mouths.

Children are not the only ones who are frightened to tears when they walk into the Temple of the Patriarch; even a young man in his prime enters very respectfully, as if to show that even though he is in the prime of his life, if that clay idol were to take it into its head to walk over and fight with him, the man would surely come out on the short end. And so, whoever kowtows in the Temple of the Patriarch, where the clay idols are so tall and powerful, does so with greater piety.

When they go to the Temple of the Immortal Matron, the people also kowtow, though they have the feeling that there's nothing very spectacular about the Matron.

The people who cast the clay idols were men, and they fashioned the female figures with an obedient appearance, as though out of respect to women. The male figures they fashioned with a savage, malignant appearance, as though in condemnation of men's dispositions. That, however, is not the case. Throughout the world, no matter how fiercely savage, there has probably never been a single man with flaming eyes. Take Occidentals, for instance: though their eyes are unlike those of the Chinese, it is simply that theirs are a limpid blue, somewhat resembling those of cats, but by no means flaming. The race of people with flaming eyes has never appeared on the face of the earth. Then why have the people who cast the clay idols made them look that way? For the simple reason that a single glance will strike fear into someone, who will not only kowtow, but will do so with absolute conviction. Upon completing his kowtows, when he rises and takes another look, there will never be the slightest regret; the thought that he has just prostrated himself before an ordinary or unremarkable individual would simply not occur to him. And why have the idol-makers cast the female figures with such obedient appearances? So as to tell everyone that obedience indicates a trusting nature, and that the trusting are easily taken advantage of; they are telling everyone to hurry up and take advantage of them!

If someone is trusting, not only do members of the opposite sex take advantage of her, but even members of the same sex show no compassion. To illustrate: When a woman goes to worship at the Temple of the Immortal Matron, all she does is ask for some sons and grandsons. Her prayers ended, she rises and leaves, and no manifestations of respect are apparent. She has the feeling that the Matron of Sons and Grandsons is nothing but a common, ordinary woman who just happens to have a surplus of children.

Then when men hit their wives they can say:

"The Immortal Matron is supposed to be in constant fear of being beaten by the Patriarch, so what makes a gossipy woman like you different?"

It is obvious that for a man to beat a woman is a Heaven-ordained right, which holds true for gods and demons alike. No wonder the idols in the Temple of the Immortal Matron have such obedient looks about them—that comes from having been beaten so often. It becomes apparent that obedience is not the exceptionally fine natural trait it has been thought to be, but rather the result of being beaten, or perhaps an invitation to receive beatings in the future.

After they've worshiped at the two temples, the people come out and crowd into the streets, where there are peddlers of all types of toys, most of which are suited for the smaller children. There are clay roosters with two red chicken feathers stuck on to make a tail, causing the toys to look far better than the real thing. Anyone with children will be forced to buy one, especially since it will make a loud whistling noise when put to the mouth and blown. After they've bought the clay rooster, the children spy some little clay men with holes in their backs in which reeds can be inserted to make whistles. The sound they make is not very pleasing to the ear—almost like a cry of grievance—but the children like it, so their mothers have to buy them.

Of the remaining toys—the whistles, reed flutes, metal butterflies, and tumbler dolls—it is the tumbler dolls that are the most popular and the ones made with the greatest care. Every family buys one—bigger dolls for the well-to-do families, smaller ones for poorer families. The big ones are nearly two feet in height, and the small ones can be as tiny as a duck's egg. But big or small, they are all very lively. They right themselves the moment they're pushed over, quickly and without fail. Prospective buyers test them on the spot; occasionally, if a doll has been made by an inexperienced hand, the bottom will be too large and the doll will not fall over, while others will fall over and not right themselves. So before they buy the tumbler dolls, the people invariably reach out and push them all over together, then buy whichever one rights itself first. This process of knocking them down and watching them right themselves produces a great deal of hilarity among the children who surround the peddler's stand to laugh at the goings-on.

A tumbler doll is very attractive, so white and plump, and though it is called "the old man who won't fall down," this is just a name, and the toy looks nothing like an old man. In fact, it is a fat little child, and the ones that have been made with a little more care even have a few strands of hair to represent a child's hair. The ones with hair sell for ten strings of cash more than those without, and many of the children are adamant in wanting a doll with hair. Not wishing to make this additional expense, the child's mother offers to take it home and add a few hairs she can cut off the family dog. But the child insists on having one with hair already on it, so he picks one of them up and refuses to put it back. Seeing that there's nothing she can do, the mother buys it. The child carries the doll with him on the road back home, happy as can be, but by the time he arrives home, he discovers that the tuft of hair has fallen off somewhere along the way, and he begins to wail. His mother quickly cuts a few hairs from the family dog and sticks them onto the doll, but the child cannot help but feel that this hair is not the real thing and doesn't look nearly as good as the original. Now the original hair may very well have been dog hair too, for that matter, and worse looking than what's on the doll now, but the child is not content with it, and is dejected for the rest of the day.

By the afternoon, the festival is concluded; but the temple doors remain open, and there are still people inside burning incense and worshiping the Matron. Women who have no sons remain inside the Temple of the Immortal Matron to play some little tricks: they stick buttons onto the back of the Matron of Sons and Grandsons, tie red sashes around her feet, and hang earrings on her ears. They fit her with eyeglasses, then steal off with one of the clay infants that have been placed beside her, in the belief that they themselves will then produce sons the following year.

There are many peddlers of sashes at the gate to the Temple of the Immortal Matron, and the women flock to buy them, believing that this purchase will bring a son into the family. If an unmarried girl should inadvertently buy one, she becomes the object of a great deal of raucous laughter.

Once the temple festival is over, each family is in possession of a tumbler doll, even those who live as far away from the city as eighteen li. When they get home they place the doll just inside the front door so that other people can see it at a glance and know that this family now has a tumbler doll of its very own. This is incontrovertible proof that the family was not left behind during the time of the festival, but clearly had participated in the "stroll."

There is a local song that goes:

> Dear young woman, take your temple stroll.
> A graceful walk, a charming gait;
> And don't forget to buy a tumbler doll.

V

All these special occasions are designed for ghosts, certainly not for people. Although the people do get to watch some opera and take their temple strolls, these are really only incidental benefits they receive.

The dance of the sorceress is all about ghosts; the great opera is sung for the benefit of the Dragon King; the river lanterns are released on the fifteenth day of the seventh lunar month to be used by ghosts, so they can light the road to transmigration by carrying them over their heads; the lighting of incense and kowtowing on the eighteenth day of the fourth lunar month is also to honor ghosts.

Only the harvest dances are performed for the benefit of the living and not for ghosts. These dances are performed on the fifteenth day of the new year, during the season of rest for those who work the land. They take advantage of the New Year's festivities to masquerade themselves, with men making themselves up as women, presenting a comical scene that delights everyone.

Lion dances, dragon-lantern dances, land-boat dances, and the like also seem to be in honor of ghosts, though there are so many different kinds it's hard to give a clear account of them all.

CHAPTER THREE   I

The town of Hulan River is where my granddad lived. When I was born, Granddad was already past sixty, and by the time I was four or five, he was approaching seventy.

Our house had a large garden that was populated by insects of all types—bees, butterflies, dragonflies, and grasshoppers. There were white butterflies and yellow ones; but these varieties were quite small and not very pretty. The really attractive butterflies were the scarlet ones whose entire bodies were covered with a fine golden powder.

The dragonflies were gold in color, the grasshoppers green. The bees buzzed everywhere, their bodies covered with a fine layer of down, and when they landed on flowers, their plump little round bodies appeared to be motionless balls of fur.

The garden was bright and cheerful, deriving its freshness and beauty from all the reds and greens. I heard it had once been a fruit orchard that was planted because of Grandmother's fondness for fruit. But Grandmother had also been fond of raising goats, and they had stripped the bark from her fruit trees, killing them. From the time of my earliest recollection, the garden had only a single cherry tree and a single plum tree, and since neither bore much fruit, I wasn't really aware of their existence. When I was a child I felt that a tall elm was the only tree in our garden. This tree, which was in the northwest corner of the garden, was the first to rustle in the wind and the first to give off clouds of mist when it rained. Then when the sun came out, its leaves shone radiantly, sparkling like the mother-of-pearl found on a sandbar.

Granddad spent most of the day in the rear garden, and I spent my time there with him. Granddad wore a large straw hat, I wore a small one; when Granddad planted flowers, so did I, and when Granddad pulled weeds, that's what I did too. When he planted cabbage seeds, I tagged along behind him filling in each of the little holes with my foot. But with my random and careless footwork, there was no way in the world I could have made a neat job of it. Some of the time not only did

I fail to cover the seeds with dirt, I actually sent them flying with my foot.

The Chinese cabbages grew so quickly that sprouts began appearing within a few days, and in no time they were ready to be picked and eaten.

When Granddad hoed the ground, so did I, but since I was too small to manage the long handle of the hoe, Granddad removed it and let me do my hoeing using only the head. Actually, there wasn't much hoeing involved in it, as I just crawled along on the ground chopping and digging at will with the head of my hoe, not bothering to differentiate between the sprouts and the grass. Invariably, I mistook leeks for weeds and pulled them all out together by their roots, leaving the foxtails, which I'd mistaken for grain stalks, in the ground. When Granddad discovered that the plot of ground I'd been hoeing was covered only with foxtails, he asked me:

"What's all that?"

"Grain," I answered.

He started to laugh, and when he'd finished, he pulled up a foxtail and asked me:

"Is this what you've been eating every day?"

"Yes."

Seeing that he was still laughing, I added:

"If you don't believe me, I'll go inside and get some to show you."

So I ran inside and got a handful of grain from the birdcage, which I threw to Granddad from a distance, saying:

"Isn't this the same thing?"

Granddad called me over and explained patiently that the grain stalks have beards, while the foxtails have only clusters that look very much like real foxes' tails. But although he was teaching me something new, I wasn't really paying any attention, and only made a cursory acknowledgment of what he was saying. Then, raising my head, I spotted a ripe cucumber and ran over, picked it, and began to eat. But before I'd finished, a large dragonfly darting past me caught my eye, so I threw down the cucumber and chased after it. Really, how could I expect to catch a dragonfly that flew that fast? The nice part about it was, I never really had any intention of catching it, and only got to my feet, ran a few steps, then started doing something else.

At such times I'd pluck a pumpkin flower or catch a big green grasshopper and tie one of its legs with a piece of thread. After a while, the leg might snap off, so there'd be a leg dangling from the piece of thread, while the grasshopper from which it had come was nowhere to be found.

After I grew tired of playing, I'd run back over to where Granddad was and dash about noisily for a while. If he was watering the plants, I'd grab the watering gourd away from him and do it myself, though in a peculiar fashion: instead of sprinkling water on the vegetables themselves, I'd fling the water into the air with all my might and shout:

"It's raining, it's raining!"

The sun was particularly strong in the garden, and there was a very high sky above. The sun's rays beat down so brightly I could barely keep my eyes open; it was so bright that worms dared not bore up through the ground, and bats dared not emerge from their dark hiding places. Everything touched by the sunlight was healthy and beautiful, and when I smacked the trunk of the big elm tree with my hand, it resounded; when I shouted, it seemed as if even the earthen wall standing opposite me was answering my shouts.

When the flowers bloomed, it was as if they were awakening from a slumber. When the birds flew, it was as if they were climbing up to the heavens. When the insects chirped, it was as if they were talking to each other. All these things were alive. There was no limit to their abilities, and whatever they wanted to do, they had the power to do it. They did as they willed in complete freedom.

If the pumpkins felt like climbing up the trellis, they did so, and if they felt like climbing up the side of the house, they did that. If the cucumber plant wanted to bring forth an abortive flower, it did so, and if it wanted to bear a cucumber, it did that; if it wanted none of these, then not a single cucumber nor a single flower appeared, and no one would question its decision. The cornstalks grew as tall as they wished, and if they felt like reaching up to the heavens, no one would give it a second thought. Butterflies flew wherever they desired; one moment there'd be a pair of yellow butterflies flying over from the other side of the wall, the next moment a solitary white butterfly flying off from this side of the wall. Whose house had they just left? Whose house were they flying to? Even the sun didn't know the answers to such questions.

There was only the deep blue sky, lofty and far, far away.

But when white clouds drew near they looked like great etched silver ingots, and as they passed over Granddad's head they were so low they seemed about to press down and touch his straw hat.

When I'd grown tired from all my playing I searched for a cool, shady place near the house and went to sleep. I didn't need a pillow or a grass mat, but simply covered my face with my straw hat and fell asleep.

II

Granddad had smiling eyes and the hearty laugh of a child. He was a tall man of robust health who liked to carry a cane when he walked. Never without a pipe in his mouth, whenever he met children, he loved to tease them by saying:

"Look at that sparrow up in the sky."

Then, when the child was looking skyward, he'd snatch the child's cap off his head. Sometimes he stuck it up under his long gown, other times he hid it up his wide sleeve; then he'd say:

"The sparrow has flown away with your cap."

The children all knew this trick of Granddad's and were never fooled by it; they'd wrap their arms around his legs and try to get their caps back by feeling around inside his sleeve or by opening up the inner lapel of his gown until they found what they were looking for.

Granddad often did this, and he always hid the caps in the same places—either up his sleeve or inside the lapel of his gown, and there wasn't a single child who didn't find his cap in Granddad's clothing. It was as if he'd made an agreement with them: "Now I'll just put it here and you try to find it."

I don't know how many times he did this, but it was a lot like an old woman who is forever telling the story of "Tiger Hunting on the Mountain" to the children; even if they've already heard it five hundred times, the listeners clap their hands and shout appreciatively each and every time.

Whenever Granddad played this little trick, both he and the children laughed loud and long, as if it were the very first time.

Other people who saw Granddad do this usually laughed too, but not in appreciation of his sleight-of-hand; rather, they laughed because he used the same method each and every day to snatch away the children's caps, and this was a comical thing as far as they were concerned.

Granddad wasn't much good at financial matters, and all the household affairs were handled by my grandmother. He simply passed his day relaxing to his heart's content, and I felt it was a good thing I'd grown up—I was three. Otherwise, how lonely he'd have been. I could walk . . . I could run. When I was too tired to walk, Granddad carried me, and then when I felt like walking again, he held my hand. Day in and day out, inside or out-of-doors, I never left his side; for the most part, Granddad was in the rear garden, and so that's where I was too.

When I was little, I had no playmates to speak of; I was my mother's first-born. I can remember things from my very early childhood, including a time when I was three years old, when my grandmother used a needle to prick my finger. I disliked her a great deal because of it.

The windows in our house had paper stuck up on all four borders, with an inlay of glass in the center. Grandmother had an obsession with cleanliness, and the paper in the window of her room was always the cleanest in the house. Whenever anyone carried me into her room and put me down on the edge of the *kang*, I'd dash over to the window beside the *kang*, reach out to touch the carved lattice of the white paper window and poke holes in it with my finger. If no one interfered, there'd soon be a whole line of little holes; but if they tried to stop me, I'd hurriedly poke one or two final holes before stopping. That paper was as tight as a drumhead, so it popped each time my finger poked through. The more holes I made, the more pleased I was with myself, and I was even happier when Grandmother came and tried to chase me away—I'd laugh, clap my hands, and jump up and down.

One day, when Grandmother saw me coming, she picked up a needle and went around to the outside of the window to wait for me. The moment I poked my finger through, it began to hurt like the dickens, and I screamed in pain. Grandmother had pricked my finger with the needle. From that time on, I never forgot what she'd done, and I disliked her because of it.

She sometimes gave me candy and shared her pork kidney with me when she prepared kidney and Sichuan fritillary for her cough, but after I'd finished the kidney, I still didn't like her.

Once, when her illness was at its worst, not long before she died, I gave her a real scare. She was sitting alone on the edge of the *kang*, cooking medicine in a kettle resting on a charcoal brazier beside her. The room was so quiet I could hear the medicine bubbling in the kettle. Grandmother lived in two rooms, one inner and one outer, and by a happy coincidence, that day there was no one else in either the outer or the inner room—she was all alone. She didn't hear me open the door, so I rapped loudly with my fist on the wooden partition: *Bang bang*! I heard her blurt out "Oh!" and the steel tongs crashed to the floor. As I looked inside, she saw me and began cursing. She looked like she was going to climb down and chase after me, so I ran off laughing.

Frightening Grandmother like that wasn't something I'd done for revenge; I was just an ignorant little five-year-old and probably thought it would be fun.

All day long Granddad was idle, as Grandmother was unwilling to give him any jobs to do. There was just one thing: on a chest on the floor there were some pewter ornaments, which Granddad regularly polished. I'm not sure if she gave him this assignment or if it was something he undertook to do on his own. But whenever he began to polish them, I was unhappy, partly because this meant he couldn't take me out to play in the rear garden, and also because he'd often be yelled at; Grandmother would scold him for being lazy and for not doing a good job of polishing. And whenever she began to scold him, somehow or other even I got yelled at.

When Grandmother started to scold Granddad, I took him by the hand and started walking out with him.

"Let's go out to the garden," I'd say.

Maybe that's why Grandmother started scolding me too. She'd curse at Granddad, calling him a "useless old bag of bones," and then call me a "useless little bag of bones."

I'd lead Granddad out into the garden, and the minute we got there, we were in a different world. We were no longer in the confined, cramped environment of the room, but in a spacious world where we were at one with heaven and earth. The sky above and the ground below were vast, stretching far, far into the distance; try though we might, we couldn't touch the sky with our outstretched hands. And the earth around us was so luxuriant with growing things we couldn't take it all in at a single glance, which made us feel that we were surrounded by a vast layer of fresh greenery.

As soon as I stepped into the rear garden, I began aimlessly running to and fro. It may have looked as if I was running after something that had caught my eye, or that there was something just waiting for my arrival, but I actually seldom had any objective in mind at all; I simply felt that absolutely everything in the garden was so alive I was powerless to keep my legs from jumping. When Granddad called to me to stop before I wore myself out, if I hadn't yet exhausted my energy, I'd have none of it, and in fact, the more he called for me to stop, the worse I behaved.

I'd sit down to rest only when I was too tired to move, but my respites were very brief: I'd sit down in the middle of a vegetable bed, pick a cucumber, and eat it. Then after this brief rest, I'd be up and running again.

Obvious though it might have been that there was no fruit on the cherry tree, I'd still climb up it to look for cherries. The plum tree was already half dead and had long since stopped bearing fruit, but still I went looking for plums. As I searched, I shouted out questions to Granddad:

"Granddad, why aren't there any cherries on the cherry tree?"

"There aren't any cherries because there are no flowers," Granddad would answer from afar.

"Why aren't there any flowers?"

"There aren't any flowers on the tree because you have such a greedy mouth."

As soon as I heard this, I'd know he was teasing me, and I would virtually fly over to where he was standing, pretending I was angry. But when he looked down at me, I could see there was no trace of malice in his eyes, and I'd break out laughing. I'd laugh for the longest time before I could stop. Just where all this happiness came from, I couldn't say. I don't know how loud my laughter was during such hell-raising in the garden, but it seemed even to me to be earsplitting.

There was a rosebush in our garden that bloomed every June and stayed in bloom until July. Each blossom was as big as a soy sauce plate, and they were in such great profusion that the bush was covered with them. Their fragrance attracted great numbers of bees to the rosebush, around which they swarmed with a great buzzing noise. When I'd tired of playing with everything else, I'd be reminded of this rosebush and its flowers and would pick a great many of them to put into the overturned crown of my straw hat. There were two things that frightened me about picking roses: first I was afraid that I might be stung by a bee, and second that I might prick my fingers on a thorn. One time I picked a large bunch of the flowers, which was no easy task for me, but then found I didn't know what to do with them. Suddenly a brilliant idea came to me: Wouldn't Granddad look terrific wearing these flowers?

He was kneeling on the ground pulling weeds, so I began adorning him with flowers, and though he was aware that I was playing with his hat, he didn't know for sure just what I was up to. I decorated his hat with a wreath of twenty or thirty bright red flowers, laughing all the while.

"The spring rains have been heavy this year," he said. "The flowers on that rosebush of ours are so fragrant you can smell them a couple of li away."

I was so convulsed with laughter when I heard him say this that I was barely able to continue sticking the flowers in, and even after I'd finished, Granddad was still blissfully unaware of what was happening. He just kept pulling up weeds from a little mound of earth. I ran off some distance and stood there, not daring to look over where he was, in order to keep from laughing. I took the opportunity to go inside the house to get something to eat; even before I could return to the garden, Granddad followed me into the house.

The moment he stepped inside, Grandmother noticed the bright red flowers covering his head. She didn't say a word when she saw them, but just broke out laughing. My father and mother started to laugh too, though I was laughing the hardest of anyone and rolling around on the *kang*.

Then Granddad took off his hat, looked at it, and found that the source of the fragrance of the roses wasn't a result of heavy spring rains, but rather because his head was covered with a wreath of flowers. He put his hat down and laughed for a full ten minutes or more without stopping; after a while, he thought about it again and broke out laughing. Then just when he seemed to have forgotten the incident, I reminded him:

"Granddad, the spring rains this year have sure been heavy."

With this reminder, his laughter returned, and I started rolling around on the *kang* again.

This is how it went, day in and day out: Granddad, the garden, and me—the inseparable trio. I don't know how windy or rainy days affected Granddad, but I always felt extremely lonesome. With no place to go and nothing to do, such a day seemed to me to last several days.

III

Hard though I may have wished it otherwise, the rear garden was sealed off once every year. Following the autumn rains, it would begin to languish; the flowers would yellow and fall, and it seemed that they would soon wither and die, almost as if someone were crushing and destroying them. None of them appeared as hardy as before—it was as if they were worn out and needed rest, and were thus putting their affairs in order before returning to the place from which they'd come.

The big elm tree was also shedding its leaves, and on those occasions when Granddad and I sat beneath the tree, its leaves fell upon my face. Soon the rear garden was blanketed with the fallen leaves.

Before too long, heavy snows would begin to fall, burying the garden. The door leading into the garden was sealed with a thick layer of mud, and frost and icicles hung from it throughout the winter.

There were five rooms in our house, two for my grandparents and two for my parents. My grandparents occupied the rooms to the west, my parents the ones to the east. The five rooms of the main house were arranged in a line, the middle one being the kitchen; the rooms all had glass windows, dark green brick walls, and tile roofs.

My grandparents had an outer and an inner room. The former was furnished with a large oblong chest, a rectangular table, and an armchair. There was a red cushion on the armchair, a vermilion vase atop the oblong chest, and a desk clock on the rectangular table. Hat stands stood on either side of the clock, though instead of being used for hats, they were decorated with peacock feathers. As a child I was intrigued by those peacock feathers; I used to say they had gold eyes, and I was forever wanting to play with them. But Grandmother wouldn't let me touch them—she was obsessed with cleanliness.

The desk clock atop the oblong chest was a strange-looking timepiece on which was painted the lifelike figure of a young maiden in ancient costume. Whenever I was in Grandmother's room alone, this young maiden glowered at me; I told Granddad about this several times, but he always said:

"She's just a painted figure; she can't stare at you."

But I was convinced that she could, and I told him that as far as I was concerned, her eyeballs moved.

The oblong chest in Grandmother's room was also decorated from end to end with carved human figures, each wearing ancient costume—wide-sleeved gowns, officials' caps, and peacock feathers. The chest was virtually covered with the figures—there must have been twenty or thirty of them; some were drinking wine, others were eating, and still others were in the act of bowing.

I was forever trying to get a closer look at the figures, but Grandmother wouldn't let me get within arm's length of the chest, saying to me as I stood off at a distance:

"Don't you dare touch it with your filthy hands!"

On the wall of Grandmother's inner room hung a strange clock with two metal cornhusks suspended by chains beneath it. The metal cornhusks were a lot bigger than real ones, and looked to be so heavy that you could kill a person if you hit him with one. The inside of the clock was even stranger and more curious; there was a figure of a little blue-eyed girl inside, and every second those eyes of hers moved in concert with the ticking of the clock.

The differences between that little girl with her yellow hair and blue eyes and me were enormous, and even though Granddad told me it was the figure of a *maozi ren* or "hairy one," I wouldn't accept the notion that she was supposed to be a real person. Each time I looked at that wall clock, I stared so long I began to look dazed. I thought to myself: "Doesn't that *maozi ren* do anything but stay inside that clock? Won't she ever come down and play?"

In the slang of Hulan River, Caucasian foreigners were called *maozi ren*. When I was four or five, I'd yet to see my first *maozi ren*, and I thought this girl was called a "hairy one" because she had such curly hair.

There were a lot of other things besides these in Grandmother's room, but since none of them really interested me in those days, I can only remember these few items.

My mother's rooms had none of these kinds of unusual curios, only commonplace items like a gold-bordered wardrobe and a variety of hat stands and flower vases—nothing remarkable enough to linger in my memory.

In addition to these five rooms—four serving as living quarters plus a kitchen—there were two incredibly small, dark rooms in the rear of the house, one for my grandparents and one for my parents. These rooms were filled with lots of stuff, since they were used as storerooms: clay jugs and pitchers, chests and wardrobes, baskets and hampers— besides the things that belonged to our family, there were objects that other people had left there for safekeeping.

It was so dark inside the rooms I could see only if I carried a lantern in with me. The air inside these rat- and cobweb-infested rooms was pretty bad, and there was always a medicinal odor that assailed my nose. I loved playing in those storerooms, since any chest I opened was invariably filled with a number of good-looking things like colorful silk thread, colorful strips of silk, perfume satchels, waistband pouches, trouser legs, detachable over sleeves, and embroidered collars, all of them antique-looking, their colors blending together beautifully. Often I'd also find jadeite earrings or rings in the chests, and when I did, I was so insistent about wanting one to play with that Mother would usually toss it over to me.

Then there were desk drawers that yielded up even more interesting items: copper rings, a wooden knife, bamboo measuring sticks, and the white material we called Guanyin powder. These were all things I'd never seen anywhere else, and the best part of all was that the drawers were never locked. So I opened them pretty much whenever I felt like it, digging out whatever was inside without being the slightest bit selective. Holding the wooden knife in my left hand and some Guanyin powder in my right, I chopped here and daubed there. Then I came across a little saw, and I began destroying things right and left with it, sawing on objects like chair legs and the edges of our *kangs*. I even ruined my little wooden knife by sawing on it. I carried these things with me whether I was eating or sleeping. At meals I used my little saw to cut open steamed buns, and when I dreamed at night, I'd shout out:

"Where did my little saw go?"

The storerooms became in a way the scenes of my explorations. Often, when Mother was not in her room, I'd grab the opportunity to open the door and go inside. There was a window at the rear of the storeroom through which a little light filtered in during the afternoons. I used to take advantage of this light to open the drawers, all of which I eventually rummaged through completely, until there was nothing new to be found inside them. I'd go through them again until I lost interest, then emerge from the room. In the end, I even dug out a lump of resin and a little piece of string, at which time I'd picked all five of the desk drawers absolutely clean.

In addition to these drawers, there were some cages and trunks, but I didn't have the nerve to touch them, since they were all so dark and covered with who knows how much dust and how many layers of cobwebs that I never gave a thought to touching them.

I remember that once when I went to the farthest and darkest recess of this unlighted room, my foot bumped against something with a thud. I picked it up and carried it over to the light, where I discovered it was a lantern. I scraped off some of the dust with my finger, revealing that it was made of red glass. The chances are that when I was one or two years old, I'd seen this lantern before, but by the time I'd reached four or five, I no longer recognized it and didn't really know what to call this object I was holding in my hand. I carried it outside to ask Granddad what it was. After he'd cleaned it up for me, he stuck a piece of candle inside. I was so delighted with it I carried it all around the room, and, in fact, ran around with it for several days until I finally dropped it, breaking it into little pieces.

Once I also bumped into a piece of wood in the unlighted room. The top part had carvings on it and was rough to the touch. I took it outside and began sawing on it with my little saw, until Granddad spotted me:

"That's an engraving block for printing currency certificates," he said.

I had no idea what a currency certificate was, so he smeared a little ink on it and printed one to show me. I could only see that it had a few human figures, plus some motley designs and written characters.

"When we operated the distillery, we used this to make the currency certificates we issued," he told me. "This one is for a thousand strings of cash. We also had them for five hundred and one hundred." He printed up a bunch of them for me, and even printed some using red ink.

I also found and tried on a tasseled hat worn during the Qing Dynasty, and I fanned myself with a great big goose-feather fan that had been around for years. During my rummaging, I came across a little *sharen*, which was a medicine for stomach ailments. Mother took some, and I took some right along with her.

Before too long, I'd brought all these ancient relics out into the open; some had been put there for safekeeping by my grandmother, while others had been stored by aunts of mine who had married and left home. They had lain in that storeroom for years, touched by no one. Some of the things were falling apart, and others were infested by bugs, owing to the fact that they'd long been neglected by their owners. It was as if they no longer existed on the face of the earth. Suddenly, here they all were, right in front of everyone's eyes, and the memories of these things came rushing back to them with a start.

Each time I brought out some new item, Grandmother would say to me:

"This goes back a lot of years. Your eldest aunt played with this when she was living at home."

If Granddad saw something, he might say:

"Your second aunt used this when she was living at home," or: "This was your eldest aunt's fan. Those embroidered shoes belonged to your third aunt." Everything had a history of its own. The problem was, I didn't know who my third aunt or eldest aunt were. Maybe I'd seen them when I was one or two years old, but I'd forgotten them by the time I was four or five.

My grandmother had three daughters, though by the time I was old enough to know about such things, they had all married and left home. Obviously, for some twenty or thirty years there had been no children around, and now there was only one—me. Actually, I had a younger brother, but at the time he was no more than a year old, so he didn't count.

All these things had been put away in the house years before and left untouched. The people led their lives, looking neither ahead nor behind; that which was in their past was forgotten, while they held out no great hope for the future. They simply passed their days in stolid fashion, uncomplainingly accepting the lot handed down to them by their ancestors.

My birth had proved a source of inestimable joy to my Granddad, and as I grew up, I was the apple of his eye. As for me, I felt that all I needed in this world was Granddad, and with him by my side I had nothing to fear. Even the cold attitude of my father, my mother's mean words and nasty looks, and the incident in which my Grandmother pricked my finger with a needle faded into insignificance. If that weren't enough, there was also the rear garden! And even though the garden was sealed off by ice and snow some of the time, I had discovered the storerooms. Just about everything conceivable could be found inside, and the treasures they held were often things I had never imagined could even exist. I was struck by the thought of how many things there must be in this world! And all of them fun and unique.

For example, once I dug up a package of dye—Chinese dark green— and although it gave off a gold sheen when I looked at it, the moment I dabbed some on my fingernail, the fingernail turned green; then when I rubbed a little on my arm, it looked as if a green leaf had landed on the spot. It was both highly attractive and highly confusing, and I was secretly delighted to think that I might have stumbled onto a real treasure.

I came across a chunk of Guanyin powder. When I scratched this powder on the door, a white streak appeared on it, and when I scratched it across the window, it left a white streak there too. This was very strange; probably what Granddad used when he wrote was black ink, I thought, and what I had here was white ink.

I also discovered a round piece of glass that Granddad called a "magnifying glass." Holding it under the sun, I found it could light the tobacco in his pipe.

How happy things like this could make me, as each and every one of them underwent some sort of change. Someone might call a certain thing a piece of scrap metal, but who was to say it might not prove useful? To illustrate: Once I picked up a square piece of metal that had a small hole on the top, into which Granddad placed a hazelnut, cracked it, then gave it to me to eat. Breaking the hazelnut open in that hole was unbelievably faster than using his teeth to open it. Besides,

Granddad was an old man, and most of his teeth weren't much good anyway.

Every day I moved objects out of that dark room, and every day there was something new. I would carry out a load of things and play with them until I broke or grew tired of them, then go and get some more. All this caused a lot of sighing on the part of my grandparents. They told me how old a certain thing was, that it had been in our house before my third aunt was even born. They then told me how old something else was, that it had been brought into our house when my great-grandfather's inheritance was divided up. Then there was this thing or that, given to us by someone whose family had by this time died off without a trace, and yet this object was still around.

I remember the wicker bracelet I used to play with. Grandmother told me that she'd worn this bracelet, and that one summer she was riding to her mother's house in a small carriage, carrying my eldest aunt in her arms, when she encountered some bandits on the road. They took her gold earrings from her, but not this bracelet. Had it been made of gold or silver, probably they'd have taken it too.

After hearing this story I asked her:

"Where's my eldest aunt now?"

Granddad chuckled as Grandmother answered me:

"Your eldest aunt's children are all older than you."

So this incident had happened some forty years earlier—no wonder I wasn't aware of it! Yet here I was, wearing that very same wicker bracelet, so I raised my arm and twirled it, making it look like some kind of windmill as it slithered up my arm—you see, the bracelet was too big and my arm too thin.

Grandmother often scolded me when she saw me moving the things from the past out of the room:

"There's nothing you won't play with, child! You'll never amount to anything."

Though this was what she was saying, still she seemed to gain some satisfaction from the reminiscences this opportunity to see these objects from her past in broad daylight afforded her. Consequently, her scolding wasn't particularly harsh at all, and naturally I paid no heed, but went right on picking up whatever I pleased.

As a result, these things in our house that had not seen the light of day for the longest time reappeared only because I had brought them out. Afterwards they either wound up broken or discarded, until they all finally ceased to exist.

This was how I passed the first winter I can remember. Although I didn't actually feel lonely, it could never be as much fun as playing in the rear garden. But then, children forget easily and can make the best of any situation.

IV

The following summer we planted leeks in the rear garden because Grandmother liked to eat dumplings stuffed with them. But by the time the leeks began to appear, she had become seriously ill and couldn't eat them; and since no one else in the family ate leeks, they were left neglected in the garden.

Owing to Grandmother's illness, the house was all a-bustle; my eldest aunt and my second aunt both came.

Second Aunt came in a carriage owned by her husband's family and pulled by a donkey with a bell around its neck that tinkled loudly as it stood beneath the window.

First out of the carriage was a child who hopped down onto the ground. This child, who was my second aunt's son, was a little taller than I. His nickname was Little Orchid, and Granddad told me to call him Orchid Brother. I don't remember what else happened, and I only recall that before long I was leading him out into the rear garden. I told him that this was a rosebush, this was called a foxtail, and the cherry tree no longer bore any fruit.

I didn't know if he'd ever seen me before, but I was sure I'd never laid eyes on him. As I was leading him over to look at the plum tree in the southeast corner, he said as we approached it:

"This tree died the year before last."

I was surprised by what he said. How did he know that this tree had died? I began to experience pangs of jealousy, as I felt that this garden belonged to me and to Granddad, and that other people had no right to know anything about it.

"Then you've been to our house before?" I asked him.

He answered that he had.

This made me even angrier. Why wasn't I informed that he'd been here before?

"When were you here?"

He said it had been the year before last, and that he'd brought me a little stuffed monkey.

"Don't you remember? After you grabbed the stuffed monkey and ran off, you fell down and started to bawl!"

Hard as I tried, I couldn't remember the incident. But at any rate, considering that he'd given me a stuffed monkey and was nice to me, I could no longer be angry at him.

From then on, we played together every day. He was eight years old—three years my senior—and he told me he was studying in school. He'd even brought a few books along with him, which he took out and showed me in the evenings beneath the light of a kerosene lamp. The words for "people," "scissors," and "house" were printed inside, and since there were illustrations for all of them, I was confident I could read the words the moment I saw them. So I said:

"This is *jiandao*, for 'scissors,' and this is *fangzi*, for 'house.'"

"No," he corrected me, "this is the single character *jian*, and this is *fang*."

I pulled the book over and looked closely. Sure enough, there was only one character given for each, not two; I'd been going by the illustrations, and I was wrong.

I also had a box of flashcards with illustrations on one side and the characters on the other, so I brought them out and showed them to him.

From that time on, we played together all day long, every day. I was no longer aware of the state of Grandmother's illness, although I noticed that a few days before she died, they put a set of new clothes on her, as if she were going visiting. They said they were afraid that if she died, there wouldn't be enough time to dress her in new clothing.

Because of the seriousness of Grandmother's illness, there was a great deal of activity at our house, with many relatives coming to call, all of them busily doing one thing or another. Some were noisily tearing up strips and patches of white cloth; off to the side, others were sewing these patches together; while still others were filling small jars with rice and sealing the mouths with red cloth. Someone else went out into the rear garden to set up a fire for frying wheat cakes.

"What are those?" I asked her.

"These are cakes to ward off dogs."

She told me there are eighteen check stations in the nether world, and when you reach the station of the canines, the dogs there will come up to try and bite you. But if you throw out some of those cakes, the dogs will eat them instead of attacking. It seemed to me that she was just talking to hear herself talk, so I didn't pay any attention to what she was saying.

The more people who came to our house, the lonelier I got. I'd walk into a room to ask about this or that, but it was all beyond my comprehension. Even Granddad seemed to have forgotten me. Once, after catching an especially large grasshopper in the garden, which I took in to show him, he said without even looking:

"That's good, that's very good. Now go out and play in the garden, all right?"

On days when Orchid Brother wasn't with me, I played in the garden alone.

V

Grandmother was now dead, and everyone else had already attended the funeral rites at the Dragon King Temple and returned; as for me, I was still playing in the garden.

A light rain started to fall there, so I decided to go inside and get my straw hat. As I walked by the pickling vat (at our house the pickling vat was located in the rear garden), I noticed a couple of drops of water land noisily on the lid, and it occurred to me that since the lid was so large, it would keep the rain off me a lot better than my straw hat. So I flipped it over onto the ground where it rolled around a bit, just as the rain started falling heavily. With considerably difficulty, I managed to find a way to squeeze myself under the lid, which was really too big for me to handle—it was almost as tall as I was.

I stood up and walked a few steps with it on my head, but I couldn't see a thing; it was so heavy it made walking very difficult. I had no idea where my steps were taking me, and all I noticed was the pitter-patter of rain over my head. Then I looked down at my feet and discovered that I was standing in a patch of foxtails and leeks. When I found a spot thick with leek plants, I sat down and was immediately pinned to the ground by the lid, which now must have looked like a little roofed cottage. This was a lot better than standing, because I no longer had to carry the lid on my head—it was now supported by the patch of ground where the leeks were growing. But inside it was so pitch dark I couldn't see a thing.

Meanwhile, all the noises I heard seemed to be coming from far away. The big tree was rustling in the wind and rain, but it sounded as if it had been moved over into someone else's yard. The leeks had been planted at the base of the north wall, and I was sitting on them. Since the north wall was a long way from the house, the noise of activity inside the house seemed to be coming to me from a great distance.

I listened very carefully for a while, but, unable to distinguish any of the sounds, I just kept sitting there inside that little cottage of mine.

What a great little cottage it was, safe from the wind and the rain. When I stood up, I walked off supporting my roof on my head, which made me as carefree as can be. Actually, it was quite heavy and made walking very difficult.

I felt my way along, propping up the lid of the vat as I walked over to the back door of the house with the idea of showing Granddad what I was carrying on my head. The threshold of our back door was quite high off the ground, and since the vat lid was so big and heavy, I couldn't step over it. I didn't even have the strength to lift my legs. But with a great deal of effort I was finally able to lift them over with my hands, and I had more or less stepped across. Having entered the house, I still didn't know which way to go to find Granddad, so I shouted at the top of my voice. But before the sound had died out, my father gave me a kick that sent me sprawling, nearly knocking me into the wood fire burning in the stove. The vat lid crashed to the ground, where it was rolling around.

After being helped to my feet, I looked around: something was very wrong here—everyone was dressed in white clothing. Another look, and I could see that Grandmother was sleeping, but not on her *kang*; she was laid out on top of a long piece of wood.

From that day on Grandmother was dead.

VI

Following Grandmother's death, a continuous stream of relatives came to our house. Some brought incense and paper money with them, went over, and wailed beside the corpse for a moment, then left to return home. Some came with bundles of all sizes and stayed over with us.

While trumpets blared by the main gate, a mourning tent was erected in the courtyard; wailing sounds filled the air throughout the whole noisy affair, which lasted for more days than I could count. Buddhist monks and Taoist priests were brought over, and the commotion of all that eating, drinking, talking, and laughing lasted late into the night.

It was fun for me too, and I was happy then, especially since now I had some playmates, where before I'd had none. Altogether there were four or five of them, some older than I, some younger. We climbed the tree and clambered up onto the walls, and nearly climbed up onto the roof of the house. They took me to catch pigeons on top of the small gate and moved the ladder over under the house eaves so we could catch some sparrows. Spacious as my rear garden was, it was no longer big enough to hold me.

I went with them over to the edge of the well and looked down inside. I'd never seen just how deep that well was. When I shouted into it, someone down inside answered me; then I threw down a pebble, and the noise it made when it hit the bottom came from far away. They also took me over to a grain storeroom and to a grain mill, and on occasion they even took me out onto the street. I'd left the confines of my home, and not in the company of any adults in the family. I'd never gone so far before.

The fact that there were bigger places than my own garden had never occurred to me, and as I stood there at the side of the street, I was not so much looking at all the activity or at the people, animals, and carts, but wondering if someday I could travel as far as this all by myself.

One day they took me to the south bank of the river, which wasn't all that far from my house—probably less than a li—but since it was the first time I'd ever gone there, it seemed to me that it was a long way off, and I worked up a sweat getting there. On the way we passed a loess pit and a military barracks with soldiers standing guard at the entrance. The courtyard in front of the barracks building looked much too big to me, bigger than it had any right to be. The yard at our house was already big enough, so how could theirs be so much bigger? It was so big it had an unappealing look about it, and even after we'd passed by, I kept turning my head back to look at it.

Then we passed a house on the road where the owners had placed some potted plants along the top of the wall. This didn't seem like such a good idea to me, because someone might come along and steal them when no one was looking.

I also saw a small Western-style house that looked ten times better than our house. If you'd asked me what was so good about it, I couldn't have told you, but to my eyes it looked new from top to bottom and not at all worn-down, like our place. I'd traveled no more than half a li or so, but I'd already seen an awful lot, which fortified my belief that the south bank of the river must be a long way off.

"Are we there yet?"

"Just about," they answered. "We're almost there."

And just as they'd promised, as soon as we rounded the corner of the barracks wall, the river came into view. This was the first time I'd ever seen the river, and I was at a loss to figure out where its waters came from and how many years they'd flowed here. It seemed enormous. I scooped up some sand along the bank and threw it into the water without dirtying it even a tiny bit. There were a few boats on the river heading either east or west, some of them being rowed to the apparently deserted opposite shore, which was lined with willow trees. I looked off even farther, but I didn't know what places I was seeing, since there weren't any people or houses or roads over there, and no sounds to be heard. I wondered whether someday I could go to that deserted place myself and take a look around.

Beyond the rear garden at my house was a wide street; beyond the street was a wide river; beyond the river was a willow grove; and beyond the willow grove were places even farther away, deserted places where there was nothing to be seen and no sounds to be heard. What else might there be beyond these places? The more I pondered this, the harder it was to come up with an answer.

Without mentioning all the things I hadn't seen in my life, let's just talk of the courtyard and potted plants: we had a yard and potted plants at my house too, but the barracks courtyard was much bigger than ours, and at our house we put the potted plants in the garden, while others put theirs on the tops of walls. Obviously, there was a lot I didn't know.

And so I lost a grandmother, but gained some wisdom.

VII

After Grandmother died, I began to study poetry with Granddad.

Now that Granddad's room was empty, I caused a big scene with my demand to sleep in there with him.

I recited poems in the mornings and in the evenings, and I even recited them when I woke up in the middle of the night. I would recite for a little while until I was drowsy, then go back to sleep. Granddad taught me the verses in the *Thousand Poet Classic*, though we didn't use a book, but relied instead on his memory. He'd recite a line and then I'd recite it after him.

Granddad would recite:

> I left home young, I return an old man . . .

Then I'd recite:

> I left home young, I return an old man . . .

I couldn't have told you what the words meant, but they sounded good when I said them, so I shouted them gleefully along with Granddad, and I was always louder than he was.

Whenever I recited poems, I could be heard in every room in the house, and since Granddad was afraid I'd injure my voice with all that shouting, he often said:

"You're going to blow the roof right off the house!"

I'd smile at his little joke for a moment, but before long I was shouting again.

In the evening, I shouted, as always, until Mother scared me by saying if I kept it up she'd spank me. Even Granddad said:

"No one recites poetry like you do. That isn't 'reciting' poetry, it's just a lot of screaming."

But there was no way I could change my habit of screaming, and if I couldn't shout, what was the use in reciting them anyway? Whenever Granddad started to teach me a new poem, if I didn't like the way it sounded, right away I said:

"I'm not going to learn that one."

Then he'd choose another one, and if it didn't please me either, I'd say no to it too.

> I slept in spring not conscious of the dawn,
> But heard the gay birds chattering all around.
> I remember, there was a storm at night;
> I know not how many blossoms fell to the ground.

I really liked this poem, and whenever I got to the second line, "But heard the gay birds chattering all around," the words *chu chu*, for "all around" pleased me no end. I really thought this poem had a nice ring to it, especially the words for "all around."

There was another poem, "Flower Shadows," which I liked even better:

> Layer upon layer they cover the steps;
> The servant, summoned often, still cannot sweep them away.
> Taken from sight with the setting of the sun,
> The moon brings them back at the close of day.

I had no idea what the words, "The servant, summoned often, still cannot sweep them away" meant, and I always said, "Serving some off the sill cannot sweep them away."

The more I recited it the better it sounded to me, and my interest grew with each recitation. Whenever we had company in our home, Granddad had me recite my poems, and this is the one I liked doing the most. I don't know if the guests understood what I was saying, but they nodded their heads and complimented me.

VIII

Just memorizing a lot of poems without any understanding of their meaning wasn't the long-range plan, and after I'd memorized dozens of them, Granddad explained to me what they meant.

> I left home young, I return an old man;
> The speech is the same; though my hair is thin.

"This is about someone who left home to go out into the world when he was young and returned when he was an old man," Granddad explained. "'The speech is the same, though my hair-is thin' means that the accent of his hometown remains the same even though his beard has turned white."

"Why did he leave home when he was young?" I asked. "Where was he going?"

"Well, it would be just like your Granddad here leaving home when he was about your age, then returning as old as he is now. Who'd know him after all that time? 'The children see me, not knowing who I am/They smile and ask: "Stranger, where do you come from?"' You see, he's met by the children, who call out to him: 'Say, where have you come from, white-bearded old man?'"

I didn't like what I was hearing, so I quickly asked Granddad:

"Will I be leaving home, Granddad? Won't even you recognize me when I come home with a long white beard?"

My heart was filled with foreboding, but Granddad laughed and said:

"Do you think your Granddad will still be around when you get old?"

After he said this, he could see I was unhappy, so he quickly added:

"You won't be leaving home . . . how could you leave home? Now, hurry up and recite another poem! Let's hear 'Slept in spring not conscious of the dawn'!"

As soon as I began reciting "I slept in spring not conscious of the dawn," out came the shouts again, and my contentment returned. I couldn't have been happier, and everything else was forgotten.

But from then on, I made sure that every new poem was explained to me first, and I made sure also that the ones I'd already learned were explained. It seemed like my habit of shouting and screaming had changed a little for the better.

> Two yellow orioles sing in the green willows,
> A line of egrets climbs into the blue sky.

At first I liked this poem a great deal, because I mistook the word for "orioles" as the word for "pears," and pears were one of my favorite fruits. But after Granddad explained that this poem was about a couple of birds, I completely lost interest in it.

> This time last year behind this gate
>   The face and the blossoms glowed in the peach trees.
> Now the face is no more; only the blossoms
>   still smile in the spring breeze.

I didn't understand this poem either when Granddad recited it for me, but I liked it anyway. That was because peach blossoms were mentioned. After all, don't peach blossoms bloom just before the fruit appears? And aren't peaches good to eat?

So each time I finished reciting this poem, I asked Granddad: "Will there be any flowers on our cherry tree this year?"

IX

Next to reciting poetry, my favorite activity was eating.

I recall that the family who lived to the east of the main gate raised pigs, and there was always a bunch of little pigs following behind their sow. One day one of the little pigs fell down the well, and although someone fished it out with a soil basket, it was dead by then. A lot of people had gathered round the sides of the well to see what the commotion was all about, and Granddad and I were there to join in the excitement.

As soon as they'd gotten the little pig out of the well, Granddad said he wanted it. He carried it home, where he packed it in yellow clay, then stuck it into the stove and cooked it. When it was done, he gave it to me. I stood beside the *kang* with the whole little pig lying there in front of my eyes; then when Granddad split it open, oil oozed out. It was so fragrant—I'd never had anything that smelled as good in my whole life, and I'd never eaten anything so delicious.

The next time it was a duck that fell down the well. Granddad packed it too in yellow clay and cooked it for me. I helped him do the cooking—that is, I helped him with the yellow clay, yelling and shouting all the while, like a cheerleader rooting him on.

The duck tasted even better than the pig because there wasn't much fat on it, and so duck became my favorite food.

Granddad sat beside me watching as I ate, but he wouldn't take any for himself until after I'd finished. He said that I had small teeth, which made it harder to chew, so he wanted me to eat the tenderest portions first, then he'd finish what was left.

Granddad sort of nodded his head with each swallow I took and made lighthearted comments like: "What a greedy little thing you are," or "This little thing of ours sure eats fast."

My hands dripped with oil, which I rubbed on my lapels as I ate. But Granddad never got angry with me for doing that; he just said: 'Hurry, add a little salt and some leeks. You shouldn't eat that without something else, or before you know it, you'll have a tummy ache . . ." So saying, he picked up a pinch of salt and put it on the piece of duck meat I was holding. I opened my mouth and stuffed the whole thing in.

The more Granddad praised my appetite, the more I ate. Starting to worry that I might eat too much, he finally told me to stop, and I put it down. I knew I couldn't eat another bite, but still I said:

"Even a whole duck isn't enough for me!"

From that time on, I thought a great deal about eating duck, but the longest time went by without another duck falling into the well. On one occasion I saw a flock of them in the vicinity of the well, so I picked up a stick and tried to drive them into it. But they just scattered and ran around the mouth of the well making loud quacking noises, and none of them fell in. I yelled out to the kids nearby who were watching all the fun:

"Give me a hand here!"

While we were shouting and running around, Granddad hurried over and asked:

"What are you doing?"

"I'm driving the ducks over to the well so one of them will fall in. Then we can fish it out and cook and eat it."

"There's no need to do that. Granddad will catch one for you and take it home and cook it."

But instead of listening to him, I kept chasing after the ducks. He stepped in front to stop me, then picked me up in his arms and wiped the sweat off me.

"You come home with me now," he said. "I'll get a duck and cook it for you."

I thought to myself: Since you can't catch a duck unless it's fallen into the well, does he expect one of them to just walk over and allow itself to be packed in yellow clay and cooked? I struggled to get down out of Granddad's arms.

"I want one that's fallen down the well!" I screamed. "I want one that's fallen down the well!"

Granddad could barely hold me.

CHAPTER FOUR

I

By the time summer arrived, the mugwort had grown as high as an adult's waist and was over my head; if the yellow dog ran in among it, we couldn't see a trace of him. The mugwort rustled in the night winds, and since it virtually covered the courtyard, the rustling was especially loud, as big clumps moved noisily with each gust. When it rained, clouds of mist rose from the tips of the stalks, and even if the rainfall was actually a light one, it seemed to be quite heavy to anyone who was looking at the mugwort. During light drizzles the mugwort took on a hazy, indistinct appearance, as if covered by a layer of fog or an overcast sky. The scene was one of a frosty morning where everything is blurred under a pall of rising vapor.

The courtyard turned dreary with the coming of the winds and rain, and even on a clear day, with the sun shining brightly in the sky, the yard remained dreary looking. There were no dazzling or eye-catching decorations there, nor a trace of any manmade objects. Everything just followed its own nature: if it wanted to grow this way, it grew this way, and if it wanted to grow that way, it grew that way. A natural, primitive scene would have been maintained if only it had been left alone; but something was wrong here. What sort of scenery was this? Off to the east there was a pile of rotten wood, while off to the west the ground was covered with firewood; to the left of the gate a layer of old bricks, to the right a pile of clay drying in the sun.

The cook had used the clay to put up the kitchen stove, and he had dumped the remainder beside the gate. If someone had asked him whether or not the leftover clay could serve any purpose, I doubt that he could have come up with any, and he had probably just forgotten all about it.

I hadn't the slightest idea what the old bricks were for, as they had been there for a long time, buffeted by the wind, baked by the sun, and drenched by the rain. But since bricks are impervious to water, it really didn't matter that they got rained on. As a result, no one gave them a moment's thought, and they just let them get rained on. In fact, there was no reason to bother about them; if it happened that the stove or the opening beneath one of the *kangs* was in need of repair, they could still be used for the job. There they were, right in front of us—we merely had to reach out and pick them up, and what could be handier than that? At any rate, the stove seldom needed fixing, and the *kang* openings were well put together. I don't know where they found such competent workmen, but the *kang* openings held up for at least a year. If they were repaired in September, by the middle of the following year they were still holding up, and then when September rolled around again, a plasterer and a bricklayer were called, who had to use a metal knife to remove and replace the bricks one at a time. And so that pile of bricks by the side of the gate served little purpose the year round. It remained there year after year, though it most likely grew smaller as time went on, with this family taking one to use as a base for a flowerpot, and that family taking one for something or other. If the reverse had been true—that the pile had grown bigger as time went on—things would have been in a sad state, for wouldn't they have gradually blocked the entire gate?

But, in fact, the pile did grow smaller. With no interference by man, the natural course of events would see to it that the pile would disappear within two or three years. At the time, however, it was still there in front of us, soaking up the sun just like the pile of clay nearby; the two piles kept each other company.

Additionally, there were the splintered remains of a large vat that had been tossed over by the base of the wall and an earthen jar with a chipped and broken mouth that rested on the ground alongside it. The jar had been put out there empty but was now half-filled with rainwater; if I took it by the lip and shook it, I could see a tiny world of living creatures swimming around. Looking a little like fish and a little like insects, they were actually neither, and I couldn't tell just what they were. Looking at the big vat that was already splintered and standing precariously, threatening to topple over, I could see there was nothing at all inside it. Actually, I shouldn't be saying "inside," since it was split wide open, and there was no longer any "inside" or "outside" to speak of; let's just call it a "vat pedestal." This vat pedestal, minus the vat itself, was delightfully smooth and shiny, and it made a resounding noise when I slapped it. When I was young, I liked to move it over, for I was always fascinated by what I found: beneath the pedestal were swarms of sow bugs. When I first saw them, I was startled into running away, but after running off some distance, I'd stop, turn back, and take a long look, watching the sow bugs scurry around for a moment before they crawled back under the pedestal.

Then why wasn't this vat pedestal thrown away? Probably it had been left there for the purpose of raising sow bugs.

Opposite the vat pedestal stood an overturned hog trough. I don't know how many years this trough had lain there upside down, but it was already rotting away. The bottom was covered with dark-colored mushrooms, small ones that didn't look as if they were edible, and I never could figure out what they were growing there for. A rusty old steel plow lay in the grass beside the trough.

Strange as it may sound, everything at our house seemed to come in twos; there were only pairs, no single items: The bricks lying in the sun had the clay to keep them company, the broken jar was matched with the splintered vat, and the hog trough was accompanied by the steel plow. It was as if they were paired or mated to each other. Not only that, each couple brought new life into the world. There were, for example, the fishlike creatures in the jar, the sow bugs beneath the vat, the mushrooms that grew on the hog trough, and so on.

I don't know why, but the steel plow didn't look as if any new life was associated with it, as it fell apart and was covered with rust. Nothing was born of it, nothing grew from it—it just lay there turning rusty. If I touched it with my finger, flakes fell to the ground, and although it was made of steel, it had by this time deteriorated so much that it looked as if it were made of clay that was on the verge of crumbling to pieces. When viewed alongside its mate, the wooden trough, there was absolutely no comparison—it was covered with shame. If this plow had been a person, it would doubtless have wept and wailed loudly: "I'm made of better stuff than the rest of you, so why has my condition weakened to its present state?"

Not only was it deteriorating and rusting, but when it rained, the rusty pigment that covered it began to run, spreading with the rainwater over to its companion, the hog trough, the bottom half of which had already been stained the color of rust. The fingers of murky water spread farther and farther away, staining the ground they touched the color of rusty yellow.

II

My home was a dreary one.

Just inside the front gate, along the eastern wall of the covered gateway, were three dilapidated old buildings, and along the western wall were three more. With the covered gateway in the middle, they gave the appearance of seven buildings standing in a line. From the outside they looked to be very imposing, with their tall roofs and sturdy frames of thick, solid wood. The posts were so thick a child couldn't wrap his arms around one. They were all roofed with tiles, and the ridges were adorned with tile decorations that were a delight to behold when the sun glinted off them. Each end of the house ridge was finished off with a pigeon, which was probably also made of tile. They remained there all year long, never moving. From the outside they didn't look bad.

But to my eyes there was an emptiness about them.

Our family used the three buildings to the west to store grain—there wasn't all that much grain kept in them, but there were hordes of rats. Holes had been chewed through the granary floors by the rats, whole families of which were eating the grain. And while down below it was being consumed by rats, up above it was being eaten by sparrows. A rank, moldy odor filled the buildings. The broken windows had been boarded up; the dilapidated doors shook on their hinges when they were opened.

The three buildings along the eastern wall beside the covered gateway were rented out to a family of hog farmers. Inside and out, it was all about hogs—grown hogs and newborn hogs, hog troughs and hog feed. The only people who came and went were hog dealers; the buildings, the people, everything was permeated with a horrible stench.

Come to speak of it, that family didn't raise all that many hogs, perhaps eight or ten. Every day at dusk people far and near could hear the sounds of their hog calls as they banged on the troughs and the tops of the sties. They would shout a few times, then stop; their voices rose and fell, and in the solemn evening air it sounded like they were complaining of the loneliness of their lives.

There were, in addition to these seven rooms standing in a row, six more dilapidated buildings—three run-down huts and three milling sheds.

The three milling sheds were rented out to the family of hog farmers, since they were located next to the sties.

The three run-down huts, which were in the southwest corner of the compound, had run off by themselves a long way from everything else and stood there all alone, squalid-looking and leaning to one side or the other.

The roofs of these buildings were covered with lichens and from a distance appeared as an eye-catching patch of green. When it rained, mushrooms grew on the roofs, which the people climbed up to pick, as if they were foraging for mushrooms on a mountain. There was always a bumper crop. Rooftops that produced mushrooms were a rare sight indeed, and of the thirty or so buildings my family owned, none of the others could boast this distinction. So whenever the people who lived there took their baskets up onto the roof to pick mushrooms, everyone in the compound would begin to comment enviously:

"Those mushrooms are certainly nice and fresh, so much better than the dried ones we have. If you killed a young chicken and fried it along with them, it would be simply delicious!"

"Fried bean curd and mushrooms—my, wouldn't that be tasty!"

"Even a baby chick isn't as tender as rain-fed mushrooms."

"If you fried chicken with some of those mushrooms, everyone would eat the mushrooms and leave the chicken."

"If you cooked some noodles with those mushrooms, everyone would drink the soup and forget the noodles."

"It would be quite a feat if someone could even remember his name while he ate those mushrooms."

"If you steamed them and added some sliced ginger, you could eat at least eight bowls of steamed rice along with them."

"It'd be a mistake to treat something like those mushrooms lightly, because they're an unexpected windfall!"

The envious people who shared the compound hated themselves for not having the good fortune to live in those huts, and if they'd known that a crop of mushrooms went with the buildings, they'd have insisted that they be rented to them. Whoever heard of such luck—renting a house with mushrooms thrown into the bargain? They stood there sighing and commiserating with one another.

Then, of course, what glory came to the person who was standing on the roof picking mushrooms under the scrutiny of all those eyes!

He picked them slowly, so that a job that should have taken no longer than the time it takes to smoke a pipeful was stretched out to perhaps half the time it takes to eat a meal. Not only that, he purposefully picked several of the larger ones and threw them to the ground.

"Just look at those, will you?" he said. "Have you ever seen cleaner mushrooms than those? There isn't another rooftop around with mushrooms like these."

The people down below had no way of knowing the size of the rest of the mushrooms on the roof, so they had to assume that they were all as big as the ones thrown down, which increased their astonishment no end. They hastily bent over, picked them up, and carried them home; then at dinnertime, when the bean curd peddler came around, they splurged several coins on a little piece of bean curd to cook up with the mushrooms. But owing to his smugness, the fellow on the roof had forgotten that there were several bad spots, some of which had even sprung holes, and in a careless moment he put his foot completely through the roof. He pulled his foot back up through the hole, only to discover that his shoe was missing.

It had fallen from the ceiling straight down into a pot in which water was just then being boiled, and so his shoe was cooked in the pot. The people sifting bean flour alongside the pot were both intrigued and amused by the sight of a toe bobbing around in the boiling water; a murky substance oozed from the sole of the shoe, turning the bean noodles that had already been sifted a yellowish color. But still they didn't fish the shoe out of the pot, their explanation being that the noodles were to be sold anyway and weren't intended for their own consumption.

The roof over this house could produce mushrooms, but it couldn't keep out the rain, and each time it rained, the room filled up like a jar. Everything was wet to the touch. Fortunately, the people who lived there were all coarse individuals. There was a child with a crooked nose and bulging eyes whose nickname was Iron Child. He held an iron shovel in his hands all day long, which he used to chop things in a long trough. But what exactly was he chopping? When you first entered the place, you couldn't see clearly because of the clouds of steam that filled the room and prevented you from discerning what anyone was doing there. Only when you had a chance to look more closely would you see that he was chopping potatoes. The trough was filled with potatoes.

This particular hut was rented out as a shop where noodles were made out of bean flour. The people there were a coarse lot who couldn't afford to wear good shoes or socks and owned no decent bedding. There wasn't much difference between them and pigs, so that living in this type of building was very appropriate—if they'd lived in a nice house, they'd probably have turned it into a sty in no time. Then, of course, their diet was enhanced by the addition of mushrooms whenever it rained.

When the people who lived there had mushrooms, they mixed them with the bean flour they milled: they had stir-fried mushrooms and noodles, stewed mushrooms and noodles, and boiled mushrooms and noodles. When there was no soup, they called it stir-fried; when there was soup, they called it boiled; and when there was slightly less soup, they called it stewed.

Often, after making such a meal, they brought a large bowlful over to Granddad. He'd wait for the boy with the crooked nose and staring eyes to leave, then say:

"We can't eat this. If there were any toadstools among those mushrooms, we'd die if we ate it."

But no one at the noodle shop ever died of toadstool poisoning, and, as a matter of fact, they spent the day singing as they sifted the bean flour.

A rack several feet tall had been erected in front of the shop, from which shiny lengths of bean noodles hung like cascading waterfalls. All the time the people were hanging out the noodles, they sang to themselves, and after the noodles had dried in the sun, they gathered them in, still singing as they worked. Their songs were not an expression of the joys of their work; rather, they were the sounds of someone laughing with tears in his eyes.

Stoically they accepted their hardships: "You say that the life I live is a pitiable one? Well, that's all right with me. In your eyes I'm in mortal danger, but my life gives me satisfaction. And if I wasn't satisfied, so what? Isn't life made up more of pain than pleasure anyway?"

The songs that emerged from that noodle shop were like a red flower blooming atop a wall—the brighter and lovelier it was, the more desolate the feeling it evoked.

On the fifteenth day of the very first month
Lanterns are hung by one and all;
While others' husbands are reunited at home,
Meng Jiangnü's spouse labors on the Great Wall.

On clear days, as the bean noodles were hung out to dry, this song could always be heard. Inasmuch as the hut was located in the southwest corner, the sounds of the singing were rather distant. Once in a while, someone imitating a woman singing "Daybreak Lament" could be heard.

The hut they lived in was certainly beyond repair. Every time there was a heavy rain, a new support had to be placed on the northern side of the building, and eventually there were as many as seven or eight such struts; but still the house leaned farther and farther to the north each day. The lean grew more and more pronounced, until it frightened me just to look at it. I could imagine it collapsing to the ground as I was passing by and pinning me beneath it. No question about it, the hut was in sad shape: the windows, which had originally been square, had been twisted out of shape by the lean of the building. The doorframe was so awry they couldn't close the door, and the tie beams above the wall seemed in danger of crashing to the ground and leaping out of the building. The central beam of the roof ridge moved a little farther north each day, since the tenons had already broken loose from the mortises, and there was nothing left to control it. It was now moving as a free agent. As for the smaller beams that had been nailed to the ridge pole, those that were able to keep up with it just followed along this northward journey as a river follows its course; those that couldn't keep up simply wrested their nails loose and sagged downward, hanging precariously over the heads of the people inside. They didn't fall because the other ends were anchored by the eaves, so they just sagged and creaked.

I just had to go in and see how they sifted the bean flour, but I didn't dare survey the scene too closely, for fear that the beams would fall in on top of me.

When winds arose, the building creaked and groaned; the beams, the timbers, the doors, the windows—everything strained and moaned.

The rains, too, caused the building to creak, and in the nighttime, even if there was no wind or rain, there were still creaking noises. As night deepened and people noises died out, the creatures of the night began their chorus. How then could this building, whose nature it was to creak, be expected to keep silent?

In fact, its creaking noises could be heard above all else. The other sounds, though audible if you strained to listen, were less discernible, and not very reliable. Perhaps the people's ears were playing tricks on them, and the sounds were not there at all, for these were not the noises that one expected to hear, unlike the sounds of animate creatures like cats, dogs, and insects.

Has anyone ever heard of a building crying out in the night? Whose house could cry out like that, making the plaintive sounds of a living creature, and so loud it often awakened whoever was sleeping inside? But the person who'd been awakened merely turned over and said:

"The house is on the move again."

He truly seemed to be talking about a living thing, saying that the building was retaking itself to a new site. Now, since the building was off to a new location, wouldn't you think that the person sleeping inside would get out of bed? But no, he just rolled over and went back to sleep.

The people who lived in this hut felt no sense of danger regarding the possibility of its collapsing. They viewed it with such trust and confidence that one might suppose there was a blood relationship between them. It was as if even if the building did collapse someday, it would not fall on their heads, and even on the chance that it did, their lives would be spared—there was absolutely no danger of losing one's life. I don't know the origin of this extreme self-assurance, but perhaps the people who lived there were made not of flesh and bones, but of iron. Either that or they were like a suicide squad who placed little value on their own lives. Otherwise, how could they be so brave that they scoffed at death?

On second thought, it may be inaccurate to say that they scoffed at death, for on those occasions when the pole from which one of them was taking down strips of bean noodles drying in the sun crashed to the ground, that person was frightened speechless.

The noodles had been smashed to pieces, but he had escaped being hit, and as he scooped up the noodles, he couldn't take his eyes off the pole. After a momentary reflection, he said:

"Could it be . . ."

The more he thought, the more bizarre it seemed to him—how could he have missed getting hit, while the noodles were shattered? He picked up the pole and put it back in place, then stood off a bit and sized it up, experiencing an ever-increasing apprehension.

"Goodness! If that had fallen on of my head . . ."

That truly was too alarming a prospect to imagine, and as he rubbed his head, he realized how fortunate he had been and vowed to be more careful next time.

The truth of the matter is, the pole wasn't as thick as the house's roof beams, but the mere sight of it gave him a scare. From then on, each time he hung noodles out to dry, he shied away from the pole, to the point of refusing to even walk by it, keeping a wary eye on it at all times. He forgot the incident only after the passage of many days.

During thunderstorms the people inside always doused their lights, for according to them, fire attracts lightning, and they were afraid of being struck. Whenever they crossed the river, they first threw two copper coins into the water, for legend has it that the river spirit is a rapacious one who often causes people to drown. But if copper coins are thrown in, he is appeased and will spare them.

All this goes to prove that the people who lived in this creaky hut were just as timorous as anyone else and, like others, spent their days on earth in mortal fear. That being the case, why then were they unafraid of the prospect of their house's collapsing on top of them?

According to Old Zhao, the steamed bun peddler:

"That teetering building just happens to be the very one they want!"

According to the boy with the crooked nose and bulging eyes who lived there:

"This is only a place to live. You don't have to look for perfection, as you would in choosing a wife."

According to the two gentry youths from the Zhou family who shared our compound:

"You couldn't find a more fitting place for coarse people like that to live in."

And according to Second Uncle You:

"They're only interested in the cheapest place they can find. Since there are good houses all over the town of Hulan River, you wonder why they don't just move, don't you? Well, a good house would cost money, not like this place of ours. Here they can live for ten or twenty catties of dry noodles a year, and that's it—why, it's the same as free rent. If your Second Uncle had a family, he'd look for a place just like that one."

Maybe there was some truth in what Second Uncle You said.

It had long been Granddad's plan to tear that building down, but the tenants came en masse to persuade him not to, and thus it remained standing. As for the questions of whether or not the building would someday collapse and whether it would bring good fortune or ill to those inside, that was considered by everyone something too far in the future to warrant any thought.

III

Our compound was a dreary one.

The occupants were bean-flour sifters who lived on one side and hog farmers who lived on the other. There was also a miller who lived in one of the side rooms belonging to the hog farmers. This miller would strike his wooden clappers at night, the whole night through. Among the family of hog farmers were several individuals with time on their hands and little to do, who often got together to sing their Shaanxi opera to the accompaniment of a two-stringed instrument called a *huqin*. On clear days the flour sifter in the southwest corner of our compound liked to sing "Daybreak Lament."

Now, although they played their *huqin*, struck wooden clappers, and sang this song, one must not be misled into believing that these were indications of prosperity or progress; it was certainly not that they could see a bright future ahead of them, nor even that they entertained any hopes for such a future—it meant none of these things. They could see nothing that could be considered bright, nor would they have recognized it for what it was even if they had. They were like a blind man standing in the sun who, though unable to see it above him, can nonetheless feel its warmth on his head.

These people were like that: they didn't know where the brightness was, but they were fully aware of the cold that enveloped their bodies. It was the struggle to break free from this cold that brought them to grief. Ushered into this world by their mothers with no real expectations, they could only hope to eat their fill and dress warmly. But they were forever hungry and cold.

Foully the affairs came; fairly they were accepted. Not in the course of their lifetimes did affairs ever come fairly.

The sounds of wooden clappers being struck at night in the mill shed often increased in intensity as the night deepened, and the more vigorously they were struck, the more desolate the sound. That was because they were the lone sounds in the night—there were no others to accompany them.

IV

Our compound was a dreary one.

A carter and his family lived in one of the side rooms attached to the noodle mill. The dance of the sorceress was frequently performed for this family's benefit, so drumbeats and chants often arose from that place. The sound of drums generally lasted late into the night, accompanied by talk of fairies and ghosts and the ritual of dialogue between the sorceress and her attendant; they were mournful, distant sounds that confused all sense of time. The old woman of this family was sick the year round, and the dance of the sorceress was performed for her benefit.

This family was more blessed than any other in the compound, with its three generations living together. Their family traditions were the best defined and the neatest: they treated one another with respect, there was mutual understanding and good feelings among the siblings, and a great deal of love between parent and child. No one in the family was an idler or had time on his hands. No similarity existed between them and the people who lived in the noodle mill or the mill shed, who spent so much of their time singing or weeping as the feeling moved them. No, their home was forever quiet and tranquil. Not counting, of course, the dance of the sorceress.

The grandmother—the old woman who was always sick—had two sons, each of whom was a carter. Both sons had wives: the elder son's wife was a plump woman in her fifties; the younger son's wife a slim woman in her forties. In addition, the old woman had two grandsons: the elder grandson belonged to the woman's younger son, while the younger grandson belonged to her elder son.

As a consequence, there was some small degree of disharmony insofar as relations between the two daughters-in-law were concerned, although it was not all that apparent, and perhaps only the two of them were aware of it. The wife of the elder son felt that the wife of the younger son treated her with less obedience and respect than might be called for, an attitude whose origin she suspected was the fact that her sister-in-law's son was older than her own. The younger daughter-in-law, on the other hand, felt that her sister-in-law was trying to ride herd over her, since her son was too young to have a wife. To her, this meant that the elder woman was upset that she herself had no daughter-in-law to control.

With two sons and two grandsons, the old woman was unreservedly pleased with her life. How could the family fail to prosper with such an equitable arrangement for the distribution of family chores?

One need look no further than the operation of the big cart; there was enough combined strength here to handle it completely, and who else could boast of a cart handled by four men of the same family? Everyone—from the one holding the whip to those seated in the rear of the cart—was named Hu, so no outsider was needed. And whatever the occasional domestic conflict that might arise, they presented themselves to the outside world as a close-knit family. For this reason the old woman had an optimistic view of life, though she was constantly ill; but even that could be put out of her mind with the performing of the sorceress' dance. She felt that even if she should die, she would do so with her mind at peace and free of misgivings. But for the moment, there was still life in her, which meant that she could continue to watch the labors of her sons with her own two eyes.

Her daughters-in-law also treated her quite well, spending whatever was necessary from time to time to engage the sorceress to do her dance.

Each time the sorceress danced, the old woman reclined on her *kang*, her head resting on a pillow; as she strained to sit up, she'd say to the women and girls who had gathered to watch what was going on: "The arrangements this time were made by my elder daughter-in-law," or "The arrangements this time were made by my younger daughter-in-law." Saying this always gave her a sense of pride and satisfaction, so she said it over and over, until she no longer had the strength to sit. Since she was afflicted with paralysis, she'd quickly call for her daughters-in-law to come help her lie down, an effort that would leave her momentarily breathless.

Not a single one of those who had gathered to watch the excitement failed to comment on the kindliness of the old woman and the filial behavior of her daughters-in-law.

And so each time the sorceress visited her, people came from far and near, from the east and west compounds and all the neighboring streets. The one thing they could not do was reserve a spot, so the early arrivals sat on benches and on the edge of the *kang*, while those who came later had to stand.

The Hu family suddenly enjoyed a position of leadership in the community, owing to the filial conduct of its members, who served as models for other women.

Men, as well as women, made their views known:

"Providence has smiled on old Hu's family, and one day wealth will come to them as well."

"Of the three factors—weather, land, and morale—morale is the most important. If there is high morale, even if the weather is bad, or if the land is no good, it's still all right."

"You wait and see—today they are a family of carters, but in another five years, if they aren't a second-class family, they'll be at least a third-class one."

Second Uncle You's comment was:

"You mark my word—before many years have passed, they'll own a stableful of donkeys and horses. Don't be fooled by the fact that they only own a single cart now."

There were no new developments in the disharmonious relationship between the two daughters-in-law, though it never completely worked itself out either.

The wife of the elder grandson, a ruddy-faced woman, was capable and obedient. She was neither too fat nor too thin, neither tall nor short, and when she spoke, her voice was neither loud nor soft. She was perfectly suited to this family. When the cart returned, she led the horse over to the well to drink, and before the horse and cart left the compound, she fed the animal. To look at her you wouldn't have thought she was made for this type of rough life, but when she worked, she seemed no frailer than anyone else and suffered little in comparison even with the men.

After she'd finished her work outside, she began her domestic chores, all of which she handled quite capably. Whether it was needlework, mending, or what have you, she managed everything just as you would expect it to be managed. And though there were no silks or satins in their house to work with, still the coarse materials had to be sewn with fine, even stitches.

Then, as New Year's approached, no matter how busy she might be, she nonetheless found time to make embroidered shoes for the old grandmother, her mother-in-law, and her aunt. She had to make do without dainty shoe tops, but even if she had only a piece of plain blue cloth to work with, the needlework still had to be delicately done. Since she had no silk thread, she used cotton thread instead, yet she still managed to make the color combination fresh and crisp. The shoes she made for her husband's grandmother were embroidered with large pink lotus petals, those for her aunt were festooned with peonies, and the pair for her mother-in-law was decorated with elegantly simple green-leafed orchids.

Whenever this young woman returned to her parents' home, she was asked how things were at the home of her husband. Her response was that everything was just fine, and that the family was destined someday to make its fortune. She told of her uncle's cautious and attentive nature, and how hardworking and capable of enduring hardship her father-in-law was. "The grandmother," she said, "is a good woman, as is my aunt. In fact, there isn't a thing there that isn't good." Everything was just as she'd have wished it, and families like that don't come easily to a woman.

Granted, her husband might beat her, but as she said: "What man doesn't beat his wife?" And so this did nothing to lessen her satisfaction with how things had turned out.

When the grandmother was presented with the finished embroidered shoes, the fine workmanship caused her to experience a sense of guilt in her treatment of this wife of her grandson. She felt that with her ability to do such fine needlework, it was an insult to have her spend each day slopping the hogs and kicking the dogs. She reached out and took the shoes, but not knowing what to say, she merely held them gently in her hands and nodded, a smile on her ashen face.

We've seen what a good wife the elder grandson had. As for the younger grandson, even though a wife had been chosen for him, he was still too young for the marriage to take place.

The fact that this girl hadn't yet been brought into the family was the cause of the ill feelings between the two daughters-in-law. The girl's prospective mother-in-law proposed that she be brought over as a child bride, while the younger daughter-in-law objected, since the girl was too young to do anything but eat, and what good would that do them? They argued over this for some time without resolving the issue; it was always: "Wait till the next time we have the sorceress over for the old woman, and we'll ask her opinion."

V

My home was a dreary one.

Roosters crowed before the sun was up, and the sound of the wooden clappers from the mill continued even after daybreak. Once the sky turned light, flocks of crows appeared in the sky. I slept beside Granddad, and as soon as he woke up, I asked him to recite some poems; and so he began:

> I slept in spring not conscious of the dawn,
> But heard the gay birds chattering all around.
> I remember, there was a storm at night;
> I know not how many blossoms fell to the ground.

"Someone sleeping on a spring morning slowly awakens to the new day, and the first thing he hears is the sound of birds all around. His thoughts return to the rainstorm of the night before, but he doesn't know how many fallen flowers are on the ground today."

Each reading of a poem was followed by an explanation, for this is what I'd demanded.

As Granddad was explaining the poem to me, our family cook was up and around. I could hear him coughing as he carried the water bucket out to the well to fetch water. Our well was quite far from the rooms where we slept, too far for us to be able to hear the sound of the well rope being pulled up during the day; but in the early morning the sound came through loud and clear.

Even after the old cook had fetched his water, the others in the house were still asleep. Then came the sounds of the old cook scraping the pot. After he'd scraped the pot clean, he boiled some water for us to wash up, and still no one else was out of bed. Granddad and I continued to recite poems until the sun rose in the sky.

"Let's get up." Granddad said.

"One more poem."

"One more and then we've got to get up."

So we did one more, and when we'd finished, I stalled by saying that that one didn't count, and I wanted to do one more.

Every morning we carried on like that. Once the door was opened, out we went into the garden, which by then was flooded with golden light. The sun baked down on us as it climbed overhead. Granddad walked over to the chicken coop to let the chickens out, so that's where I went too; Granddad went over to the duck pen to let the ducks out, and I followed right behind him. I tagged along behind him with the big yellow dog on my heels. I was hopping and jumping; the big yellow dog was wagging his tail.

The dog's head was the size of a small washbasin. He was a large dog, and round, and I was forever trying to ride him as I would a horse, though Granddad wouldn't allow it. Nonetheless, the big yellow dog liked me and I loved him.

The chickens and the ducks came out of their coops, shook out their feathers, and began to run around the yard, cackling and quacking noisily. Granddad scattered some kernels of bright red sorghum on the ground, and then the golden kernels of some other grains. Immediately the air was filled with the pecking sounds of chickens as they ate the feed on the ground.

After the chickens had been fed, we looked up at the sky to see that the sun had climbed even higher. Granddad and I returned to the house, where we set up a small table; Granddad ate a bowl of rice porridge with sugar sprinkled on top. But I didn't eat any. I wanted some baked corn, so he took me back out into the rear garden; then, walking on the dew-covered ground, he went over to the clump of corn stalks and pulled off an ear of corn for me. Our shoes and socks were soaked through by the time he'd broken off the ear of corn.

Granddad told the cook to bake the corn for me, but by the time it was ready, I'd already eaten two bowls or more of sugared rice porridge. I took the corn, ate a few kernels, and complained that it wasn't any good—you see, I was by then already full. So what I did was take the corn out into the garden to feed Big Yellow. "Big Yellow" was the dog's name.

From out on the street beyond the wall came the voices of all the different peddlers: There was the bean curd peddler, the steamed bun peddler, and vegetable peddlers.

A vegetable peddler was calling out the things he had to sell—eggplants, cucumbers, various legumes, and scallions. After he'd passed with his basket of produce, another followed; but instead of eggplants and cucumbers, this one had celery, leeks, and cabbage.

There was a good deal of noise and commotion out on the street, while our house remained quiet.

The mugwort-covered yard was the hiding place of hordes of chirping insects, as well as all sorts of discarded objects.

One would assume that my house was quiet because the day had just begun. But the truth of the matter was, there were a great many buildings, a large compound, and few people living there. For that matter, even at high noon my house was still placid.

Each autumn smartweed flowers covered the tops of the mugwort, bringing forth great numbers of dragonflies and butterflies that darted back and forth atop the dreary stretch of mugwort. But instead of investing the area with luxuriance, as one might expect, their presence increased the sense of gloom and loneliness one felt there.

CHAPTER FIVE   I

Except for the time I spent playing in our rear garden, accompanied by Granddad, I was left to my own devices to find amusement. Sometimes I pitched a makeshift tent beneath the eaves, then, after playing for a while, fell asleep there.

We had removable windows in our house that, when taken down, would stand up only if they were propped up against a wall, making a nice little lean-to. This I called my "little hut." I often took naps there in my little hut.

Our compound was covered with mugwort, over which swarms of dragonflies flew, attracted by the fragrance of the red smartweed flowers. I amused myself by catching dragonflies until I wore myself out, after which I lay down in the mugwort and went to sleep.

Clumps of wild berries grew among the mugwort, resembling mountain grapes, and quite delicious. I foraged for berries among the mugwort, and when I grew weary of that, I lay down beside the berry bushes and went to sleep. The dense mugwort served as a kind of mattress, and I enjoyed the shade the tall grass offered.

One day, just before suppertime, as the sun was setting in the west, I lay dreaming on my bed of mugwort. I must not have been sleeping all that soundly, for I thought I heard lots of people talking nearby. They were chatting and laughing with real gusto, but I couldn't quite make out just what was happening. I could only sense that they were standing off in the southwest corner, either inside the compound or just beyond it—whether it was inside the compound or not, I simply couldn't tell—and out there somewhere there was quite a bit of excitement. I lay there half awake for a while, and the noise eventually died out; most likely I'd fallen asleep again.

After I woke up, I went into the house, where I was given the news by our old cook:

"The Hu family's child bride arrived, and you weren't even aware of it. Hurry up and eat so you can go have a look at her!"

The old cook was busier than usual that day. He was carrying a platter of sliced cucumbers into Granddad's room, and his brief but animated conversation with me nearly caused him to drop the plate to the floor. In fact, the cucumber slices did slide off the platter.

I walked into Granddad's room, where I found him sitting alone at the table with all the dishes laid out before him. There was no one else there to eat with him; Mother and Father hadn't come to supper, nor had Second Uncle You. Granddad saw me come in and asked:

"How does the child bride look?"

He apparently thought I'd just come from taking a look at her. I told him I didn't know, that I'd just come in after eating wild berries amid the mugwort.

"Your mother and the others have all gone to look at the child bride over at old Hu's house—you know, the one where the sorceress is always doing her dance." When he finished, Granddad called out to the old cook to hurry up with the plate of cucumbers.

The cucumbers, lying in vinegar sauce and topped by hot-pepper oil, were an eye-catching mixture of greens and reds. I was sure he'd had to slice another plateful, since I'd seen the original one scattered on the kitchen floor. The moment the cucumber dish arrived, Granddad said:

"Hurry up and eat, so we can go have a look at the child bride."

The old cook stood off to the side, wiping his sweaty face with his apron. Every time he spoke he blinked his eyes and spurted saliva from his mouth.

"There certainly are a lot of people going over to see the child bride!" he said. "Even the second wife of the grain shop owner took her kids over. Little Pockface from the compound behind us is over there too, and several members of old Yang's family from west compound, who climbed over the wall to get there."

He said he'd seen all this as he was drawing water from the well.

Exhilarated by this news of his, I said:

"Granddad, I don't want to eat now. I want to go see the child bride."

But Granddad was steadfast in wanting me to eat before he'd take me over, though I was in such a hurry I didn't eat much. I'd never in my life seen a child bride, whom I imagined be beautiful beyond words. The more I dwelled upon it, the more I was convinced that she must indeed be beautiful, and the more anxious I grew, the stronger was my conviction that she must be a rare beauty. Otherwise, why was everyone so eager to see her? Otherwise, why would even Mother miss her supper?

I grew more and more fidgety, since I was sure that the best part of the show was already over. Now if I left right away, at the very least I'd be able to see something worthwhile, but I was afraid I'd be too late if I waited much longer. So I pressed Granddad:

"Hurry, hurry up and eat, Granddad, please hurry."

The old cook was still standing off to the side talking a blue streak, while Granddad asked him a question every once in a while. I could see that the cook was interrupting Granddad's meal, but even though I tried to get him to stop talking, he wasn't about to listen to me. He kept on chuckling and laughing, so finally I got down from my chair and literally pushed him from the room.

Granddad still hadn't finished when Third Granny from old Zhou's house came over to report that their rooster kept running over to our house, and that she'd come to fetch it. But instead of leaving after she had her rooster, she came to the window and notified Granddad:

"The little child bride has already arrived at old Hu's. Aren't you going over to see her? Lots of people are over there taking a look, and I plan to go after supper." Granddad told her he was going over after supper too, but it seemed to me that he'd never finish his meal. First he asked for some more hot-pepper oil, then he wanted some salt. I could see that I wasn't the only one who was growing impatient—the old cook could barely contain himself; his brow was sweating and his eyes were blinking nonstop.

The moment Granddad put his rice bowl down, I began dragging him along with me over to the southwest corner of the wall without even letting him light up his pipe. As we hurried along, I experienced feelings of regret every time I saw someone coming back from watching all the fun. Why had I had to wait for Granddad anyway? Couldn't I have run over there by myself a long time ago? The recollection that I'd heard some excitement coming from over here while I was lying in the mugwort added to my displeasure. Honestly, the more I thought about it, the stronger my regrets grew. This affair had already taken up half the afternoon, and I just knew that the good part was over, that I was too late. Coming now was a waste of time—there'd be nothing more to see. Why hadn't I rushed over to take a look the second I heard all that talking and laughing while I was lying in the grass? My regrets grew so strong that I began to get angry at myself, and just as I'd feared, when we drew up next to old Hu's window, there wasn't a sound. I was so mad I nearly cried.

When we walked in the door, it wasn't at all as I'd been led to expect. Mother, Third Granny Zhou and several people I didn't know were there, and everything was contrary to what I'd imagined; there was nothing worth seeing here. Where was the child bride? I didn't see her anywhere until the others pointed and nodded; then I saw her. This was no bride, she was just a girl! I lost interest the moment I saw her, and started pulling Granddad toward the door.

"Let's go home, Granddad."

The next morning I saw her when she came out to draw water to wash up. Her long black hair was combed into a thick braid; unlike most young girls, whose braids hung down to about their waists, hers came down nearly to her knees. Her complexion was dark, and she had a hearty laugh.

After the people in the compound had all taken a look at the child bride of old Hu's family, they agreed that apparently there was nothing particularly wrong with her, except that she seemed a little too proud-spirited and didn't look or act much like a child bride.

Third Granny Zhou said:

"She isn't at all shy around people."

Old Mrs. Yang from the next compound agreed:

"She isn't a bit shy. Her first day at her mother-in-law's house she ate three bowls of rice!"

Then Third Granny Zhou said:

"Gracious! I've never seen the likes of it. Even if she weren't a child bride, but someone who came to the house already married to the boy, she'd still have to get to know what the people are like her first few days in the house. Gracious! She's such a big girl, she must be well into her teens!"

"I hear she's fourteen!"

"How could a fourteen-year-old be that tall? She must be lying about her age!"

"Maybe not. Some people develop early."

"But how are they going to handle the sleeping arrangements?"

"Good point. There are three generations of family and only three small *kangs*."

This last response to Third Granny Zhou came from old Mrs. Yang, who was leaning over the wall.

As for my family, Mother was also of the opinion that the girl was not at all like a child bride ought to be.

Our old cook said:

"I've never seen the likes of her, with such a proud bearing and eyes that look right at you."

To which Second Uncle You added:

"What's the world coming to when a child bride doesn't look like a child bride ought to?"

Only Granddad had nothing to say on the subject, so I asked him:

"What do you think of that child bride?"

"She's quite all right," he said.

So I felt she was quite all right too.

Every day she led their horse to the well to drink, and I saw her on many of these occasions. No one properly introduced us, but she smiled when she saw me, and I smiled back and asked her how old she was.

"Twelve," she replied.

I told her she must be wrong: "You're fourteen—everybody says so."

"They think I'm too tall," she said, "and they're afraid people will laugh if they know I'm only twelve, so they told me to say I'm fourteen."

I couldn't figure out how being very tall would cause people to laugh at her.

"How about coming over to play in the grass with me?" I asked her.

"No," she said. "They won't allow it."

II

Before many days had passed, the child bride's in-laws began to beat her. They beat her so severely her cries could be heard far and wide, and since none of the other families in the entire compound had any children, cries or shouts were seldom heard there.

As a result, this became *the* topic of conversation throughout the neighborhood. The consensus was that she'd deserved a beating from the start, for whoever heard of a child bride with no trace of shyness, one who sat up straight as a rod wherever she was, and who walked with a brisk, carefree step?

Her mother-in-law, having led the family horse up to the well to drink one day, said to Third Granny Zhou:

"We have to be harsh with her from the outset. You mark my word, I'm going to have to beat her when I go back to the house. This little child bride of ours is really a handful! I've never seen the likes of her. If I pinch her on the thigh, she turns and bites me, or says she's going home to her mother."

From then on the sounds of crying filled our compound daily—loud, bitter cries accompanied by shouts.

Granddad went over to old Hu's house several times to try to stop them from beating her, saying she was just a girl who didn't know much, and if there were problems in her behavior, he recommended trying to educate her. But as time went on, the beatings grew more severe, day and night, and even when I woke up in the middle of the night to recite my poems with Granddad, I could hear the sounds of crying and shouting coming from the southwest corner.

"That's the child bride crying, isn't it?" I'd ask Granddad.

To keep me from being frightened, he'd answer:

"No, it's someone outside the compound."

"What could they be crying about in the middle of the night?" I'd ask him.

"Don't concern yourself about that," he'd say. "Just keep reciting your poems."

I got up very early, and just as I was reciting, "I slept in spring, not conscious of the dawn," the crying sounds from the southwest corner started in again. This continued for the longest time, and only when winter arrived did the sounds of her crying finally come to an end.

III

The sounds of weeping were replaced by those of the sorceress, who came to the southwest corner every night to do her dance. The staccato drumbeats resounded in the air, as the sorceress first chanted a line, and was then answered by her attendant. Since it was nighttime, the words came through loud and clear, and I soon memorized every line.

There were things like: "Little spirit flower," and "May the genie let her 'come forth.'" Just about every day the sorceress chanted these kinds of things.

Right after I got up in the mornings, I started to mimic her chants:

"Little spirit flower, may the Genie let her 'come forth . . .'" Then I went *bong bong, bang bang,* imitating the drumbeat.

"Little spirit flower" was the young girl; the "Genie" was supposed to be a fox spirit. To "come forth" meant to become a sorceress.

The sorceress performed her dances for nearly the whole winter, until she finally succeeded in causing the child bride to fall ill. The child bride soon had an unhealthy look, but even though her complexion was no longer as dark as it had been when she'd first arrived that summer, she retained her hearty laugh.

When Granddad took me over with him to visit the family, the child bride even came over and filled his pipe for him. When she looked at me, she smiled, but on the sly, as if afraid her mother-in-law might see her. She didn't speak to me.

She still wore her hair in a thick braid, but her mother-in-law told us she was ill and that the sorceress had been engaged to drive the evil spirits away. As Granddad was leaving their house, the mother-in-law walked out with him, saying softly:

"I'm afraid this child bride isn't going to make it. She's being claimed by a fox spirit that's determined to have her come forth."

Granddad would have liked to ask them to move, but here in Hulan there's a custom that the time for moving in the spring is March and in the autumn, September. Once those months have passed, it's no longer the time for moving.

Each time we were startled out of our sleep in the middle of the night by the sorceress' dance, Granddad would say:

"I'm going to ask them to move next March."

I heard him say this on any number of occasions. Whenever I imitated the shouts and cries of the sorceress and chanted "Little spirit flower," Granddad said the same thing—he'd ask them to move next March.

IV

In the meantime, the commotion emanating from the southwest corner grew in intensity. They invited one sorceress and quite a few attendants, and the drumbeats resounded the day long. It was said that if they allowed the little child bride to "come forth," her life would be in peril, so they invited many attendants in order to wrest her from the sorceress' clutches.

Whereupon many people volunteered their opinions to the family, for who would not come to the rescue of someone facing death? Every person of conscience and good will extended a helping hand; he would offer a special potion, she would share her magical charms.

Some advocated making a straw figure for the girl, to be burned in the big pit to the south.

Some advocated going to the ornament shop and having them make a paper figure called a "proxy doll," which could then be burned as a surrogate.

Some advocated painting a hideous face on the girl, then inviting the sorceress over, with the expectation that when the sorceress saw her, she'd find her too ugly and reject her as a disciple; that way she would not have to "come forth."

But Third Granny Zhou advocated that she be made to eat a whole, unplucked rooster—feathers, feet, and all—on a given star-filled night, then be covered with a quilt. She should be made to sweat it out until cockcrow of the following morning before allowing her to emerge from under the quilt. For after she ate a whole rooster and sweated profusely, a rooster would forever exist in her soul, and spirits, ghosts, fox spirits, and the like would not dare try to possess her body. Legend has it that ghosts are afraid of roosters.

Third Granny Zhou told of her own great-grandmother, who had fallen under the power of a fox spirit and was in the throes of this agony for a full three years, on the verge of death. Eventually, she was cured by this very method, and was never again ill for the rest of her life. Whenever she was having a bad dream during the night, one that nearly frightened her to death, the rooster in her soul would come to her rescue by crowing and waking her from the nightmare. She was not ill another day in her life and, strange as it sounds, even her death was extraordinary. She died at the age of eighty-two, and even at that advanced age she was still able to do embroidery work. At the time, she was busy embroidering a child's apron for her grandson, and after sitting on a wooden stool and embroidering for a while she felt tired, so she leaned back against the door and dozed off. She died in her sleep.

Someone asked Third Granny Zhou:

"Were you there to see it?"

"I certainly was," she replied. "Just listen: For three days and nights after she died, she could not be laid out, and eventually there was nothing to do but make a special coffin and seat her inside it. Her cheeks were still pink, just as if she were still alive."

"Did you see that too?" someone else asked.

"Gracious! What a strange question," she replied. "It was passed from mouth to mouth. With all the tales of things that have happened in this world, how many can a person witness in one lifetime? How else can we know about things unless we're told?" She appeared somewhat put out by the question.

And then there was old Mrs. Yang from the west compound, who also had a tonic: She said you needed two ounces of rhizome and half a catty of pork, both finely chopped and cured over a piece of tile, then pounded into powder and divided into five portions. Each portion was to be wrapped in red paper and taken individually. This potion's specialty was curing convulsions and a drifting soul.

Her prescription was simple enough, though the child bride's illness was neither convulsions nor a drifting soul, and there seemed to be some disparity between the disease and the cure. But then, what harm could it do to give it a try—after all, it only called for two ounces of rhizome and half a catty of pork. Besides, here in Hulan there was often some cheap pork available. And even though the pork was said to be plague-ridden and not entirely dependable, this was, after all, a matter of curing an illness, not eating a meal, so what difference could it make?

"Go ahead and buy half a catty of pork and see how it works on her."

"Anyway, even if it doesn't cure her, it certainly can't do any harm," a bystander said approvingly.

"We have to try," her mother-in-law said, "because where there's life there's hope!"

And so the child bride began her cure by eating half a catty of pork and two ounces of rhizome.

Her mother-in-law personally prepared the prescription, but the slicing of the pork was the job of the elder grandson's wife. The pork was dark and discolored, but there was a portion of bright red meat in the center, which the elder grandson's wife secretly held back. She figured that it had been four or five months since her husband's grandmother had eaten any meat, so she used this piece of pork she'd held back to make a large bowl of pork noodle soup for the old woman.

"Where did this pork come from?" the grandmother asked her.

"Why not just enjoy it as something your grandson's wife prepared especially for you?"

Meanwhile, the child bride's mother-in-law was curing the medicine on a piece of tile over the fire in the stove, saying as she did so:

"What I have here is half a catty of pork, not a fraction less."

The pork smelled better each minute it was being cured, its odor eventually attracting a kitten that came over to snatch a piece. But when it stretched out a paw to take it, the child bride's mother-in-law reached over and swatted it.

"So you think you can get your paws on this, do you! You greedy little thing, this is someone's medicine—a full half catty of pork—so what makes you think you deserve a bite? If I gave you a piece, there wouldn't be enough medicine to work the cure. Then the responsibility for the girl's death would be yours. Don't you know any better? There's exactly half a catty of pork here—no more, no less."

After the prescription was prepared, it was pulverized and given to the child bride with water.

Two portions were to be taken each day. She managed all right on the first day, but on the morning of the second, when the people who had prescribed the remedy came over, there were still three portions lying on the altar where the kitchen god was placed. Someone present questioned the wisdom of eating rhizome, for it was, after all, a cold ingredient, and if someone like her, who experienced night sweats, ate rhizome, her vital energy would be driven out. How could a person survive after her vital energy has been driven out?

"She can't take that!" someone agreed. "Within two days after she's eaten it she'll have passed on to the nether world."

"What'll we do now?" the child bride's mother-in-law exclaimed.

"Has she already taken some?" the man asked apprehensively.

Just as the mother-in-law of the child bride opened her mouth to answer, the clever wife of the elder grandson cut her short:

"No, she hasn't—not yet," she said.

"Well, since she hasn't taken any yet," the man replied, "there's nothing to worry about. The Hu family is certainly blessed. Your lucky star is watching over you, for you came awfully close to throwing away a human life!"

The man then offered a potion of his own, which, according to him, was actually not a potion at all, but simply a cure-all that the proprietor of the Li Yongchun Pharmacy on Road Two East often prescribed. The medicine was so effective that a hundred uses resulted in a hundred cures, and it worked for everyone—man, woman, young, and old—every single time. It didn't matter what the symptoms were—headaches, aching feet, stomachaches, visceral disorders, falls, broken bones, cuts, boils, carbuncles, rashes—whatever the illness, it vanished with one application of this remedy.

What was this remedy? The more the people heard of the great results it produced, the more eager they were to learn just what it was.

"If an elderly person takes it," he said, "his dimming eyesight will be restored to what it was during his youth.

"If a young man takes it, his strength will be great enough to move Mount Tai.

"If a woman takes it, her complexion will be the color of peach blossoms without the aid of rouge or powder.

"If a child takes it, an eight-year-old can draw a bow, a nine-year-old can shoot an arrow, and a twelve-year-old will become a *zhuangyuan*, first on the list at the official examinations."

When he began, everyone in old Hu's family was amazed and awed, but toward the end, his discourse somehow lost its effect on them. After all, the men of old Hu's family had always been carters, and there'd never been a *zhuangyuan* among them.

The elder grandson's wife asked the onlookers to move back a bit, then she walked over to the vanity and took out a willow charcoal stick for painting eyebrows

"Won't you please write down the ingredients of this prescription for us," she said, "so we can go to the pharmacy right away and get some of that remedy?"

Now the person who was telling them about this prescription had at one time been the cook at the Li Yongchun Pharmacy, but had not worked there for three years, ever since the woman with whom he had been having an affair had run out on him, taking with her the little savings he'd managed to accumulate over half a lifetime. He'd been in such a rage over this that he'd developed a touch of insanity. But even though he was slightly mad, he hadn't completely forgotten the names of the medicines he'd committed to memory during his employment at Li Yongchun. Since he was illiterate, he gave a verbal listing of the ingredients:

"Two-tenths of an ounce of plantain, two-tenths of an ounce of angelica, two-tenths of an ounce of fresh rehmannia, two-tenths of an ounce of Tibetan safflower, two-tenths of an ounce of Sichuan fritillary, two-tenths of an ounce of atractylis, two-tenths of an ounce of Siberian milkwort, two-tenths of an ounce of placenta . . ."

At this point he was unable to recall the remaining ingredients, and nervous beads of sweat began to dot his forehead. So he blurted out:

". . . and two catties of brown sugar . . ." The prescription was complete.

Once finished, he asked the Hu family for something to drink:

"Do you have any liquor? I could use a couple of bowlfuls."

Everyone in Hulan River knew this slightly mad fellow well, everyone, that is, but the members of old Hu's family. Having moved here from somewhere else, they were taken in by him. Since they had no liquor in the house, they gave him twenty strings of cash to go out and buy his own. As for the remedy he'd prescribed, it was absolutely useless, a product of his wild imagination.

The child bride grew more seriously ill with each passing day and, according to her family, she often sat bolt upright as she slept during the night. The sight of another person threw a terrible fright into her, and her eyes invariably brimmed with tears. It seemed inevitable that this child bride was fated to "come forth," and if she were not allowed to do so, there was little hope she'd ever be well again.

Once the news of her plight spread throughout the area, all the people living nearby came forth with suggestions: How, they said, could we not come to the rescue of someone at death's door? Some believed that she should simply be allowed to "come forth," and let that be the end of it. Others were of the opposite opinion, for if someone of such tender years were to "come forth," she would be a sorceress for many, many years.

Her mother-in-law adamantly refused to let her "come forth."

"Now don't any of you get the wrong idea that I'm opposed to letting her 'come forth' only because of the money spent when I arranged for the engagement," she said. "Like the rest of you, I feel that if someone so young were to 'come forth,' she'd be a sorceress for a very long time."

Everyone promptly agreed that it would be best not to allow her to "come forth," so they turned their collective energies to finding the right prescription or engaging the right sorceress, each extolling the virtues of his own plan.

Finally there came a soothsayer.

This soothsayer told them he'd come unhesitatingly from the countryside a great distance away as soon as the news reached him that old Hu's family had recently brought a child bride into their home, one who had fallen ill shortly after her arrival and remained so even after being seen by many eminent physicians and mystics. He had made the trip into town expressly to have a look for himself, for if he could perform some service that might spare her life, then the trip would have been worth making.

Everyone was moved by this speech of his. He was invited into the house, where he was asked to sit on the grandmother's *kang*, was given tea, and was offered a pipeful of tobacco.

The elder grandson's wife was the first to approach him:

"This sister-in-law of mine is actually only twelve years old, but since she's so tall, she tells everyone she's fourteen. She's a cheerful, sociable girl who up to now was never sick a day in her life. But ever since she came to our house she's grown thinner and paler every day. Recently she lost her appetite for food and drink, her eyes stay open all night, and she's easily startled. We've given her every imaginable remedy and have burned incense of every kind for her benefit, but nothing has worked."

Before she'd finished, the girl's mother-in-law interrupted her:

"I haven't abused her all the time she's been in my house. Where will you find another family that hasn't abused its child bride by giving her beatings and tongue-lashings all day long? Now I may have beaten her a little, but just to get her started off on the right foot, and I only did that for a little over a month. Maybe I beat her pretty severely sometimes, but how was I expected to make a well-mannered girl out of her without being severe once in a while? Believe me, I didn't enjoy beating her so hard, what with all her screaming and carrying on. But I was doing it for her own good, because if I didn't beat her hard, she'd never be good for anything.

"There were a few times when I strung her up from the rafters and had her uncle give her a few hard lashes with a leather whip, and since he got a little carried away, she usually passed out. But it only lasted for about the time it takes to smoke a pipeful, and then we always managed to revive her by dousing her face with cold water. We did give her some pretty severe beatings that turned her body black and blue and occasionally drew blood, but we always broke open some eggs right away and rubbed egg whites on the spots. The swellings, which were never too bad, always went down in ten days or a couple of weeks.

"This child is such a stubborn one. The moment I started beating her, she threatened to return to her home. So I asked her, Just where do you think your home is? What is this, if not your home? But she refused to give in. She said she wanted to go to her own home. And that made me madder than ever. You know how people are when they get mad—nothing else seems to matter—so I took a red-hot flatiron and branded the soles of her feet. Maybe I beat her soul right out of her body, or maybe I just scared it away—I don't know which—but from then on, whenever she said she wanted to go home, instead of beating her, all I had to do was threaten to chain her up if she even tried, and she'd start screaming with fright. When the Sorceress saw this, she said she should be allowed to 'come forth.'

"It costs a lot of money to bring a girl into a family as a child bride. Figure it out for yourself: The engagement was arranged when she was eight years old, when we had to hand over eight ounces of silver. After that there was the money we spent for her trousseau, and finally we had all the expenses of bringing her here by train from far-off Liao-yang. Then once she got here, it was a steady series of exorcists, incense, and one potion after another. If she'd gotten better as time went on, then everything would have been fine, but nothing seemed to work. Who knows eventually . . . what the outcome will be . . .?"

The soothsayer, who had come unhesitatingly from so far away, was a proper and serious man who showed signs of much travel. He wore a long blue gown under a short lined coat, while on his head he wore a cap with earflaps. He was a man whom others treated with the respect due a master the moment they saw him.

Accordingly, the grandmother said:

"Please draw a lot for my second grandson's child bride and tell us what her fate will be."

The soothsayer could tell at a glance that this was a very sincere family, so he removed his leather cap with the earflaps. The moment he took off the cap, everyone noticed that his hair was combed into a topknot and that he was wearing Taoist headwear. They knew at once that this was no run-of-the-mill individual. Before anyone could even utter the questions they wanted to ask, he volunteered the information that he was a Taoist priest from such-and-such a mountain, and that he had come down to make a pilgrimage to the sacred Mount Tai in Shandong. But how could he have foreseen that midway on his journey he'd have to cut his trip short for lack of traveling expenses? He had drifted to the Hulan River area, where he had been for no less than half a year.

Someone asked him why, if he was a Taoist, he wasn't wearing Taoist garb.

"There's something you people don't know," he replied. "Each of the 360 trades in this world of ours has its share of miseries. The police around here are terrible; the minute they see someone dressed as a Taoist, the interrogation begins, and since they are disbelievers of the Taoist creed who won't listen to reason, they are all too ready to take one of us into custody."

This man had a nickname—the Wayfaring Immortal—and people far and near knew of whom you were speaking when you mentioned his name. Whatever the disease or discomfort, whether the signs were good or evil, life and death was settled for all time with the drawing of one of his lots. He told them he'd learned his divining skills from the head priest of the Taoists himself, Zhang Daoling, Master Zhang.

He did not have many divining lots—four in all—which he removed from the pocket of his gown one at a time. The first lot he brought forth was wrapped in red paper, as was the second; in fact, all four were wrapped in red paper. He informed everyone that there were no words written on his divining lots, nor were there any images; inside each there was only a packet of medicinal powder—one red, one green, one blue, and one yellow. The yellow one foretold the wealth of gold, the red one foretold ruddy-cheeked old age. Now if the green one were drawn, that was bad, for it represented the devil's fire. The blue one wasn't very good either, for it meant the cold face of death, and Master Zhang himself had said that the cold face of death must come to meet Yama, the king of the nether world, whether the person be dead or alive.

Once the soothsayer had finished reciting his chants, he called for someone in the afflicted person's family to reach out and draw a lot. The child bride's mother-in-law figured this to be an easy, uncomplicated task, so she decided to quickly choose one and get some idea of whether it was the girl's fate to live or die. But she had overlooked something, for the moment she reached her hand out, the Wayfaring Immortal said:

"Each lot will cost you one hundred strings of cash. If you choose the blue one and are unhappy with it, you can choose another . . . one hundred strings of cash each . . ."

Suddenly the child bride's mother-in-law understood everything: these drawings weren't free after all, and at a hundred strings of cash apiece, it was not something to be taken lightly. For ten strings of cash she could buy twenty cakes of bean curd. Now if she bought one cake every three days, then with twenty cakes—since two threes are six—that would be enough bean curd for sixty days. But if one cake were bought only every ten days—that's three cakes a month—then there would be enough bean curd in the house for half a year. Continuing along this line of thought, she wondered who would be so extravagant as to eat a cake of bean curd every three days. According to her, a cake a month was enough for everyone to have a taste every now and then, in which case twenty cakes of bean curd—one each month—would be sufficient for twenty months, or a year and a half plus two months.

Or let's say rather than buying bean curd, she were to buy and raise a plump little pig. If she conscientiously fed it for five or six months, until it was nice and fat, just think how much money that could bring in! And if she raised it for a whole year, then we're talking about twenty thousand strings of cash . . .

Or if she didn't buy a pig, but spent the money instead on chickens, a hundred strings of cash could buy ten or so laying hens. After the first year the chickens would begin to lay eggs, and everyone knows how much an egg is worth! Or if she didn't sell the eggs, but traded one of them for vegetables to feed the family—all three generations—for one day . . . not to mention the fact that each egg laid meant one more chicken, and by keeping the cycle going they could have an unlimited supply of chickens and an unlimited supply of eggs—wouldn't they then make their fortune!

But her thoughts weren't really so grandiose; it would be sufficient if everyone had enough to eat and enough clothes to wear. If, by living frugally, she could manage to put a little something aside in her lifetime, that would be enough for her. For even though she had a real love for money, if she'd been given the opportunity to actually make a fortune, she definitely would not have had the nerve to do so.

The numbers she was contemplating were greater than she could count, more than she could ever remember. With chickens laying eggs and eggs producing more chickens in an unbroken cycle, wouldn't the situation soon have developed where there were as many chickens as there are ants? There would be so many they'd cloud her vision, and clouded vision produces headaches.

This mother-in-law of the child bride had raised chickens in the past; in fact, it was exactly a hundred strings of cash worth—no more, no less. To her one hundred strings of cash was the ideal number. For one hundred strings of cash she was able to buy twelve chicks, a number she considered just right. If there were more, she was afraid she might lose some, but if there were fewer, then they wouldn't have been worth a hundred strings of cash.

When she was buying these newly hatched chicks she picked them up one at a time to take a close look, rejecting one after the other. She rejected all those with black claws, those with spotted wings, and those with marks on the tops of their heads. She said that her mother had become an expert at choosing chickens after raising them for a lifetime. She had raised them year after year, and although she never kept too many, she was never short of household necessities during her lifetime, managing to trade eggs the year round for anything she needed, such as needles and thread. As a result, she really knew her chickens—which would be short-lived and which could be expected to live a long time—spotting the good ones unerringly every time. She could even tell at a glance which of them would lay large eggs and which would lay small ones.

As she was buying the chicks, she constantly reprimanded herself for not having had the foresight to learn more about chickens from her mother in years past. Ai! How could young people develop an eye for the future! She was moved to sighing as she bought the chicks; having picked them out with a great deal of thought, she had done her very best in selecting. The chicken seller had over two hundred chicks for sale, every one of which she picked over; but whether the ones she chose were the best of the lot was something of which she herself was never able to be absolutely sure.

She raised chickens with a great deal of care. She was forever cautious, lest they be eaten by cats or bitten by rats, and whenever they dozed during the day, she chased the flies away, fearing that the flies might wake them up; she wanted them to get plenty of sleep, for she was concerned that they got too little. If one of them had a mosquito bite on its leg, the moment she discovered it, she immediately mixed a solution of mugwort and water and rubbed it on the bite. According to her, if she didn't rub it on right away, then if the chick later turned out to be a rooster, its growth would be stunted, and if it turned out to be a hen, it would lay small eggs. A small egg could be traded for two cakes of bean curd, while a large one would bring in three. That's what can happen to a hen. As for a rooster, they eventually wind up on the dinner table, and since everyone prefers fat ones, the stunted ones are difficult to sell.

Once her chickens had grown a bit and were ready to leave the house and go out into the courtyard and look for their own food, she put some dye on the top of each of their heads—six red and six green.

In order to determine where she should place the dye, she first took a look at her neighbors' chickens to see where they'd dyed theirs, after which she was able to decide. Her neighbors had put the dye on the tips of the chickens' wings, so she put hers on the tops of their heads. If her neighbors had dyed the tops of their chickens' heads, she'd have dyed the bellies of hers. According to her, people shouldn't dye their chickens in the same place, because then you can't tell them apart. Your chickens would run over to my house, and mine would run over to your house, and there'd be nothing but confusion.

The dyed chicks were eye-catching, with their red or green heads, as if they were wearing little colored caps, as if instead of raising a brood of chicks, she was raising a brood of children.

This mother-in-law of the child bride had even said during her chicken-raising days:

"Raising chickens is more refined than raising children. People who raise children just leave them to fend for themselves and grow up the best they can, don't they? They always wind up with mosquito bites, bedbug bites, and what have you, until there's hardly a child anywhere who doesn't carry scars all over his body. Children who don't have them will be hard to raise—they won't live long."

According to her, she didn't raise many children of her own—in fact, only the one son—but despite the small number to care for, she didn't fawn over him, and he already had more than twenty such scars here and there on his body.

"If you don't believe me," she'd say, "I'll have him take off his clothes and you can see for yourself . . . he has scars of every size on his body—even one as big as the mouth of a rice bowl. Honest, I've never spoiled him. Not counting the ones from falls and spills, some of those scars come from beatings with an axe-handle. Raising a child isn't like raising chickens or ducks. If you raise a chicken carelessly, it won't lay any eggs; a large egg is worth three cakes of bean curd, a small one's worth two, and that's nothing to laugh at, is it? It certainly isn't!"

Once her son stepped on a chick and killed it; she beat him for three solid days and nights.

"Why shouldn't I have beaten him? Each chick is worth three cakes of bean curd—chicks come from chicken eggs, you know! In order to get a chicken, you have to have a chicken's egg—half an egg isn't enough, is it? Not just half an egg, even an egg that's almost whole, but not quite, won't do. Bad eggs won't do, neither will old ones. One chicken requires one egg, and if a chicken isn't the same as three cakes of bean curd, what is it? Just imagine what a sin it would be to put three cakes of bean curd on the ground and squash them with your foot! So how could I have not beaten him? The more I thought about it, the angrier I got, and every time I thought about it, I hit him, day or night, for three days. Eventually, he fell ill from the beatings and woke up crying in the middle of the night. But I didn't let that overly concern me. I just beat on the door frame with the rice ladle to call his spirit back, and he got better on his own."

It had been years since she'd raised chickens, and in the period since making engagement arrangements for this child bride she'd spent all the little savings she'd managed to put aside. Not only that, she'd had to spend money each year on gifts and other expenses, so things had been tighter than she could ever have imagined these past few years. And so, she reluctantly gave up all plans to raise a few chickens.

Now here was this Wayfaring Immortal sitting there asking one hundred strings of cash for each lot drawn. If he hadn't mentioned money, but had just let her go ahead and draw a lot, then asked for money afterwards, that would have been a lot like a free drawing. But no, he had to mention the hundred strings of cash before he'd let her draw a lot. So the child bride's mother-in-law had a vision of all her money flying off into the distance—a hundred strings of cash each time she reached out her hand or opened her mouth. And if that wasn't throwing money out the window, what was? Without a sound or a trace it simply disappeared. It wouldn't even be the same as crossing a river and throwing money into the water, for at least when you do that, there's the splash and the ripples that spread out. But nothing came from doing it this way—it was like losing money without being aware of it or being robbed.

The child bride's mother-in-law was nearly moved to tears by the anger welling up inside. These thoughts made her feel that this was not so much drawing lots as it was paying some sort of tax. Accordingly, she drew back her hand, ran over to the washbasin, and washed her hands. This was no laughing matter—it was money, a hundred strings of cash worth! After washing her hands, she went over and knelt before the kitchen god to offer up a prayer, after which she finally drew her lot.

Her first drawing produced the green lot, and green was not good—it represented the devil's fire. So she drew again, but this one was worse—in fact, it was the worst of all; she'd drawn the one in which blue medicinal powder was wrapped, the one that meant that the person would have to come face to face with Yama, whether dead or alive.

When the child bride's mother-in-law saw that both her choices had been bad ones, by rights she should have burst into tears. But she didn't. Ever since the child bride had fallen seriously ill, she had already heard every conceivable comment regarding the prospects of living or dying. In addition, they'd engaged fox fairies and sorceresses any number of times, with all of their chants and witchery, and she'd seen a great deal of the affairs of this world during that time. She seemed to live under the impression that although it's nice to be alive, she wouldn't be particularly grieved to die either, for it seemed to her that her meeting with Yama wouldn't be taking place for the time being.

She then asked the Wayfaring Immortal if, since both lots she'd drawn were bad ones, there was some way to negate their power.

"Bring me a brush and some ink," was his answer.

Since there were no brushes in their home, the elder grandson's wife ran over to the grain shop next to the compound's main gate to borrow one.

The proprietress there asked in a heavy Shandong accent:

"What's happening over at your place?"

"We're curing our younger sister-in-law's illness," the elder grandson's wife answered.

"Your younger sister-in-law's illness must be serious. Is she at all better?"

Now the elder grandson's wife had planned to just get an ink stone and a writing brush and run back home, but since the woman seemed so concerned, it would have been impolite to ignore her; and so she was gone long enough to smoke several pipefuls before heading back.

By the time she finally arrived with the ink stone, the Wayfaring Immortal had already torn some red paper into strips. He took up the brush and wrote one large character on each of four strips of red paper; since the strips were no more than half an inch in width and an inch in length, the characters looked as if they were about to fly off the edges.

As for the four characters he wrote, inasmuch as no one in the family knew how to read—even the scrolls hanging on either side of the kitchen god altar had been written by someone at their request—they looked identical, children of the same mother, and could well have been the same character. The elder grandson's wife looked at them, but had no idea what they said; then the grandmother looked at them, but she did no better. But though they couldn't read them, they were sure they could not have bad meanings; otherwise, how could they keep anyone from having to come face to face with Yama? And so, they all nodded approvingly.

The Wayfaring Immortal then ordered them to bring some paste. Now paste was something they went without all year long, since it was so expensive—a single catty of flour cost more than a hundred strings of cash—so when they had to repair shoes they settled for kernels of cooked millet.

The elder grandson's wife went to the kitchen and scooped a gob of millet off the rice pot. The Wayfaring Immortal spread some of the gooey substance onto the strips of red paper, then lifted the tattered jacket off the head of the child bride and told her to hold out her hands, sticking one strip on each palm. Then he had her remove her stockings, after which he stuck a strip onto the sole of each foot.

When the Wayfaring Immortal noticed the white scars on the soles of her feet, he reckoned they must be from the branding the mother-in-law had been talking about a short time before. But he feigned ignorance and asked:

"What sort of malady did she have here on the soles of her feet?"

The child bride's mother-in-law quickly reminded him:

"Didn't I just say I branded her with a flatiron? This girl refuses to admit the error of her ways. She walks like she's on the top of the world and soon forgets all the beatings I gave her, so I had to brand her. Fortunately, it wasn't serious—after all, young people's skin is so resilient—and after being laid up for ten days or a couple of weeks, she was just fine."

The Wayfaring Immortal mulled this over for a moment, then decided to throw a scare into the woman by saying that although he'd stuck paper strips onto the scarred soles of her feet, he was afraid they might not hold; nothing, he went on, escaped Yama's attention, and these distinctive scars might just stick in his mind, which could really mess up their plans.

He looked to see if he'd succeeded in scaring them or not; deciding that he'd fallen a bit short, he continued in an even graver tone:

"If these scars aren't gotten rid of, Yama will be able to find her within a period of three days, and the moment he finds her, he'll snatch her away, even though she still be alive. The last lot you drew a while ago was infallible, so these red stickers are useless."

The Wayfaring Immortal could not have imagined that this chilling prospect would still not noticeably frighten any of them, from the grandmother down to the grandson's wife, and so he continued:

"Not only will Yama snatch the child bride away, he'll likewise come after her mother-in-law to seek retribution. For what is branding the soles of someone's feet, if not a form of abuse? A woman who abuses her prospective daughter-in-law will be consigned to a vat of boiling oil, and since the child bride of the Hu family has been abused by her prospective mother . . ."

His voice grew louder as he went along, until he was on the verge of screaming; it was as if he were a gallant crusader attacking injustice—his demeanor had undergone a transformation since his arrival. When he reached this point, there wasn't a single member of the Hu family—young or old—who wasn't in the grip of fear. Trembling from head to toe, they felt as if an evil demon had infiltrated their household. The mother-in-law was more frightened than any of the others; mumbling incoherently over these ghastly prospects, she couldn't imagine that anyone on the face of the earth could actually abuse their own daughter-in-law. She quickly fell to her knees and, with tears streaming down her face, said to the Wayfaring Immortal:

"This is a result of a lifetime of accumulating no virtues, and my sins are being visited upon my children. I implore the Wayfaring Immortal to break this terrible spell, to use his divine methods to snatch my daughter-in-law from the jaws of death!"

The Wayfaring Immortal changed his tune immediately, saying that he had an infallible means of keeping the daughter-in-law from coming face to face with Yama—a guaranteed method. It was extremely simple: The child bride need only remove her stockings once again, and he would place a mark with his brush over the scars, making them invisible to Yama. So the stockings were removed, and he made his mark on the soles of her feet, chanting as he did so. Seen as an extremely simple act by those who witnessed it, nonetheless, it cost the Wayfaring Immortal such great effort that beads of perspiration dotted his forehead. He performed the act with a deliberate gnashing of teeth, wrinkled brows, and staring eyes, as if making these marks had taken a great deal out of him, that, in fact, it had been much the same as scaling a mountain of knives. Then, having made his marks, he tallied up his fee: two hundred strings of cash for the drawn lots, four strips of red paper stuck to the palms of his hands and soles of her feet, at fifty strings apiece—half the normal rate—which amounted to two hundred strings; and finally the two marks he'd made (the usual rate was a hundred strings per mark, but he'd cut his fee in half), at fifty apiece, making another hundred. Two hundred plus two hundred, and another hundred, made a total of five hundred strings of cash.

Accepting his fee of five hundred strings of cash, the Wayfaring Immortal departed the scene in high spirits.

Just prior to the time the mother-in-law of the child bride had drawn the first lot, her heart had been gripped by an excruciating pain as she learned that each would cost her a hundred strings of cash. Thoughts of how she could have put that money to work raising chickens or raising hogs had crossed her mind. But now that the five hundred strings had been handed over, she thought no longer about raising chickens or raising hogs. For she figured that when things had reached this point, she had no choice but to hand it over. The lots had been drawn, the characters written, and it would have been out of the question to withhold payment. What was a person expected to do when things had reached this point? Even if it had been a thousand rather than five hundred, what choice did she have but to hand it over?

And so, with a sense of resignation, she handed over the five hundred strings of cash, part of the earnings from the sale of a quarter peck of soybeans that she'd foraged in the fields in the autumn. She'd sold the beans for less than a thousand strings of cash. Foraging soybeans in the field was hard work for these people, since after the landlord's harvesting, there were precious few left on the surface of that vast plot of land. And yet there were hordes of poor people—children, women, old ladies—engaged in the same task, with the result that competition for each bean was fierce. A grand total of a quarter peck of beans had required two or three weeks of foraging on her knees, until her back ached and her legs were sore. Ai! On account of those few beans, the mother-in-law of the child bride had visited the Li Yongchun Pharmacy to buy two ounces of safflower. That she'd been forced to do because the thorn of a bean plant had pricked her under her fingernail while she was crawling along the ground looking for beans. She hadn't given it any thought at the time, but had merely removed the thorn and gone on about her business. Since she was there to forage beans, forage is what she'd do. But for some unknown reason, after a night's sleep, she woke up to find her finger swollen to the size of a small eggplant.

Even this didn't concern her much; since she wasn't royalty, she wasn't used to being pampered. Besides, for those whose lives are at Heaven's mercy, who hasn't occasionally experienced Heaven's wrath? But after suffering with this hand for several days, until she could no longer sleep at night for the searing pain, she finally bought the two ounces of safflower.

That's what she should have done at the outset. Urged to do so by the grandmother, she chose not to; prompted by the elder grandson's wife to buy some, still she refused. Her own son, out of a sense of filial responsibility, tried to force the issue with his mother, demanding that he be allowed to go buy some for her. He was rewarded for his troubles by a blow on the head from the bowl of her pipe, which raised a lump the size of an egg.

"You little scamp, are you trying to bring the family to ruin? Your mother isn't even in the grave, and already you're acting like the head of the family! You little devil, now let's see if you've got the nerve to bring up the subject of buying safflower again. We'll see if this pest of mine has the nerve!" All the while she was cursing she was hitting him with the bowl of her pipe.

But, in fact, she eventually did buy some, most likely because the neighbors had by then heard about the argument; now that everyone was talking about it, how would it look if she didn't buy some safflower? Everyone would be gossiping about the wife of the elder son of the Hu family: Any money she accumulated throughout the year would be hidden away, they'd say, as if it had fallen through a crack in the earth the moment it touched her hand; once it had come to her there was no chance it would ever reemerge. Now this was not the sort of talk that did a family any good. Besides, after selling the beans she'd picked for a price of nearly a thousand strings of cash, if it was necessary to part with twenty or thirty for a little safflower, then so be it. All she had to do was clench her teeth and buy two ounces of safflower and rub it on.

But even though she gave it some serious thought, she still could not make up her mind to go ahead. She put it off for several days, never quite able to bring herself to "clench her teeth."

Ultimately, she did buy some. She chose a day when her condition was at its most serious—not only was her finger affected, but the whole hand had begun to swell. A finger that had originally puffed up to the size of a small eggplant was now as big as a small melon, and even the palm of her hand was so huge and puffy it looked like a winnowing basket. For years she'd bemoaned the fact that she was too thin, saying that people who were too thin had less than their share of good fortune. This was especially true for those with skinny arms and legs, an obvious sign of a lack of blessings, and even more so for those with bony hands; looking like claws, they were a sure indication of ill fortune.

Now she had the plump hand she coveted, but not the way she'd hoped to get it. On top of that, she'd come down with a fever, her eyes and mouth were dry, and her face was flushed; experiencing hot and cold flashes all over her body, she commented:

"Is this hand going to bring me to grief? This hand of mine . . ."

She said the same thing over and over from the moment she got up one morning. She could no longer even move the hand, which had grown to the size of a winnowing basket. As if it were a big cat or the head of a small child, she laid it beside her on the pillow as she lay down.

"I'm afraid this hand of mine is going to bring me to grief!" This she said as her son walked up beside her; from the tone of her voice, he got the impression that this time she was prepared to buy some safflower. So he ran to see his grandmother to discuss the purchase.

Since their home was arranged with two *kangs* opposite each other—one facing north and one facing south—even though they carried on the discussion in hushed tones, his mother could hear what they were saying. Yet she pretended that she couldn't, so no one could later accuse her of having been complicit in the decision to buy the safflower or say that the idea had originated with her; it most certainly wasn't she who'd asked them to go buy safflower!

Grandmother and grandson discussed the matter on the northern *kang* for a while, then the grandson said he'd ask his mother for the money.

"Use my money," his grandmother counseled. "We can talk about paying it back once your mother is well."

She intentionally raised her voice a bit as she said this, evidently wanting to make sure that her elder son's wife had heard her.

She had and, for that matter, had heard everything else as well. Yet she lay there without moving, not letting on that she was listening.

After the safflower had been purchased and brought home, the son sat down beside his mother.

"Ma," he said, "rub on some of this safflower tonic."

His mother turned her head on the pillow to face him, looking as if she'd been caught unaware by the news that some safflower had been bought.

"Well!" she exclaimed. "So this little rascal has bought some safflower for me, has he?"

But this time she refrained from hitting him with the bowl of her pipe. Instead she quietly put her puffy hand out and let him smear the safflower mixture all over it.

She wondered whether they'd paid twenty strings of cash worth for the safflower, or thirty. If it was twenty, then they'd gotten plenty for their money, but if they'd paid thirty, then it was a bit high. Now if she'd gone to buy it herself, she most certainly wouldn't have bought so much; after all, wasn't it only some safflower! Safflower was merely something red, and who could say whether or not it had any medicinal qualities, or if it was anything more than a little psychological comfort?

These thoughts occupied her for a while, until the coolness of the tonic on her hand, the fragrant aroma of the heated mixture, and the strong medicinal aroma of the safflower combined to make her feel drowsy. She was feeling better now, and the moment she closed her eyes, she began to dream.

She dreamed she'd bought two cakes of bean curd—big, white ones. Where had she gotten the money to buy it? It had been paid for with money left over after buying the safflower; in her dream it was she who had bought the safflower, and she hadn't spent thirty strings of cash, not even twenty—she'd spent only ten. Figuring it all up in her dream, not only could she eat two cakes of bean curd that very day, but eat two more any day she felt like it! For she'd spent only ten of thirty strings of cash on the safflower.

And yet she'd just handed over five hundred strings of cash to the Wayfaring Immortal. Put in terms of her way of looking at things, just think how much bean curd she could have bought with that much money! But these thoughts did not occur to her now. On the one hand, there was her prospective daughter-in-law, whose illness had involved them all inextricably and had already been a huge drain on their finances; on the other hand, there was the Wayfaring Immortal with his powers, who had just accused her of abusing the child bride. Giving him the money and letting him get the hell out of there had been the best way to handle it, after all.

Having a sick individual in the house exposes a person to all sorts of unpleasantness. As the child bride's mother-in-law thought about this unexpected calamity, it kept growing in her mind. She felt terribly put upon and wronged: wanting to vent her anger, there was no one to rail at; feeling like crying, she found herself unable to; wanting to strike out at someone, there was no one within reach.

Of course there was always the child bride, but she couldn't withstand another beating. Now if she'd just then arrived at their house, of course her mother-in-law could have grabbed her, administered a beating, and let the chips fall where they may. When the mother-in-law broke a rice bowl, she grabbed the child bride and gave her a beating; when she lost a needle, again she grabbed the child bride and gave her a beating; when she fell, tearing a hole in the knee of her unlined trousers, once again she grabbed the child bride and gave her a beating. Whatever the situation, when things were not going well with her, her reaction was to hit someone. Who would that someone be? Who could she get away with hitting? The answer was always the child bride.

She couldn't hit anyone whose mother was nearby, and she didn't really have the heart to beat her own son. She could hit the cat, but was afraid she might never see it again, or she could hit the dog, but was afraid it might run away. If she hit one of the pigs, it might lose a few pounds of weight, and if she hit one of the chickens, it might stop laying eggs. The only one she could hit with impunity was the child bride. She wouldn't disappear from sight or run away, she didn't lay eggs, and, unlike a pig, if she lost a few pounds it wouldn't make any difference, since she was never weighed anyway. But as soon as this prospective daughter-in-law started getting beaten, she lost her appetite. Now a lost appetite is nothing to be too concerned about, since she could always drink a little water left over from boiling rice; after all, leftover rice water was normally fed to the pigs.

But these moments of personal glory were all in the past, and it didn't look as if such days of freedom would return in the foreseeable future. Not only was beating out of the question now, she couldn't even administer much of a tongue-lashing to her anymore. All the woman's worries were now subordinated to her fear of the girl's dying. Her heart was in the grip of a dark terror: her prospective daughter-in-law simply mustn't die on her!

So she mustered her self-control to overcome all her own personal difficulties, clenching her teeth with determination, fighting back tears, and restraining herself from cursing and beating. She would not allow herself to cry, even though she experienced enormous sorrow and grief, often at the same time. She thought that maybe the reason she was burdened with such trouble in this life was because she herself had done nothing good in a previous one. Otherwise, how could she be fated not to have a child bride in the family?

She reflected that she'd done nothing evil in her life; with a kindly look on her face and a heart brimming with benevolence, she'd always given way before others, allowing herself to get the worst of all matters. Granted that she had not abstained from eating meat altogether and had neglected to chant her sutras, but still she had gone without meat on the first and fifteenth days of each lunar month ever since she was a child. And granted that she'd often been remiss in going to the temple to worship and light incense, but still she'd never once stayed home from the temple festival on the eighteenth day of the fourth lunar month, at which time she always lit incense at the Temple of the Immortal Matron and performed her three kowtows at the Temple of the Patriarch. Every year, without fail, she'd done what was expected, burning incense and performing her kowtows. Granted, furthermore, that she hadn't learned to read when she was young and didn't know her characters, nonetheless she was able to recite the *Diamond Sutra* and had memorized the prayer to the kitchen god. And granted that she had never performed such charitable acts as donating money to mend a road or repair a bridge, yet she always gave her leftover soup and uneaten rice to beggars who came around over New Year's or other holidays. Finally, granted that she had not lived a particularly frugal life, still she had never eaten a single cake of bean curd more than she should have. She could live with herself, for she had a clear conscience. Why then, in Heaven's name, had the seeds of disaster been planted on her, of all people?

The more she puzzled over this, the more troubled and agitated she became.

"Things have turned out this way in my present life because I never performed good deeds in a former one."

When her thoughts came to this juncture, she let them go no further; since matters had already reached this point, what good could come of a lot of foolish thoughts and ideas? So she convinced herself that she must fight back her tears, clench her teeth, and simply part with the modest sum of money she had so diligently put aside after raising hogs and performing other menial tasks. It was a matter of ten strings of cash here, ten more there; fifty for this, a hundred more for that.

One neighbor recommended the burning of incense and paper money, another prescribed a rare remedy to be taken. She'd tried them all—remedies, herbal medicines, sorceresses, exorcists, incense divination, and prophecy boards—and although she'd spent untold sums of money, nothing seemed to have produced much in the way of results.

The child bride talked in her sleep at night and ran a fever during the day. During the night as she slept, she talked only of going home.

In the eyes of the girl's mother-in-law the words "go home" were the most disquieting of all, for she imagined that the girl might be a reincarnated daughter who was being summoned home by the Queen of Hell herself. And so she sent for a reader of dreams, whose explanation was just as she'd feared: "Go home" did, in fact, mean return to the nether world.

Thus, whenever the child bride dreamed of being beaten by her mother-in-law, or of being bound and strung up from the rafters, or of being branded on the soles of her feet, or even of having her fingertips pricked with a needle, she began to wail and scream, shouting that she wanted to "go home." And the moment her mother-in-law heard her scream that she wanted to go home, she reached out and pinched her on the leg. As the days went by, and one pinch followed another, the child bride's thighs became a welt of black and blue bruises, making her look like a reindeer.

Now the woman's intentions were completely benevolent: fearing that the girl would really be returning to the nether world, she wanted to quickly rouse her from her sleep. But the child bride, heavy with slumber, always imagined that she was being beaten by her mother-in-law, and as a result, would scream more loudly, roll over on the *kang*, and jump to the ground. No one could hold or control her. At such times her strength was astonishing and her shouts fearfully loud, further strengthening her mother-in-law's conviction that she was seeing ghosts and being visited by devils.

The certainty that this child was possessed by a demon was felt not only by the mother-in-law—the whole family believed it to be true. Hearing what was going on, who could not believe? Shattering the late night calm with her shouts of going home, she then jumped to the floor upon being awakened, eyes bulging, mouth agape; wailing and shouting, she was more powerful than an ox, her shouts like those of a pig being slaughtered.

Who could doubt it, especially when the girl's mother-in-law added the information that her eyeballs had turned green, like demon fires, and that her screams were more like an animal's roar than the cries of a human being?

And so the talk spread, until there was no one in the neighborhood who doubted. As a result, several people of good conscience felt pity for this young girl who had suffered enough torture by a demon. Was there ever a child not born of mother, a person not made of flesh and blood? All people care for their elders and educate their young ... the people's natural compassion was aroused. This family's auntie knew of a rare cure, that family's auntie was privy to a miraculous remedy.

And so it went: sorceresses, exorcists, incense, prophecy boards; there was a constant clamor at the home of the Hu family. It became the main attraction throughout the area, and anyone who didn't come to watch the dance of the sorceress or the rites of the exorcist was considered ignorant. So many sorceress dances were performed for the Hu family that it was a historic time—never had there been such activity. This record-breaking episode had ushered in a new age of sorceress dancing, and if a person failed to see it for himself, his ears and eyes would henceforth be forever closed.

But these grand events went unrecorded, since the town was without a local newspaper. If a person were to suffer partial paralysis, or palsy, or a disease that kept him permanently bedridden, it was considered nothing less than the misfortune of his lifetime, and he was pitied by all. Such a person was feared to be forever cut off from the rest of the world, for he had been unable to witness such a momentous occasion.

This place, Hulan River, was much too closed off from the outside world, and there wasn't much culture to speak of. Nonetheless, the local officials and gentry were in the main satisfied, and a Hanlin scholar of the Qing dynasty had been asked to pen a lyric about the place, which went:

> Natural forests along the Hulan,
> Since antiquity the abundant source of rare timber.

This lyric had been set to a melody imported from the Eastern Sea [Japan] and was sung by all elementary school children. Actually there was more to the song than just these two lines, but it was considered quite good enough just to sing the two. By good I mean they were sufficient to instill feelings of self-importance in anyone who heard them. To illustrate: During the Qingming Festival, when trees were planted at the gravesites of ancestors, the children from many of the elementary schools made a procession through town, singing this melody as they passed by. When the citizenry along the route heard their singing, they felt that Hulan River was a truly magnificent place and spoke of it as "this Hulan River of ours." Even the child who collected animal droppings for fertilizer would talk of "this Hulan River of ours" as he walked along with his dung rake. I could never figure out, though, just what Hulan River had ever done for him. Maybe the dung rake he carried was Hulan River's gift to him.

This place, Hulan River, may very well have been blessed with rare "timber," but it was still too closed off—it couldn't even support a newspaper. And so the curious tales and strange events that occurred here went unrecorded, simply carried away on the wind.

The dance of the sorceress at the home of the Hu family was a novel event, as was the bath that the child bride was given in a large vat in full view of everyone. As news of these unusual spectacles spread, people came in droves to get an eyeful. As for the paralyzed and the palsied, while no one gave much thought to the tragedy of their physical incapacitation, the fact that they were thus incapable of personally witnessing the public bathing given to the Hu's child bride was, in their eyes, the calamity of a lifetime.

V

Dawn was ushered in by the beating of drums at the Hu house. All was in readiness: the vat, the boiling water, and the rooster. The rooster had been caught and brought forward, the water heated to a running boil, and the vat placed there ready for use.

People came in an unbroken stream to watch the activities, and Granddad and I came with them. I went up to the dark-skinned child bride with the hearty laugh as she lay on the *kang* and gave her a marble and a little platter. Commenting that it was a pretty little platter, she held it up in front of her eyes to study it more closely. Then she said that the marble would be fun to play with as she flipped it with her finger. Seeing that her mother-in-law was not there beside us, she sat up with the idea that she'd play with the marble on the *kang*. But before she even began, her mother-in-law entered and said:

"You really don't know what's good for you! What are you up to now?"

She walked up and covered her again with the tattered coat so that no part of her head—not even her face—was sticking out.

I asked Granddad why the woman wouldn't let her play.

"She's sick," he said.

"No, she isn't; she's fine."

I climbed up onto the *kang* and removed the coat from her head.

The moment her face was visible, I saw that her eyes were wide open. She asked whether or not her mother-in-law was gone, and when I answered that she was, she sat up again. But no sooner had she sat up than her mother-in-law reappeared, and once again she covered the girl up, saying:

"Don't you even care that people will laugh at you? You're so sick we've had to invite sorceresses and exorcists over. Who ever heard of such a thing—sitting up any old time you feel like it!"

After saying this very quietly to the girl, the mother-in-law turned to the gathered crowd and commented:

"We have to keep her out of a draft, because even a slight one will make her sick." As the clamor spawned by all this entertainment grew and grew, the child bride said to me:

"Just wait and see—they're going to give me a bath soon."

She said it as if she were talking about someone else.

Before long, just as she'd predicted, the bathing began, accompanied by a chorus of screams and shouts. The sorceress started beating her drum and ordered that the girl be stripped naked in full view of the crowd. But she resisted their efforts to take her clothes off, forcing her mother-in-law to wrap her arms around her and ask for several people's assistance to come forward and rip the clothes off her body.

Now although the girl was only twelve years old, she looked more like a girl of fifteen or sixteen, so when her body was exposed, the young girls and married women who were watching all blushed.

The child bride was quickly carried over and placed inside the vat, which was brim full of hot water—scalding hot water. Once inside, she began to scream and thrash around as if her life depended upon it, while several people stood around the vat scooping up the hot water and pouring it over her head. Before long her face had turned beet red, and she ceased her struggles; standing quietly in the vat, she no longer attempted to jump out, probably sensing that it would be useless to even try. The vat was so large that when she stood up inside, only her head cleared the top.

I watched for the longest time, and eventually she stopped moving altogether; she neither cried nor smiled. Her sweat-covered face was flushed—it was the color of red paper. I turned and commented to Granddad:

"The child bride isn't yelling any more."

Then I looked back at the vat to discover that she'd vanished. She'd collapsed inside the vat.

At that moment the crowd witnessing the excitement yelled in panic, thinking that the girl had died, and they rushed forward to rescue her, while those of a more compassionate nature began to weep.

A few moments earlier, when the child bride was clearly still alive and begging for help, not a single person had tried to rescue her from the hot water. But now that she was oblivious to everything and no longer seeking help, a few people decided to come to her aid. She was dragged out of the vat and doused with cold water. A moment before, when she'd lost consciousness, the crowd watching all the excitement had been moved to unbelievable compassion. Even the woman who had been shouting, "Use hot water! Pour hot water over her!" was saddened by the turn of events. How could she not be? Here was a sprightly girl whose life had abruptly ended.

The child bride was laid out on the *kang*, her body as hot as cinders. A neighbor woman reached out and touched her body; then another woman did the same. They both exclaimed:

"Gracious, her body's as hot as cinders!"

Someone said that the water had been too hot, while someone else said that they shouldn't have poured it over her head, and that anyone would lose consciousness in such scalding water.

While this discussion was going on, the mother-in-law rushed over and covered the girl with the tattered coat, exclaiming:

"How immodest can you get, lying there without a stitch of clothing on!"

Originally, the child bride had fought having her clothing taken off out of a sense of modesty, but she'd been stripped on the orders of her mother-in-law. Now here she was, oblivious to everything, with no feelings at all, and her mother-in-law was worried about how she looked.

The sorceress beat some tattoos on her drum, as the attendant said something to her, and the onlookers cast glances back and forth. None could say how this episode would end, whether the child bride was dead or alive; but whatever the outcome, they knew they had not wasted their time in coming. They had seen some eye-opening incidents, and they were a little wiser in the ways of the world—that alone made it all worthwhile.

As some of the onlookers were beginning to feel weary, they asked others whether or not the final act of these rites had drawn to a close, adding that they were ready to go home to bed. Seeing that the situation would turn sour if the crowd broke up, the sorceress gathered her energies to make sure she kept her audience. She beat a violent tattoo on her drum and sprayed several mouthfuls of wine into the child bride's face. Then she extracted a silver needle from her waistband, with which she pricked the girl's fingertip. Before long the child bride came to.

The sorceress then informed the people that three baths were required—there were still two to go. This comment injected new life into the crowd: the weary were given a second wind, renewed vigor came to those wanting to go home to bed. No fewer than thirty people were gathered there to watch the excitement; a new sparkle in their eyes, they were a hundred times more spirited than before. Let's see what happens! If she lost consciousness after one bathing, what will happen when she takes a second? The possibilities of yet a third bath were beyond their imagination. As a result, great mysteries crowded their minds.

As anticipated, the moment the child bride was carried out to the large vat and dumped into the scalding water, her eerie screams began anew. All the time she was shouting, she was holding on to the rim of the vat, trying desperately to pull herself out. Meanwhile, as some people continued to douse her with water, others pushed her head down, keeping her under control until once again she passed out and collapsed in the vat.

As she was fished out this time, she was spurting water from her mouth. As before, among the onlookers some kind people were moved to sympathize with the plight of this girl. Women from neighboring families came forward to do whatever they could to aid her. They crowded around to see whether or not she was still alive. If there was still a spark of life, then they need not worry about rescuing her. But if she was breathing her last, then they must hurriedly douse her with cool water. If there was still life in her, she'd come around on her own, but if her life was ebbing away, then they would have to do something quickly in order to bring her to. If they didn't, they'd surely lose her.

VI

The child bride was bathed three times that evening in scalding water, and each time she passed out. The commotion lasted until very late at night, when the sorceress returned home to go to bed. The onlookers, too, returned to their homes to retire.

On this winter night, the moon and stars filled the sky, ice and snow covered the ground. Snow swirled and gathered at the base of the wall, winds beat against the windowsills. Chickens were asleep in their roosts, dogs slumbered in their dens, and pigs holed up in their pens. All of Hulan River was asleep.

There were only the distant sounds of a barking dog, maybe in White Flag Village, or possibly a wild dog in the willow grove on the southern bank of the Hulan River. Whatever the case, the sound came from a great distance away and belonged to those affairs that occurred outside the town of Hulan River. The whole town of Hulan River was fast asleep.

There was no longer any hint of the dancing and drum-beating of the sorceress from earlier that evening, and it was as if the shouts and cries of the child bride had never occurred, for not a single trace of all of this remained. Every household was pitch dark, its occupants sound asleep. The child bride's mother-in-law snored as she slept.

Since the third watch had already been struck, the fourth watch was nearly upon them.

VII

The child bride slept as if in a trance the whole day following, as well as the day after and the day after that. Her eyes were neither completely open nor completely shut; a small slit remained, through which the whites of her eyes were visible.

When members of her family saw how she lay there, they said she had undergone a great struggle, but that her true soul still had a grip on her body; if that was the case, then she'd recover. This was the opinion not just of her family, but of the neighbors as well. As a result, not only did they feel no anxiety over her condition—neither eating nor drinking, and always in a sort of half stupor—but on the contrary, they felt it was something over which they should rejoice. She lay like that for four or five days, which were four or five happy days for her family; when she had lain there for six or seven days, they were six or seven happy days for her family. During this period, not a single potion was used, and not a single type of herbal medication was put to the test.

But after six or seven days had passed, she remained in a coma, neither eating nor drinking, and giving no indication that she was on the road to recovery. The sorceress was called back, but this time she said nothing about effecting a cure; she said it had now reached the point where there was no alternative but for the girl to "come forth," to become a sorceress herself.

The family then decided to apply true methods of exorcism, so they went to the ornaments shop; there they had a paper image of her made, which they dressed in cotton clothing made especially for it (the cotton clothes were to make the image more lifelike). Cosmetics were applied to the face and a colorful hankie attached to its hand; the result was a delight to behold—dressed completely in fancy clothes, it looked just like a maiden of seventeen or eighteen. The image was carried by people down to the big pit on the south bank of the river, where it was burned.

This procedure is called burning a "proxy doll," and according to legend, when this "proxy doll" is burned, it takes the place of someone's real body, sparing that person's life.

On the day the "proxy doll" was burned, the child bride's mother-in-law showed proof of her devotion by engaging musicians, who filed in behind the people hired to carry the image. The procession made its way to the big southern pit to the accompaniment of the musicians' tooting and clanging. It would be accurate to call the procession a boisterous affair, with the trumpets blaring the same tune over and over again. But it would be no less accurate to call it a mournful affair, for with the paper figure in front and three or four musicians bringing up the rear, it looked like something between a funeral procession and a somber temple rite.

Not many people came out onto the street to watch the commotion, since it was a cold day. A few folks did stick out their heads or venture out to take a look, but when they saw there wasn't much worth seeing, they shut their gates and went back inside. Therefore, the paper figure was burned in the big pit in a mournful ceremony with little fanfare.

The child bride's mother-in-law experienced pangs of regret as she burned the figure, for had she known beforehand that there weren't going to be many people looking on, she could have dispensed with dressing the figure in real clothing. She felt like going down into the pit to retrieve the clothing, but it was too late, so she just stood there watching it burn. She'd spent a total of more than a thousand strings of cash for that set of clothes, and as she watched it burn, it was as if she were watching more than a thousand strings of cash go up in smoke. There was both regret and anger in her heart. She had by then forgotten that this was a "proxy doll" for her future daughter-in-law. Her original plan had been to intone a prayerful chant during the ceremony, but it slipped her mind completely until she was on her way back home, at which time it occurred to her that she had probably burned the "proxy doll" for nothing. Whether or not it would prove effective was now anybody's guess!

VIII

Later we heard that the child bride's braid had fallen off one night as she slept. It had simply fallen off beside her pillow, and no one was quite sure how that could have happened.

Convinced that the child bride was some kind of demon, the mother-in-law kept the detached braid around to show to everyone who dropped by. It was obvious to anyone who saw it that it had been snipped off with scissors, but the mother-in-law insisted that such was not the case. She stuck to her story that it had simply fallen off by itself one night while the girl slept. Eventually, as this curious news made the rounds throughout the neighborhood and outlying areas, not only were the members of her family unwilling to have a demon among them, even others in the same compound felt that it was a terrible situation. At night, when closing their doors and windows, the people commented:

"The Hu family's child bride is a demon for sure!"

The cook at our house, a real gossip, was forever telling Granddad one thing or another about the Hu family's child bride. Now there was something new to report: the girl's braid had fallen off.

"No it didn't," I retorted. "Someone cut it off with scissors."

But as far as the old cook was concerned, I was too young, and to ridicule me, he stopped me by putting his finger over my mouth and saying:

"What do you know? That child bride is a demon!"

"No she isn't. When I asked her how her braid had fallen off, she grinned and said she didn't know!"

"A nice child like that," Granddad interjected, "and they're going to kill her."

A few days later the old cook reported:

"The Hu family is going to divorce away that little demon."

Granddad didn't hold the people in the Hu family in very high esteem.

"Come March I'm going to have them move," he said. "First they nearly kill someone else's child, then they abandon her."

IX

Before March rolled around, however, that dark-skinned child bride with the hearty laugh died. Early one morning, the elder son of the Hu family—the carter with the sickly face and big eyes—came to our

house. When he saw Granddad, he brought his hands together in front
of his chest and bowed deeply.

Granddad asked him what had happened.

"We'd like you to donate a small plot of ground to bury our child
bride."

"When did she die?" Granddad asked.

"I was out with my cart and didn't get home till daybreak," he replied. "They say she died during the night."

Granddad agreed to let them bury her on a piece of ground on the
outskirts of town. He summoned Second Uncle You and told him to
accompany them to the place. Just as Second Uncle You was about to
leave, he was joined by the old cook. I said I wanted to go along to
watch, but Granddad wouldn't allow it:

"You and I will stay home and trap some sparrows."

So I didn't go along, though I couldn't take my mind off the affair. I
waited and waited for Second Uncle You and the old cook to return so I
could hear how things had gone, but they didn't come right back. It
was after one o'clock when they finally returned, having stopped off
somewhere for some liquor and lunch. They returned with the old cook
in the lead, followed by Second Uncle You, the two of them looking like
a couple of fat ducks; hardly able to move, they walked slowly, looking
quite smug.

The old cook, who was in front, had bloodshot eyes and lips that glistened with oil. Second Uncle You, who was walking behind him, was
flushed from his ears all the way down to the thick tendon below his
neck. When they entered Granddad's room, one of them said:

"The liquor and food weren't half bad."

"The egg soup was piping hot," the other commented.

Not a word about the burying of the child bride. It was as if they'd
returned from a New Year's celebration, feeling nothing but satisfaction and happiness. I asked Second Uncle You how the child bride had
died and what had happened at the burial.

"Why ask me that? The death of a human being isn't as noteworthy
as that of a chicken . . . just stick your legs out straight and that's the
end of it."

"Second Uncle You, when are you going to die?" I asked him.

"Your Second Uncle isn't going to die . . . now you take a rich man
who lives in comfort all his life; the longer he hopes to live, the
younger he is when he dies. Not even burning incense in the temple or
going into the mountains to worship the Buddha will change the outcome. But then take someone like me who's been poor all my life; I get

stronger with each passing year. I'm like a rock that never dies! As the saying goes: 'The rich get but three measures of life, the poor hang on forever.' Second Uncle You is one of those poor ones, and King Yama won't stoop to look at the likes of me."

That evening the Hu family invited the two of them, Second Uncle You and the old cook, over again to drink some more liquor. This was how they paid them back for their help.

X

Not long after the Hu family's child bride died, the elder grandson's wife ran off with another man.

Later on the grandmother passed away.

As for the wives of the two sons of the family, one lost the sight of one eye because of the affair with the child bride; she'd cried every day over the fact that all her wealth—more than fifty thousand strings of cash—had been squandered on behalf of the child bride.

The other wife had suffered untold shame over the fact that her son's wife had run off with someone, and she spent every waking minute of each day sitting beside the stove smoking a pipe, never combing her hair or washing her face. If someone walked by when her spirits were high, she'd ask them:

"Is everyone in your family well?"

But when her spirits were low she'd spit in the person's face.

She'd become half mad.

From then on, few people ever thought about the Hu family.

XI

Behind our house was a Dragon King Temple, to the east of which there was a big bridge we called Great Eastern Bridge. The ghosts of wronged people congregated below this bridge, and during inclement weather, people crossing over it could hear the weeping sounds of those ghosts.

People were saying that the ghost of the child bride had come to this spot below Great Eastern Bridge. They said she'd been transformed into a big white rabbit that came to that place under the bridge once every few days to weep.

Someone might ask her why she was weeping.

She'd say she wanted to go home.

If the person responded with:

"I'll take you home tomorrow . . ."

The white rabbit would wipe her eyes with her big floppy ears and disappear. But if no one paid any attention to her, she'd continue to weep until roosters ushered in the new day.

CHAPTER SIX

I

Second Uncle You had an unusual temperament. If we had something to eat but wouldn't give him any, he'd curse us. But if we took some to him, he'd say: "Your Second Uncle You doesn't eat this stuff, so eat it yourself."

If we bought some things like peanuts or frozen pears and didn't want to give him any, we had to hide them from him, for if he so much as spotted them, he invariably began cursing:

"Goddamn it, you little bastards . . . rabbit whelps. There's plenty for dogs and cats, or for cockroaches, or even rats, but there's goddamn little for people . . . rabbit whelps, damned rabbit whelps . . ."

But if we took some to him, then he'd say:

"Your Second Uncle You doesn't eat this stuff, so eat it yourself."

II

Second Uncle You's temperament was strange indeed—he loved to talk to sparrows in the sky and he loved to chat with the big yellow dog. But somehow he ran out of things to say when he was with people. Or if he did have something to say, it was of such a strange nature that it left the person scratching his head in bewilderment.

On summer evenings after dinner, when we all sat in the courtyard to cool off, we talked about everything under the sun, and our spirited discussions were accompanied by the buzzing of mosquitoes and the croaking of distant frogs. Second Uncle You alone sat there without saying a word, flyswatter in hand, which he flicked from side to side. If someone asked him whether the flyswatter was made of horse's mane or horses tail, he'd answer:

"Like they say: 'Everybody has his own thing, and even the short and ugly Wu Dalang had his pet duck.' Horse's mane is costly stuff, reserved for people who wear silks and satins, with bracelets on their wrists and big rings on their fingers. Each person is matched with his own kind of stuff to play with. We poor rootless souls must not become the butts of others' laughter by forgetting our place."

There's a fable concerning the evening star: When the Kitchen God ascended to the Western Heaven on his young donkey, he carried a lantern in his hand; but because the donkey traveled so fast, in a careless moment he dropped the lantern and it got stuck in the sky, where it hangs today. I often asked Granddad how the lantern had gotten up in the sky and why it stayed there without falling to Earth. I could see he had no answer, but he knew I wouldn't be satisfied without some kind of answer. So he told me there was a lantern pole in the sky, a very tall one, on which the evening star was perched. It was, however, invisible to the human eye.

"That's not true," I'd say. "I don't believe you."

Or I'd say:

"There's no lantern pole. If there was, why can't people see it?"

"There's a long thread up in the sky, and the evening star hangs from that," Granddad would answer.

"I don't believe you. There's no thread in the sky, or else I could see it."

"How could you, since it's so fine? There isn't a person alive who can see it."

"If no one can see it, how do you know it's there?"

The others would laugh, commenting on how clever I was.

Eventually my questions would back Granddad into a corner, until there was nothing else to say. I could see that his wild fabrications were a result of my persistent questions, and I knew he really didn't have an answer. Still, the wilder his answers became, the more persistently I kept up the questioning. By the time I was finished, I'd shot holes in the theory regarding the relationship between the Kitchen God's lantern and the evening star, following which I asked Granddad just what exactly the evening star was.

The others could see that I'd reached the end of the line as far as Granddad was concerned, so someone recommended that I direct my questions to Second Uncle You.

I ran over to where he was sitting, but before I'd even opened my mouth, and had barely brushed against his flyswatter, he frightened me by shaking the flyswatter and grumbling:

"Come on, kid, move back a little."

Forced to heed his command, I moved back a bit, then asked him:

"Second Uncle You, just exactly what is that evening star up in the sky?"

He didn't answer me right away, as if he were mulling over my question. Finally he said:

"The poor concern themselves not with heavenly phenomena . . . dogs chase mice, cats watch the house . . . mind your own business!"

Thinking he'd misunderstood my question, I asked again:

"Is the evening star really the Kitchen God's lantern?"

"Though your Second Uncle has a pair of eyes, he's never seen a single thing in his whole life. And though your Second Uncle has a pair of ears, he hasn't heard a single thing in his whole life. Your Second Uncle is deaf and blind. You want to know why I say that? Take, for example, bright, shiny, tile-roofed houses. I've seen them before, but what good has it done me? They belong to other people, so I might as well never have seen them at all. The same is true for hearing things; what difference does it make if you hear something that has nothing to do with you? Everything in your Second Uncle's life has had nothing to do with him . . . stars, the moon, winds and rain, those are all Heaven's affairs that your Second Uncle knows nothing about . . ."

Second Uncle You was really strange. If his foot bumped into a brick while he was walking, stubbing his toe painfully, he'd very carefully bend over and pick the brick up, then minutely examine it to make sure it was neither too small nor too big, but just right. Then, after examining the brick, he'd begin talking to it.

"You there, little one, I guess you don't have eyes either. You're just like me, blind as a bat. Otherwise, why move over and bump into my foot? Since you've got the nerve to bump people, why not aim at the high and mighty, those with boots or shoes on their feet? Why waste your time bumping into the likes of me? You're not going to get a thing out of bumping into me . . . like a chunk of stinking mud trying to roll itself into a stone, only to find itself stinking worse every minute."

His chat with the brick finished, he'd toss it away with a flick of his wrist, giving it one final admonition as he did so:

"Next time find yourself someone who's wearing shoes and socks to bump into." The brick would crash to the ground just as he finished what he was saying; but since he hadn't thrown it very far, it would wind up in about the same place he'd found it.

If Second Uncle You was walking in the yard, and some droppings from a sparrow or swallow flying overhead landed on him, he'd stop in his tracks and simply stand there. Then he'd raise his head and begin cursing at the sparrow, which by then had already flown past. The gist of his comments would have to do with how the sparrow shouldn't have sent its droppings down on him, but should have aimed instead at someone wearing silks and satins. His comments would be punctuated by references to the sparrow's stupidity, blindness, and the like. But the sparrow, after having quickly let fly its missile, would have disappeared without a trace, so that Second Uncle You would be left with only the clear blue sky overhead as a target for his curses.

III

When Second Uncle You spoke, he pronounced "this" as "dis."
"That man is good."
"Dis man is no good."
"Dis man has the heart of a wolf and the lungs of a wild dog."
"Dis thing's worse than nothing at all."
"What kind of year is dis, with house sparrows sending their droppings down on my head?"

IV

Besides this,
Second Uncle You didn't eat mutton.

V

Granddad said that Second Uncle You had come to our home thirty years before, when he was just past the age of thirty. Second Uncle You was now over sixty.

As a child he'd been given the nickname Youzi, which meant Little You. Now, over sixty, he was still called by his pet name. Granddad would say to him: "Little You, do this," or "Little You, do that."

We called him Second Uncle You.

The old cook called him Second Master You.

When he visited the house of our land tenants, he was called Second Landlord You.

When he went to the distillery on Avenue North, he was called Second Proprietor You.

He was also called Second Proprietor You when he went to the oil store to fetch cooking oil.

He was likewise called Second Proprietor You by the people at the butcher shop when he went to buy meat.

Whenever he heard people refer to him as Second Proprietor You, he beamed. He also beamed when he was called Second Master You, Second Landlord You, or Second Uncle You. But he hated it like poison when someone called him by his nickname. Some of the neighborhood brats, for example, would throw rocks at him from behind or spray him with handfuls of dirt, loudly calling him names like: "Little Second You" or "Big Oaf You" or "Little Runt You."

In situations like this, Second Uncle You would never miss the opportunity to strike out at the kids. If he had his flyswatter in his hand, he'd swipe at them with it, and if he had his pipe in his hand, he'd hit them with that. That's because this made him as mad as a wet hen, and his eyes would turn red with rage.

But as soon as those rascally kids saw him coming at them, his fists swinging, they'd quickly call out: "Second Master You, Second Landlord You, Second Proprietor You, Second Uncle You." They'd clasp their hands in front of their chests and bow low to him. When Second Uncle You saw this new state of affairs, his face would break into a broad grin; he'd stop swinging and resume the walk that had been interrupted.

But before he'd taken more than a few steps, the kids behind him would start in again with their shouts of:

"Second Master You, the big queer."

"Second Uncle You plays with his own oar."

"Second Landlord You, out catching bastard turtles."

He'd keep walking ahead, while the kids he'd left in the distance behind him would continue with their taunts, raising clouds of dirt in the air as they shouted; and as the dust swirled in the wind, the whole chaotic scene would take on the appearance of a whirlwind.

Although no one could say whether or not Second Uncle You heard all this, the kids behind him believed he had. But Second Uncle You would walk on rather majestically, step after undaunted step, without once turning his head back.

"Second Master You," the old cook would call out. He preceded every sentence he spoke about or to him with "Second Master You."

"Second Master You's flyswatter . . ."

"Second Master You's pipe bowl . . ."

"Second Master You's tobacco pouch . . ."

"Second Master You's tobacco pouch belt . . ."

"Second Master You, dinner's ready . . ."

"Second Master You, it's raining . . ."

"Second Master You, look over there. The dogs are fighting in the yard . . ."

"Second Master You, the cat's climbed up onto the wall . . ."

"Second Master You, your flyswatter's shedding hairs."

"Second Master You, there's some sparrow droppings on the crown of your hat."

The old cook always called him "Second Master You." That is, except when they were having an argument; then the old cook would say:

"As I see it, if you took away the 'Second Master' from your name, all you'd have left is the 'You zi [word].'"

When he heard the words "You" and "zi" together it sounded to him just like his pet name, Youzi. With that, curses would fly back and forth between them, as each tried to outdo the other. Their voices would grow louder and louder, and sometimes they'd come to blows.

But before long, the two of them would be all buddy-buddy again, and once more we'd hear:

"Second Master You this" and "Second Master You that."

Whenever the old cook was in high spirits, he'd say:

"Second Master You, as I see it, if you took the word 'You' away from your name, then you'd be left with 'Second Master,' wouldn't you?"

Second Uncle You would beam.

He never got angry when Granddad called him "Youzi." Instead he'd say:

"When you speak to an emperor, you refer to yourself as a slave. There's always a high and a low: a prime minister may be high, but he must prostrate himself before the emperor. Though superior to the multitudes, he is yet inferior to one man."

Second Uncle You was a very courageous man—he feared nothing. Once I asked him whether or not he was afraid of wolves.

"What's there to fear from a wolf? When I was young, I took pigs out to pasture on a mountain where wolves were living."

I asked him if he had the nerve to walk down dark roads.

"What's there to fear from a dark road? If one has done nothing shameful, one has naught to fear from ghosts at the door."

I asked him if he had the nerve to walk across the Great Eastern Bridge alone late at night.

"Why wouldn't I? The only things your Second Uncle dares not do are shameful ones. He has the nerve to do anything else."

Second Uncle You often talked about how courageous he'd been when people were fleeing from the *maozi*, or "Hairy Ones," during the

Russo-Japanese War. The city's populace had fled, including our entire family. The "Hairy Ones," astride their horses, galloped back and forth through the streets, brandishing swords. They slaughtered countless people back then, as they pounded on all the closed doors they saw, then broke them down and butchered every person they caught.

"When the 'Hairy Ones' were galloping back and forth," Second Uncle You said, "their horses' hooves made a great racket on the streets. I was cooking some noodles when they came pounding at my door and yelling, 'Is there anyone inside?' At times like that, someone had to open the door in a hurry, or else the 'Hairy Ones' would break the door down with their swords and burst in. That was bad news, for there was sure to be bloodshed . . ."

"Second Uncle You, you must have been afraid!" I said.

"I'd just boiled some water and was putting the noodles in. The 'Hairy Ones' were outside pounding on the door, and your Second Uncle was inside eating noodles."

But I persisted:

"You were afraid, weren't you?"

"Afraid of what? "

"If the 'Hairy Ones' had come inside, wouldn't they have killed you with their swords?"

"So what if they had? After all, it's only a life!"

But every time he and Granddad were talking of the past, he sang a different tune:

"People are flesh and blood: They're all raised by their fathers and mothers! We've all got the same five organs and six bowels. Afraid? Who wouldn't be afraid? I was so scared I shook in my boots—those swords were about to fall. One slash and there'd go my life!"

So I asked him:

"But didn't you say before that you weren't afraid?"

At times like that he cursed me:

"You heartless pest, get away from me! Not afraid? Show me a person who isn't afraid . . ."

I don't know why, but he grew timid whenever he and Granddad discussed the subject of fleeing from the "Hairy Ones." The more he talked about them, the more frightened he became, on occasion even breaking into tears. He ranted on about the glint of the swords and how the "Hairy Ones" had ridden by on their horses in a frenzy of killing.

VI

Second Uncle You's bedding was a real jumble: if you touched his comforter, cotton batting oozed out of the corners; if you spread open his mat, shreds of felting skittered to and fro, making it look like a living map, with the provinces moving on their own. His pillow was filled with buckwheat husks, and every time he tried to fluff it up, a stream of husks poured from its corners or from rends in the middle.

Second Uncle You doted on this bedding of his, and when he had nothing else to do, he picked up needle and thread to mend it . . . sewing his pillow, sewing his shredded felt mat, sewing his comforter. I never knew how his things could be so fragile, but every second or third day, he had to get out his needle and thread and go to work.

Second Uncle You's hands were so coarse and thick that he had to use a gigantic needle; he said he couldn't hold a small one. His needle was so big that when it lay in the sunlight it looked more like one of the silver pins women use in their hair. It was sheer delight to watch him trying to thread this needle of his. He'd raise the needle and thread high above him, then close one eye and stare intently with the other, as if taking aim. He'd look as if he'd spotted something up in the sky that he wanted to grab, but was afraid he might miss and knock away; wanting to study the situation carefully, he was also afraid that it would be gone if he waited too long. All this anxiety would make his hands tremble, and that was quite a spectacle.

When Second Uncle You woke up in the morning, he always rolled up his bedding, then tied it with a piece of cord, giving the impression that he was about to set off on some sort of journey.

Second Uncle You didn't sleep in any one prescribed place. One night he might stay in the bean-noodle mill with its creaky beams and posts, the next night he might sleep at the foot of the herder-boy's *kang* in the home of the hog raisers, while the night after that he might just sleep on a *kang* with Harelip Feng in the mill shed behind our house. In short, he slept wherever there happened to be room for him. He carried his bedding roll on his back, and whenever the old cook saw him carrying it like that, he shouted out loudly:

"Second Master You is off to the market again."

Second Uncle You would answer from a distance:

"I'm off to the market, Old Wang. Can I get you anything?" Then he'd continue on to wherever he was going—he'd take up temporary lodging at whichever of the tenant's homes was convenient.

VII

Second Uncle You's straw hat had a crown but no brim. Since his face was swarthy black and the crown of his head snowy white, there was a clear dividing line between black and white, which occurred exactly at the point where the straw hat fit down neatly over his head. Whenever he took off his hat, the top half of his head was white, the bottom half black. Just like a melon in our rear garden—the side that faced the sun was green, the shaded side white. But the moment he put on his straw hat, none of this was apparent any longer. He put the hat on his head very accurately, fitting it down so that it reached the line dividing black from white. Neither above nor below, it rested precisely on that dividing line. Every once in a while, he'd put it on slightly higher than normal, but only very seldom, and not so that other people would notice. It just looked to them that there was a narrow white border at the juncture where hat and head met—just a single white line.

VIII

Second Uncle You wore a gown that came down to his knees. It was neither a full-length gown nor a short jacket; rather it reached just to his knees. The gown, made of marine blue cotton, had a squared-off, high-pointed collar, loose sleeves, and a row of brass-tipped hempen buttons. It was an old thing dating from the Qing dynasty that had been stored at the bottom of Granddad's chest. After Grandmother died, it eventually wound up draped over Second Uncle You's frame. And so, when Second Uncle You was out walking, it was hard to tell just what dynasty he belonged to.

The old cook often said:

"Second Master You, with those loose sleeves of yours, in the eyes of a Buddhist monk you, too, are a Buddhist monk, and in the eyes of a Taoist priest you, too, are a Taoist priest."

Second Uncle You liked to wear his pant legs rolled up, so when farmers saw him, they thought that he, too, might be a farmer, one just returning from planting rice.

IX

As for Second Uncle You's shoes, if one of the soles wasn't flapping, then a heel had dropped off. He glued the soles and nailed the heels on with his own hands, but he apparently neither nailed nor glued them very well, for within a few days the soles would invariably loosen, and the heels fall off again

When he walked, it was either with a shuffle or with a flapping sound. If the soles had loosened, the shoes had the appearance of gaping mouths, his toes looking like tongues that moved back and forth inside those gaping mouths; if the heels of his shoes had fallen off, then the heels of his feet made slapping sounds against the bottoms of the shoes as he walked.

Second Uncle You's feet never really left the ground when he walked, and Mother often said that they were weighted down with half-ton sluice gates. The old cook said that Second Uncle You's feet were locked in horse fetters.

But Second Uncle You himself said:

"Your Second uncle has foot-tie bands on his feet."

Foot-tie bands are ropes that are fastened around the feet of a dying man. That's what Second Uncle You used to say about himself.

X

Even though Second Uncle You dressed like a cross between a monkey trainer and a beggar, when he walked, he did so with solemn, quietly dignified airs; he had great strength in his heels, which smacked loudly against the ground, and he walked with extremely slow steps, like a great general. Whenever he walked into Granddad's room, the works inside the black clock that stood on the lute-shaped table jingled and whirred a time or two, then grew silent. This happened because Second Uncle You's footsteps were so heavy, like big rocks crashing to the ground and causing everything resting on the floor to bounce up and down.

XI

By chance I discovered Second Uncle You stealing things.

In the late autumn, when the tall elm tree had shed its leaves, the rear garden grew dreary, and there was nothing for me to do there. The mugwort in the front yard had withered and lay flat on the ground. A layer of frost covered the plants and stalks in the vegetable garden behind the house, and only a few sparse leaves remained on the elm tree, though the autumn winds continued to make its limbs sway.

The sky was ashen and covered with shapeless clouds, causing it to look like a water basin in which an ink stone had been washed—a mottled mixture of darks and lights. Some of the clouds carried rainwater in them, others carried fine snowflakes. During such weather, since I couldn't play outdoors, I went up into the attic above the back room, where old objects were stored.

One day, after climbing up by standing on a trunk, my hand bumped into a glass jar that was packed full of dried black dates. But when I tried to climb back down, holding onto the jar, I found I couldn't. For there stood second Uncle You, opening up the very trunk I'd used to climb up into the attic. He was opening it not with a key, but with a piece of wire.

I watched him try to open it for a long time; he was using his teeth to twist the thing in his hand—he'd cock his head and gnaw loudly on it. Then, after biting it, he'd twist it in his hands, then try it again on the lock. He obviously was unaware that I was up in the rafters watching him, and when he finally succeeded in opening the trunk, he took off his brimless straw hat and tucked the thing he'd been chewing on for such a long time into the crown. Then he rummaged through the trunk; in it were some red chair cushions, a blue embroidered apron made of coarse cotton, some women's embroidered shoes, as well as a tangled wad of multicolored silk threads. At the bottom of the trunk lay a dark yellow brass liquor flask. He pushed the embroidered shoes and tangled silk to the side with his veiny hands. Then he picked up the flask from the pile. He placed the red armchair cushions on the floor and tied his belt around them, after which he placed the flask on the lid of the trunk, which he then locked.

I thought he was going to take these things away with him, but for reasons known to him alone he walked out of the room without doing so. As soon as I saw him leave I jumped down onto the trunk and lowered myself down. But the moment my feet touched the floor, Second Uncle You reentered the room, scaring the daylights out of me. I was frightened because I was in the act of stealing some dried black dates, and if Mother had found out about it, she'd have given me a spanking for sure. Usually, when I stole something, it was merely things like eggs and steamed buns, which I took outside and shared with some of the neighbor kids. Whenever Second Uncle You saw me, he was sure to tell my mother, and she was just as sure to spank me.

He first picked up the chair cushions lying beside the door, then came over to fetch the flask from the lid of the trunk. It was only when he'd opened his gown and tucked the flask underneath it up against his belly that he looked up and saw me standing in the corner of the room.

He had a brass flask under his gown tucked up against his belly, I was holding a jar of dried black dates pressed up against mine. He was stealing, so was I, and both of us were scared.

The moment he laid eyes on me, large beads of sweat appeared on his forehead.

"You won't tell?" he asked.

"Tell what? "

"Be a good kid and don't tell," he said as he patted the top of my head.

"Then will you let me take this jar out with me?"

"Go ahead, take it," he said. He didn't try to stop me.

When I saw he wasn't going to stand in my way, I stopped by the basket beside the door, picked up four or five big steamed buns, and darted off.

Second Uncle You also stole some rice from our grain storage shed. He filled a large sack, hoisted it up onto his back, then took it over to the grain shop on the eastern side of the bridge, where he sold it.

Second Uncle You stole all sorts of things: a tin cook pot, old brass coins, pipe stems . . . As a rule, whenever something was missing from the house, he was accused of stealing it.

The cook had actually stolen some of those things, but he passed the blame on to Second Uncle You. Some I'd stolen to play with, and Second Uncle You was blamed for them, too. Then there were things like the blade of the scythe, which hadn't been stolen at all, but was simply misplaced; yet when the time came to use it, and it couldn't be found, Second Uncle You was accused of stealing it.

When Second Uncle You took me to the park, he refused to buy me anything to eat. Everything imaginable thing was for sale at the park: fried rice cakes, fragrant stuffed flat cakes, gelatined bean curd, and other delicacies, but he wouldn't buy a single one of them for me. If I merely stood for a moment near one of the stalls where those treats were sold, he'd say to me:

"Hurry up, lets keep walking." A walk in the park with him was like a forced march—he wouldn't let me pause even for a second.

There were all sorts of entertainment in the park, things like magic shows, a blind man and a dancing bear; the loud gongs and drums produced a festive atmosphere. But he wouldn't let me watch any of it. If I stopped for a moment in front of a circus performance, he'd say:

"Hurry up, let's keep walking." I don't know why, but he was always chasing me on ahead.

As we walked up to a stall with a white awning where ices were sold, I noticed two big, yellow Buddha-fingers fruit in a glass jar; since I'd never seen anything like them before, I asked Second Uncle You what they were.

All he said was: "Hurry up, let's keep walking."

It was as if someone might come up and start beating me if I looked at them even a moment longer.

Then we drew up alongside the circus grounds, where shouting and singing produced a great commotion. I was determined to go inside and take a look, but Second Uncle You was just as determined not to let me.

"There's nothing worth seeing in there."

Then he said:

"Your Second Uncle doesn't watch 'dis' kind of thing."

Then he said:

"It's time to go home and eat."

Then he said:

"If you keep it up, I'm going to hit you."

Finally he said to me:

"Your Second Uncle would like to watch it, too—who wouldn't like to watch something so entertaining? But your Second Uncle doesn't have any money, and they won't let us go in if we can't buy a ticket."

There in the park, right where we stood, I grabbed hold of his pocket and checked to see what was in it. All I came up with was a few strings of cash, not enough to buy a ticket. Again he said:

"Your Second Uncle doesn't have any money."

Growing impatient, I asked him:

"Couldn't you steal a little?"

Second Uncle You's face paled when he heard this, but in a flash the color came rushing back. With his face now flushed, a forced smile on his tiny eyes, and his lips trembling, he seemed to be on the verge of uttering a stream of his customary comments. But he didn't.

"Let's go home."

After giving it some thought, that's all he said.

Once I even saw Second Uncle You steal a bathtub.

Our yard was generally quiet the day long. Granddad was usually asleep, Father was away from home, and Mother kept herself busy with household duties and didn't see much of what was going on outside. This was especially true during the summertime at midday, when everyone was napping, including the old cook. Even the big yellow dog would find a shady spot and go to sleep.

As a result, both the front yard and the rear garden were deathly still, without a trace of people or sounds. It was on just such a day that someone walked out from the rear garden carrying a big bathtub on his shoulders.

The bathtub was made of galvanized iron that shone brightly under the sun's rays; it was longer than a person and made clanging noises as the man walked. It was scary to look at, as it reminded me of the fabled great white snake.

It was so huge that, with it over his head, Second Uncle You almost completely disappeared from sight, and only the bathtub itself was visible. It was as if the bathtub were moving along under its own power.

But more careful examination revealed that it was riding atop Second Uncle You's head.

He walked along as if he had no eyes in his head, wobbling first to the left then to the right, leaning to one side then the other. Fearing that he'd bump into me, I flattened up against the wall.

The big bathtub was so deep it covered Second Uncle You from the top of his head all the way down to his waist, which meant that he couldn't see the road ahead and had to feel with his hand as he walked along.

The scene that followed Second Uncle You's theft of the bathtub was a repetition of the one when he'd stolen the brass liquor flask. As soon as the old cook discovered the theft, he derided him daily, directing every kind of taunt he knew at Second Uncle You.

Previously, when he'd stolen the flask, every time he picked up a flask to have a drink, the old cook would say:

"Second Master You, does it taste better to drink out of brass flasks or pewter ones?"

"They're all the same to me," Second Uncle You would say. "Either way it's still liquor."

The old cook would reply:

"I don't agree. I still think brass ones are better . . ."

"What's so special about brass?"

"I guess you're right, Second Master You. We don't have any use for a brass flask, and we couldn't get anything for ours if we tried to sell it."

By this time everyone else in the room would be chuckling, but Second Uncle You still didn't know what was going on.

The old cook would then ask:

"How much can you get for a brass wine flask?"

"Don't know," Second Uncle You would answer. "I've never sold one."

After this the cook would begin guessing—five hundred strings of cash? Seven hundred?

Second Uncle You would say:

"What makes you think you'd get that much? You can't even sell a great big brass flask for more than three hundred!" At this, everyone would double up with laughter.

The old cook stopped bringing up the subject of the brass liquor flask following the theft of the bathtub; instead he began asking Second Uncle You about his bathing habits. He'd ask him how many baths he took a year or how many baths he'd taken in his lifetime. He even asked him whether people took baths in the nether world after they died.

"There's no difference between the nether world and this one," Second Uncle You said. "A poor man in this world becomes a poor ghost after he dies. King Yama of the underworld has no sympathy for a poor ghost, who's lucky if he isn't sent down to the lowest hell. There's no talk of a bath—he's afraid you'll muddy the water!"

Then the old cook said:

"Second Master You, according to you, a poor man has no need for a bathtub."

Second Uncle You seemed to be getting the drift of the conversation, so he said:

"I've never been to the nether world, so I wouldn't know."

"You wouldn't know?"

"I wouldn't know."

"I think you know very well, and you're going against your own conscience by lying," the old cook said.

At this point, a fight broke out between them.

Second Uncle You demanded that the old cook tell him when he'd ever gone against his conscience.

"I've never in my life gone against my conscience. I've walked the proper road, done the things I was supposed to do, never straying from the straight and narrow."

"Straight and narrow? That I'd like to see."

"What is it you'd like to see?"

"If I told you, you'd die of shame!"

"Die! I'm not going to die. Don't treat me like that because I'm poor. Even the poor have a desire to live."

"Yes, I suspect you aren't going to die."

"That's right, I'm not!"

"Not going to, or won't? As I see it, you're one of those old fogies who won't die."

Sometimes their arguments would last as long as a couple of days, and invariably it was Second Uncle You who got the worst of them, for the old cook would call him an "heirless old man." These three words hit Second Uncle You harder than any other, even including comments like "going to meet Yama." He'd begin to weep and mumble:

"That's exactly how it is. After I'm dead, there won't be a single person to take care of my grave. I've lived a lifetime for nothing, and when I leave this world, it'll be as if I hadn't even been here . . . no family, no property . . . when I'm dead there won't even be anyone to mourn me."

At this point, peace would reign once more between the two of them, and they would again pass their time peacefully as before, laughing and joking.

XII

Later on, we added three side rooms to the east of our five-room house. As soon as these new rooms were completed, Second Uncle You moved back into the house.

Our house was very quiet, especially at night, when the chickens and ducks had gone to roost and the pigeons on the roof and the sparrows in the eaves had returned to their nests to sleep. At such times I often heard the sounds of weeping coming from the side rooms.

Once Father beat up Second Uncle You. Father was just over thirty, while Second Uncle You was nearly sixty. As Second Uncle You got to his feet, Father knocked him back down. He got up again, and once more was knocked to the ground. Finally he could no longer get to his feet, so he just lay there in the courtyard with blood oozing from his nose, or maybe his mouth. The people in the yard watching the excitement stood off at a distance, and even the big yellow dog was frightened away, as were the chickens. As for the old cook, he continued gathering firewood and fetching water, pretending he hadn't seen what was happening.

Second Uncle You lay there in the middle of the yard, alone and neglected. His brimless straw hat had been knocked off his head, so everyone could see that the top half of his head was white, the bottom half dark, and the line that separated the black and white halves ran right across his forehead, just like the sunny and shady halves of a melon. He lay there like that for a long time, until a pair of ducks waddled over to peck at the blood splattered on the ground beside him. One of the two ducks had a multicolored neck; the top of the other's head was green.

It was on this very night that Second Uncle You tried to hang himself. At first he cursed, then he cried, and finally he stopped both his cursing and his crying. A short while later, the old cook began to shout as if he'd discovered some sort of weird apparition:

"Second Master You's hanged himself! He's hanged himself!"

Granddad put on his clothes and took me with him, but by the time we arrived at the side room, we discovered that Second Uncle You wasn't there. The old cook summoned us outside. When we got there, we noticed a rope hanging from one of the beams of the southernmost room. It was a dark night, so we couldn't see a thing until the old cook held up a lantern and showed it to us. The rope hung limply from a crossbeam affixed to the beam of the southernmost room.

Where was Second Uncle You? Looking around with the aid of the lantern, we spotted him sitting quietly at the base of the wall. He was neither crying nor cursing. When I held the lantern up to his face to take a closer look, I saw that he was glaring at me with eyes red from crying.

Not long afterwards, Second Uncle You "jumped down the well." The news came to us from the water bearer who lived in the same compound when he came banging on our window and pounding at our door. We dashed over to the well to see for ourselves, but Second Uncle You was not inside it; rather, he was sitting calmly off to the side on a pile of firewood some fifty steps distant. He was just calmly sitting on the pile of firewood. With the aid of a lantern, we could see that he was sitting there having a leisurely smoke.

The old cook, the water bearer, even the bean-flour sifter from the noodle mill had shown up—the incident had disturbed a good many of the neighbors. At first he didn't move, but when he saw that just about everyone had arrived, he broke out running toward the well. But he was caught and stopped by several of those present. They couldn't just stand by and watch him jump down the well, could they?

When he made his attempt at jumping down the well, he took his pipe and his tobacco pouch along with him. Then, when he was urged by everyone to go home, he pointed to a small candle atop the pile of firewood and said:

"Bring that candle along for me."

Later on, Second Uncle You's "jumping down the well" and "hanging" became laughing matters, and the kids in the street sang a little ditty about the incidents:

> Second Master You faced the well, but came to no harm.
> Then came his hanging, a false alarm.

The old cook said he was clinging to life out of a fear of dying, and others said he'd live forever. From then on, whenever Second Uncle You "jumped down the well" or "hanged himself," no one went to look. And Second Uncle You lived on.

XIII

The yard at my house was a dreary one. In the winter it was covered with a blanket of snow, and in the summer it was overrun by mugwort that whistled in the wind and misted when it rained. When there was neither wind nor rain, we passed our days quietly behind a closed gate.

Dogs have their kennels, chickens their roosts, and birds their nests; everything belongs somewhere. Only Second Uncle You, among all the rest, never enjoyed a good night's sleep. There in that side room of his he talked to himself at all hours of the night.

"Accuse me of being afraid of death, will they? Well, if they think I'm so full of hot air, let a couple of them come over here, and I'll find out if they've ever been around death! Those shiny swords the Russian 'Hairy Ones' carried . . . they killed and butchered at will. As for all those fearless people who disdained death, the instant they heard that the Russian 'Hairy Ones' were coming, they abandoned everything they owned and fled for their lives. If it hadn't been for this 'coward,' who took good care of their belongings for them, when they returned home after fleeing from the 'Hairy Ones' there wouldn't have been even a pair of pants left for them to wear. Now here they are today, with food to eat and clothes to keep themselves warm, but any thoughts of the outstanding debts they owe for their present situation have scattered to the farthest reaches of the universe. Their consciences are stuck between their ribs, those black hearted wretches with their faces of steel."

" . . . So they say I'm afraid of death . . . well, I'm not bragging when I say I've seen wars and weapons, thunderstorms and killer winds. Like those Russian 'Hairy Ones' with their swords, slaughtering everyone they saw. But I wasn't afraid, and anyone who says I was . . . what are the times coming to?"

A steady stream of Second Uncle You's monologues poured from the eastern side rooms. There was the time when the river overflowed its banks, and though others didn't have the nerve to cross it, Second Uncle You said he did. Then there was the time of the great fire, when everyone else fled, but Second Uncle You bravely stayed behind to save several things. Then there was the time when he was a child out on the mountain gathering firewood and he met up with a wolf, a truly vicious beast. We heard him say:

"The hearts of wolves and the lungs of wild dogs . . . the people 'dis' year all have the hearts of wolves and the lungs of wild dogs. They eat good food and drink good liquor, and anyone who tries to be a good man in times like 'dis' is a bastard and a rabbit whelp . . ."

"Rabbit whelp, rabbit whelp . . ." Sometimes, on nights when Second Uncle You couldn't sleep, he'd walk into the courtyard and begin to talk to himself in mid-sentence with "rabbit whelp this" and "rabbit whelp that."

Chickens, ducks, cats, dogs—all were asleep in the middle of the night—all, that is, except Second Uncle You.

Since the window in Granddad's room was covered by a curtain that blocked out the moon and stars, for all I knew the evening star might have fallen from the sky, or Orion's Belt might be lying on its side. All I could see was the silvery curtain through which the light from the stars and moon shone.

I woke up to hear Second Uncle You talking to himself—"Rabbit whelp this, rabbit whelp that"—and I wanted to run over and pull back the window curtain to look at him out in the yard. But Granddad wouldn't let me get up.

"Go back to sleep, and we'll get up early tomorrow morning to roast corn for breakfast."

That's the comforting tone he used to keep me from getting up.

After falling back to sleep, I dreamed I could hear sounds of a dog-fight on the southern bank of the Hulan River, or some distant spot beyond the town. Then I dreamed about a great white rabbit whose ears were as big as those of the little donkey in the mill. Having heard Second Uncle You's talk about a "rabbit whelp," I dreamed of a great white rabbit; having heard the sound of the wooden clappers from the mill, I dreamed of the little donkey that lived there. And so my dreams were of a great white rabbit with ears as big as those of the little donkey in the mill.

I hugged the great white rabbit, liking it more with every passing second. Then I laughed out loud and woke myself up. When I woke up, Second Uncle You was still sitting in the yard talking to himself: "Rabbit whelp this" and "Rabbit whelp that." The wooden clappers in the mill behind our house were still being struck loudly.

I asked Granddad if the great white rabbit in my dream was the "rabbit whelp" Second Uncle You was always talking about.

"Hurry up and go back to sleep," he said. "The middle of the night is no time to be talking." When he finished, he chuckled, then repeated himself:

"Hurry up and go back to sleep. The middle of the night is no time to be talking."

But Granddad and I didn't go right back to sleep. We listened to the far-off sounds of the dogfight as they slowly drew nearer, and to some of the neighborhood dogs that had started barking. A few carts and horses were beginning to pass along the road beyond the outer wall, signaling the fast approaching dawn. But Second Uncle You was still out there cursing those "rabbit whelps" of his, and the miller was still striking his wooden clappers in the mill out back.

XIV

As soon as I got up the following morning, I ran over to ask Second Uncle You if the "rabbit whelp" he was always talking about was my great white rabbit.

This really made him angry:

"There isn't a decent person in your whole family—you're a bunch of rats! From top to bottom, all of your consciences are stuck in your ribs. The adults are a bunch of adult rats, and the kids are all baby rats . . ."

I had no idea what he meant. I listened for a while, but couldn't comprehend what he was talking about.

CHAPTER SEVEN

I

Harelip Feng lived in the mill. He struck his wooden clappers deep into the night, night after night. It was a little better during the winter, but on summer nights he struck it with great frequency.

The window of the mill faced the rear garden of our house. Pumpkins, gourds, cucumbers, and other creepers were planted at the base of the wall that ran all around our garden, and the pumpkin plants spread to the top of the wall, where their flowers bloomed. Some had even passed over the top of the wall out onto the street, where they showed off their bright orange blossoms.

The kitchen window was covered by that tenacious climber, the cucumber, whose tendrils were as slender as fine silver threads. A single cucumber plant put forth countless numbers of these tendrils, which caught your eye as they shone in the sunlight, their tips so clean they seemed like threads that had been formed out of beeswax. But the points were coiled back around, as if to show that while they were bold enough to climb great trees, wild vegetation, walls, and window sills, still they harbored some hidden reservations.

The moment the sun came out, these tendrils, which had grown cold at night, suddenly took on a new warmth, pushing forward with increased speed—you could almost see them growing before your eyes, pushing ever forward. The cucumber plant at the base of the mill window reached the window sill in a day, by the second day it had climbed over the frame, and by the third the window frame was covered with its flowers. Within a few days, before you even realized it, the cucumber stems had climbed above the window of the mill and had reached the roof.

After that it was as if all the cucumber plants were signaling to each other as they gathered in great numbers to block out the window of the mill.

From then on, the sunlight was kept from the man who worked the mill, as there was but one window, and now it was barricaded, so that neither wind nor rain could penetrate it. With the inside of the mill thus completely darkened, there existed two separate worlds—one inside the garden and one beyond—and Harelip Feng belonged to the world beyond. But looking from the outside, that window was a wonderful sight, adorned with all those flowers and cucumbers—it was virtually covered with cucumbers.

There was also a pumpkin plant that had climbed past the window to the roof of the mill and had formed a large pumpkin above the eaves. It almost seemed as if it had grown independently of the plant, looking rather like one that someone had placed on the tiles to soak up the sun. It was a lovely scene.

On summer days as I played in the rear garden, Harelip Feng would call out to me for some cucumbers. I'd pick some and hand them in to him through the window, which was thickly overgrown with the vines. He'd force apart the leaves covering the window, reach out through the small opening he'd made, and take the cucumbers.

Sometimes he'd stop striking his wooden clappers and ask how big the cucumbers had grown or whether the tomatoes were red yet. Separated from the rear garden by only a window, it was as if he were holed up a great distance away.

When Granddad was in the garden, the two of them would have a chat. He said that the little donkey that turned the mill was limping from a lame leg. Granddad advised him to send for a veterinarian, and Harelip Feng replied that he had, but with no results. When Granddad asked what medication had been given to the donkey, Harelip Feng said it was a mash of cucumber seeds and sorghum vinegar. Harelip Feng was behind the window, Granddad was outside; Granddad couldn't see Harelip Feng, Harelip Feng couldn't see Granddad.

Sometimes Granddad would walk away and return home, leaving me to play alone as I sat at the base of the mill wall. I could hear Harelip Feng say things like:

"Haven't you been out to see the farms this year, old master?"

Sometimes, when I heard him say such things, I'd keep silent to see what would come next. Once in a while I'd be so amused by this that I couldn't keep from jumping to my feet and rapping on his window, laughing so hard I'd knock off some of the cucumbers growing there. Then I'd race home to tell Granddad what had happened. Just like me, he'd laugh until tears came to his eyes. But he always admonished me not to laugh, that I might be heard. On occasion he'd shut the back door before he started laughing, as if he was afraid Harelip Feng would be embarrassed if he heard us.

But this wasn't how the old cook handled it. Sometimes he'd be passing the time of day with Harelip Feng, then slip away in the middle of their conversation. Now since Harelip Feng couldn't see out the vine-covered window and was unaware that the other fellow had left, he'd continue the conversation alone, but with no response.

Once, when the old cook went out into the garden with a basket to gather some eggplants, he chatted with Harelip Feng as he picked them. Then without a word he slipped away back to the house, basket in hand, to begin preparing the meal.

Harelip Feng continued talking in a loud voice from inside the mill:

"The circus has come to West Park, but I haven't found the time to go see it. How about you, old Wang, have you seen it yet?"

By that time there was no one in the garden; dragonflies and butterflies were darting back and forth, and Harelip Feng's voice fell on the empty garden, where it was lost. It died away without a trace. When he discovered that old Wang had long since left the garden, he began striking his wooden clappers again and watched the donkey turn the mill.

Second Uncle You, on the other hand, never once slipped away during one of his chats with Harelip Feng. He'd ask him things like how badly the roof leaked when it rained or if there were many rats in the mill. For his part, Harelip Feng would ask whether or not a lot of rain had fallen in the garden that year and whether or not the eggplants and beans were ripe. Then, after the two of them had finished what they had to say, Second Uncle You would invite Harelip Feng to take a stroll in the garden, or Harelip Feng would invite Second Uncle You into the mill to sit for a while.

"When you've got the time, come out to the garden for a stroll."

"When you've got the time, come in to the mill and sit a spell."

Then Second Uncle You would take his leave and walk out of the garden, and Harelip Feng would recommence striking his wooden clappers.

In the autumn the garden would look drearier with each passing day, as the leaves of the elm tree yellowed and the foxtails atop the wall dried up. It was at this time that Harelip Feng's window reemerged, for the tangled cucumber vines that had blocked it withered and fell to the ground. By then I could stand in the rear garden and see Harelip Feng, and by pulling myself up to the window, I could see the donkey turning the mill, its ears straight up, blinders covering its eyes. With every third or fourth step a snort of air emerged from its nostrils as it walked lamely along; when it stopped to rest, it stood on three legs. Harelip Feng told me that the donkey had a lame leg.

Once the cucumber vines had withered and fallen away, I could see Harelip Feng every day: Harelip Feng drinking liquor, or sleeping, or striking his wooden clappers, or playing the two-stringed *huqin*, or singing opera arias, or turning the windmill—all I had to do to see these things was pull myself up to the window ledge.

Once the glutinous rice was harvested in the autumn, for every three days Harelip Feng spent working the mill he spent two making rice cakes, which he covered with a layer of beans. They were composed of one layer of yellow and one layer of red—the yellow a golden yellow, the red a fiery red. He sold the cakes for three cash apiece, or two for a large slice; he'd sprinkle on some brown sugar if you wanted, or some white sugar, at no extra cost.

When Harelip Feng pushed his wheelbarrow along the street, he'd be followed by a pack of children, some with money to spend, others just looking on.

Granddad loved these cakes, and so did Mother, but I think I liked them the best of anyone. Sometimes Mother would send the old cook to buy some, sometime she'd send me.

But there was a limit to how much we were permitted to eat. We were only allowed a slice as big as the palm of our hand, so we wouldn't upset our stomachs. As Granddad ate his, he'd say, "That's enough, that's enough," for fear I would eat too much, and when Mother had finished hers, she too would say, "That's enough," for fear I'd want more. But in all honesty, I really didn't feel that I'd had enough, and I could easily have eaten two more pieces. But once they'd said this, there was nothing I could do; I'd have felt embarrassed to keep clamoring for more, even though the truth of the matter is, I hadn't had enough.

When I was playing outside the main gate and Harelip Feng came by with his wheelbarrow, he always cut a slice off of the big piece of rice cake for me, and I always accepted it. If I was playing inside the compound and heard him passing by the other side of the wall yelling, "Rice cake, rice cake," I'd clamber up onto the earthen wall at the spot in the southwest corner, where part of it had crumbled away over the years, and look around to see Harelip Feng coming up the street, pushing his wheelbarrow along. When he came up alongside me, he'd ask:

"Want a slice?"

I'd neither give him an answer nor jump down from the wall, but would just stay there as if nothing had happened. He'd then set down his wheelbarrow, cut off a slice of the cake and hand it to me.

When winter came, Harelip Feng spent nearly every day out selling his rice cake. He needed a huge pot for making the stuff. First he'd boil water under a bamboo steamer, then spread a layer of the freshly ground rice over the steamer, followed by a layer of beans. Since he did all this inside the mill, the place was filled with hot steam. If I went inside the mill to buy some rice cake, I could hear the crackling sounds of burning firewood, but I couldn't see a soul there.

Whenever I bought some, I went over early, then waited until it was just out of the pan, piping hot. There'd be a great pall of steam inside the room, making it impossible to see anyone, so as I opened the door, I always called out:

"Hey, here I am!"

When he heard the sound of my voice, Harelip Feng would say:

"This way, I'm over here."

II

Once, when Mother sent me to buy some rice cake, it was later than usual and the cake was already out of the pan. So I hastily bought it and ran home, but as soon as I arrived, I discovered I'd mistakenly gotten some with brown sugar rather than white sugar, as Mother had wanted. I hadn't noticed it at the time, only discovering my mistake when I got it home. I ran back right away to exchange it, and Harelip Feng cut me some more slices, on top of which he sprinkled white sugar.

Then, after I'd taken the rice cake from him and was about to leave, I happened to turn and notice a curtain hanging in front of his small *kang*. I couldn't imagine what that was there for, so I ran over to take a look. I reached out, pulled the curtain back, and looked inside. Wow! There was a baby in there! I turned on my heel and ran home, where I gave Granddad the news that there was a strange woman sleeping on Harelip Feng's *kang*, and that there was a baby lying beside her under the quilt. Only the baby's head was sticking out—it was bright red.

Granddad seemed perplexed as I gave him the news, but then he told me to hurry up and eat the rice cake before it turned cold and lost its flavor. But how could I eat it then? I was much too excited—not only was there a little donkey in the mill, now there was a baby there, too.

Because of all the excitement that morning, I didn't eat any rice cake, and finally I put on my fur-lined cap and ran over to take another look. Harelip Feng was out when I went over the second time, though I didn't know where he'd gone. Apparently, he wasn't out selling his rice cake, for his wheelbarrow was lying up against the millstone. As I opened the door and went in, a gust of wind parted the white bed curtain. The woman was still lying there motionless, her baby beside her, not making a sound. I looked all around the room;

nothing had changed, except for the addition of a brass basin in which some old rags were soaking in water that had already frozen over. There were no other changes.

The little donkey that lived inside the mill during the winter was standing there placidly, its eyes covered with blinders, just as it was every day. Everything else in the mill—the windmill itself, the bolting frame, the millstone—were all right where they should have been. Even the rats at the base of the wall were scurrying back and forth wildly and squeaking as loudly as ever.

I looked around for a while, but I had no idea what was going on. Then, just as I was about to head back home, I spotted an earthenware jar on the edge of the *kang* that was so frozen it looked like a little iceberg. This reminded me just how cold the room was, and I began to shiver. Then I noticed a gaping hole in the window that gave out onto the rear garden, and I saw sky showing through holes in the tiled roof. I opened the door and ran all the way home, where the heat from the brightly burning stove hit me full in the face as I stepped through the door. Just as I was about to ask Granddad whose baby that was in the mill, Harelip Feng came walking up to the house.

You could tell it was him at a glance, wearing his four-flapped hat and the grin that always appeared before he said anything. He came into the room and sat in the armchair with the thick red cushion next to Granddad. He sat there looking like he was unable to say what was on his mind, all the while restlessly rubbing the cushion with his right hand and pulling at his left ear with the other. Several times he grinned as if he were about to speak, but each time he stopped short of saying anything. The heat from our stove was so strong it turned his face crimson.

"Old Master, I've got a problem," he said at last.

Granddad asked him what his problem was.

Fidgeting on his chair, Harelip Feng took off his dog-skin cap and fumbled with it. Then, after grinning for a long while, which indicated he was about to say something, he finally managed to utter:

"I've got a family now."

Tears came to Harelip Feng's eyes.

"Won't you please help me, old Master?" he continued. "I've got them in the mill for the time being, since there's no place else for them to stay."

As soon as he finished, I looked over at Granddad and said:

"Granddad, it's freezing in the mill. An earthenware basin on the edge of the *kang* was cracked from the cold."

Granddad nudged me away with the airs of someone engrossed in his thoughts.

"There's a baby sleeping on the *kang*!" I added.

Granddad gave his permission for them to set up temporary lodgings in a shed to the south of the mill where we stored hay.

Harelip Feng stood up.

"Thank you!" he exclaimed, "Thank you!"

Tears welled up in his eyes again as he was expressing his thanks, then he put on his dog-skin cap and walked out, tears streaming down his cheeks.

The moment Harelip Feng was out of the room, Granddad turned to me and said:

"Children should keep quiet when grownups are talking."

Since I was only six or seven at the time, I didn't understand what he meant.

"Why should I be quiet?" I asked. "Why can't I talk?"

"Didn't you see the tears in Harelip Feng's eyes? He was embarrassed."

What was there to be embarrassed about? I really didn't understand it at all.

III

Toward noon we heard a commotion in the mill.

Harelip Feng was standing silently alongside the millstone facing his boss, the proprietor, who stood there, pipe in hand, cursing him. The proprietor's wife was abusing him in a loud voice and pounding on the windmill:

"Are you trying to ruin our *fengshui*, letting that dirty bitch of yours live here in our mill?

"I suppose you think it's all right for that woman of yours to anger the spirits!

"Harelip Feng, if we don't make any money after this, I'm going to hold you accountable. Who do you think you are! Can you call yourself a human being? You've got no pride left. If you had, you wouldn't have brought this dirty bitch over for everyone to see. You get the hell out of here!"

"I was just getting ready to move them," Harelip Feng said. "They're going to move . . ."

"They're going to move!" the proprietor's wife shouted. "I don't know what kind of trash they are, but I'm telling you to get the hell out. Thanks to you, we're probably ruined!"

In the midst of this tirade, something on the *kang* caught her eye.

"What's this? You're using *our* grain sacks to cover that dirty bitch? Take them off this minute! I'm telling you, Harelip Feng, you've ruined us. You've absolutely ruined us!"

He'd covered his newborn child with four or five grain sacks while it slept, its face nearly buried under the pile.

The proprietor's wife stood off to the side and railed:

"Take them off, take them off this minute!"

So Harelip Feng walked over and removed the grain sacks, exposing the crimson hands of his child, which clenched and unclenched several times until the baby started to cry. Its breath rose white as snow in the air as it cried.

The proprietor's wife took the grain sacks from him, saying:

"I'm freezing to death! Hurry up and move; I don't have the time to stay here and fight with you."

She opened the door, hunched her shoulders, and ran home.

The proprietor, whose name was Wang Si, and who was also Harelip Feng's landlord, invited Granddad over to his house for some tea. We sat on the *kang* in his place warming ourselves by a charcoal brazier and listening to the baby's cries from the mill. Granddad asked me if my hands were warm enough yet. I told him no.

"When they're warm, we'll go back home," he said.

As we emerged from Wang Si's house, I told Granddad I wanted to go back to the mill and have another look. He said there wasn't anything to see there, but if I felt like it, he'd let me go back after I warmed up at home.

There was a thermometer at home, but none in the mill, so I asked Granddad:

"What do you think the temperature is in the mill, Granddad?"

He said it was below zero.

"How much below?" I asked.

"How can I tell without a thermometer?"

"How much below zero is it?" I persisted.

Granddad looked up at the sky and said:

"Seven or eight degrees, I expect."

"Wow, that's cold!" I said with rising spirits. "That's the same as it is outside, isn't it?"

I began racing home: past the well, past the watering trough beside it, and past a millstone by the well, beneath the big glass window of our tenant, past Old Zhou's house, then past the big chimney at our place. They all flew past me, fading into the distance as I raced by. I was running so fast it seemed to me that the houses and the chimney were the ones moving, not me. I felt like I was traveling as fast as the wind.

If the temperature inside the mill was below zero, I thought, then it was the same as being out of doors. That really amused me—the temperature inside a house being the same as outside. The more I thought about it, the funnier it seemed, and the higher my spirits rose. Shouting with glee as I ran, I finally reached home.

IV

That afternoon Harelip Feng moved his baby into the shed to the south of the mill. The baby's cries were so loud they sounded more like those of a grown child than a newborn baby. With all the noise coming from their shed, I decided to go take a peek.

This time the woman was sitting up, the quilt wrapped around her shoulders, her long braid hanging down her back. She was sitting atop a pile of hay facing the inside of the room, occupied with some task or other. She turned around as she heard the door creak, and when she did, I recognized her as the daughter of the Wang family who lived in our compound, the one we called Big Sister Wang. That was strange—how could it have been her? I was shocked when she turned to face me. I felt like turning around and running right home to tell Granddad the news and find out what this was all about. She smiled when she saw me. She had a large face and a pointed nose, which crinkled whenever she smiled. As she smiled at me now, her nose was covered with wrinkles, just like always.

Normally, when we had an excess of vegetables in our rear garden, she'd come over with a basket and pick some of the eggplants and cucumbers to take home. She was a friendly, cheerful girl, and very loud; she always greeted anyone she met with:

"Have you eaten?"

Her voice was as crisp and loud as that of a magpie perched on a roof.

Her father was a carter, and when she took the horse up to the well to drink, she drew the water faster than her father could—two or three turns of the handle and the bucket was full. People commented when they saw her:

"Someday that girl is going to be a big help to her husband's family."

Often, after she'd finished picking vegetables in our garden and was about to leave, she'd pluck a purslane flower and stick it in her hair. Her glossy braid was bound with a red ribbon at the base and a green one at the tip, all neat and clean and topped with a purslane flower above her ear, which made her look very fetching. As she walked, basket in hand, the people behind all voiced favorable comments.

To the old cook her beauty was in her large head and big eyes.

Second Uncle You said there was something auspicious in her broad shoulders and rounded waist.

As for Mother, she commented:

"I don't have a son old enough, but if I did I'd choose her for his wife—such a bright young girl."

Third Granny Zhou from our compound said:

"Gracious, this girl's as tall and large as a big sunflower. How old are you this year, girl?"

Every time she saw Big Sister Wang, Third Granny Zhou asked her how old she was. I don't know how many times she asked, but it nearly became a ritual; it was as though, if she didn't ask, she'd have nothing to say.

"Twenty," Big Sister Wang would reply every time.

"Twenty! Then it's time to find you a husband."

Or she'd say:

"Let's see who the lucky family will be. We'll just have to wait and see."

Whenever old Mrs. Yang from the next compound climbed up the wall to look at her, she said:

"That girl's cheeks are as red as fire!"

But now, although her nose crinkled as she smiled, her face was somewhat gaunt and her complexion much paler than before.

She was holding her baby in her arms. As I stood there looking at her, she grew embarrassed, and so did I. My feelings of embarrassment stemmed from my not having seen her for so long, and I guess the same must have been true for her. I wanted to leave, but would have felt awkward doing so right away; yet, if I stayed, I didn't know what to say.

So I just stood there quietly for a while watching her put her baby down on the *kang* and cover him with some hay. Actually there wasn't any *kang* to be seen, just piles of hay all over the room, on the floor, and on the *kang* stacked in bales nearly to the rafters. The *kang* wasn't a very big one to begin with, and now it was completely covered with bales of hay. She'd made a little nest for her baby, where he slept on a bed of hay and was covered by a blanket of hay.

The longer I looked, the more amused I was by the sight of this baby sleeping in what looked like a magpie nest. Come evening, I gave Granddad a complete account of all I'd seen. He didn't say a word, but I could see from his face that he knew a lot more about what was going on than I did.

"She covers her baby with hay!"

"Uh-huh."

"She's Big Sister Wang, isn't she?"

"Uh-huh."

Granddad was evidently in no mood to ask questions or listen to me. But that night, as the family gathered round the kerosene lamp, the conversation turned lively. How the tongues wagged! Big Sister Wang such-and-such, one would say; Big Sister Wang thus-and-so, someone else would add. Back and forth it went, getting more vicious by the minute. The more they talked, the worse she sounded. Everyone was of the opinion that her voice was too loud, proof positive that she was no good. No respectable girl would talk so loud.

"What's 'dis' world coming to," Second Uncle You commented, "when a nice girl like that falls for a man who works a mill?"

"A man's supposed to be rough and tough, but a woman's supposed to be dainty," said the old cook. "Who ever heard of a young woman who looks like a coolie laborer?"

To which Second Uncle You added:

"You're right there! The Patriarch looks like a Patriarch, and the Immortal Matron looks like an Immortal Matron. Haven't you been on temple strolls on the eighteenth day of the fourth month? You know how awesome and stern the Patriarch in the Temple of the Patriarch is and how gentle and refined the Matron in the Temple of the Immortal Matron is."

The old cook continued:

"Who ever heard of such a thing, a girl who can draw water better than an able-bodied man? I've never seen a girl as strong as that one."

"She's done for now," Second Uncle You lamented. "She was born to poverty, right down to her bones. Instead of falling for someone wearing silks or satins, she had to get hooked up with a grimy miller. Well, to each his own."

By the following day, everyone in the neighborhood knew that Big Sister Wang had had a baby. When Third Granny Zhou ran over to our house to get all the news, Mother told her she could go take a look for herself in the shed. But she replied:

"Gracious, I don't have the time to spend on seamy affairs like that."

Old Mrs. Yang from the west compound also came over when the news reached her ears. She was wearing a starched and shiny blue gown, a silver pin in her hair, and a white copper ring on her finger. The moment she stepped into the room, Mother told her that Harelip Feng had a son, but old Mrs. Yang quickly protested:

"I certainly didn't come over to ask about things like that. I only want to find out what the interest rate at the Guanghe Bank is these days. You see, my second son wrote home from Xihuang yesterday that his father-in-law wants to deposit a large sum of money for a relative."

With that she seated herself with great dignity.

Since our house was much too hot, old Mrs. Yang's face flushed a bright crimson almost as soon as she walked in, so Mother hurriedly opened the ventilation window on the north side. The moment it was opened, the sounds of the baby's cries carried into the room from the shed—loud, harsh cries.

"Just listen," Mother said. "That's Harelip Feng's son."

"Well, well. I could have told you that Big Sister Wang was no good. And you mark my word, she'll never come to any good, either. Some time ago, when she upped and disappeared, I asked her mother: 'Where's your daughter gone to?' She told me she'd gone to visit her grandmother, but I was a little suspicious, since she'd been gone so long."

"Big Sister Wang cried so much during the summer her eyes were constantly red," Mother said. "Her mother told me she has a bad temper, and her eyes are red from all their fights."

Folding her arms, old Mrs. Yang exclaimed:

"She sure does have a temper! But now she's disgraced herself, and I'm surprised that temper hasn't killed her. She's no good. Just look at those eyes, how big they are! I said long ago that she'd never come to any good."

Then she whispered something in Mother's ear and walked off laughing and muttering. Apparently, she'd forgotten her original purpose in coming over, which had been to inquire about interest rates, because she walked out the door without ever again mentioning Guanghe Bank.

Old Mrs. Yang, Third Granny Zhou, even the people in the bean mill—everyone was saying Big Sister Wang was no good. Some said there was something wrong with her eyes, others said she was too strong, and still others said her braid was too thick.

V

Once this affair became known, the entire compound was obsessed with Big Sister Wang: people discussed her, gossiped about her, even recorded her daily activities.

According to one story, she'd been raised by her maternal grandmother, spending nearly the whole of every day with boys, until she herself became a tomboy. Once she'd even injured one of her cousins by hitting him with a pair of tongs. Another time during a windstorm she'd stolen more than twenty of her grandmother's duck eggs and eaten every last one of them. Then on another occasion she'd gone down to the stream to gather water chestnuts, but most of the ones she'd brought back in her basket were other peoples', which she'd claimed as her own. She was said to be unreasonable, and no one dared try talking sense to her; when they did, she'd curse and hit them.

The woman who spread these tales told them as though she'd witnessed everything with her own eyes. She said that on the twenty-third day of the twelfth month, during the pre-New Year's festivities, the girl had even hit her own grandmother because she'd been given one piece of meat less than she'd expected; then she'd run home.

"You see what a greedy little thing she is!" Everyone laughed. This self-appointed biographer of Big Sister Wang had collected a wealth of material for her stories.

Ever since the death of the child bride, the compound had suffered a long spell of boredom, and now, although the atmosphere couldn't be called lively, there was at least full participation in the goings-on. Even though there was no sorceress dancing or drum-beating, everyone felt that it was a good opportunity to have a little fun. So all the gossips and busybodies donned their fur-lined caps and felt boots and stood outside Harelip Feng's window on snowy evenings, waiting to pick up so tidbit. Even if the news they gleaned was so small it would of a needle, as far as they were concerned, the wait in the er had been worth it, for that was the only way there'd r the next day.

e next few days there was always a group of news outside Harelip Feng's window. These news-gatherers, none of whom was educated, were natural gossips and busybodies. Our old cook, for example, went over to gather some information, then came back and reported:

"It's mighty cold in that shed! The wind howls right through it. The baby isn't making a sound, and I'll bet it's dead from the cold. Hurry up, go see for yourselves!"

Beside himself with glee, the old cook was waving his arms and jumping around. Before long, he put on his dog-skin cap again and went out to gather some more tidbits, but this time when he came back, he reported:

"Damn it to hell, the little pest isn't dead after all! It's at its mother's breast."

All this news was being made a mere fifty steps from our house, but the news-gatherers twisted it all out of proportion and made a big sensation out of it.

Someone spotted a coil of rope on Harelip Feng's *kang* and quickly spread the rumor that he was planning to hang himself

Talk of a "hanging" was a powerful stimulant. Women fastened on their scarves and men put on their felt boots; it's hard to tell just how many there were who came to watch the fun or who were making plans to come.

There were more than thirty people, not counting the children, in old Yang's family from the west compound, and with the children there were more than forty. If just the thirty adults had come over to watch Harelip Feng hang himself, they'd have crushed our little shed to pieces! Figuring that among them there were some who were too old or too sick to come, let's say that only ten turned out. That would make ten from old Yang's family in the west compound and three from old Zhou's family in our compound—Third Granny, Fourth Daughter-in-Law, and Eldest Daughter-in-Law, plus the child Fourth Daughter-in-Law carried with her and the child Eldest Daughter-in-Law dragged along, as they customarily did—which means there were five people altogether representing three generations of the Zhou family.

Then there were quite a few of the men—how many exactly is not known—who made bean noodles, stoked the furnace, or ran errands for the mill. At any rate, no less than twenty or thirty from our compound went to watch the fun. They were joined by countless others from the neighborhood, who came as soon as the word reached them.

"A hanging! Why should a good man choose not to live, but prefer to hang himself? Hurry up and see! Besides, what harm is there in looking? After all, it isn't like a circus, where you have to pay admission

That's why crowds always gather when a woman in the town of Hu-lan River jumps down a well or into the river, or when a man hangs himself. I don't know if this is true all over China, but at least it's true where I come from.

A woman who throws herself into the river is not buried immediately upon recovery of her body. Rather, her corpse is left on the bank for a couple of days for everyone to see. A woman who jumps down a well is not buried when her body is pulled out, either, but is displayed to the curious eyes of eager spectators like an exhibition of native products.

And yet these are not pleasant things to see. If Harelip Feng had hanged himself, it would have been a gruesome sight. Timid women cannot sleep for several nights after seeing the corpse of a suicide. But the next time some unfortunate person takes his own life, they flock around just the same. The fearful and vivid impression they take home causes them to once again lose sleep and appetite, but, as if under some strange compulsion, they go a third time, even though it frightens them nearly out of their wits. They buy yellow paper money and a bundle of incense sticks to burn at The Crossroads, then kowtow three times each toward the north, south, east, and west, imploring the evil spirits:

"Don't take possession of me! I've sent you off properly with incense and paper money!"

One girl died of fright after seeing a hanged corpse, and I heard of another who died of fright after seeing a body brought up from a well. She fell ill from the shock, and no doctors were able to save her.

Yet people choose to look, and men, perhaps because they are bolder, are not afraid. Most women are more timid, but they screw up their courage and go. Some women even take their children along. Long before they've even grown up, they're taken along, perhaps to accustom them to this exciting world of ours; that way they won't be totally inexperienced in the area of suicides.

One of the news-gatherers saw Harelip Feng buy a meat cleaver and quickly spread the word that he was going to cut his throat.

VI

Feng neither hanged himself nor cut his throat; he got ⁿn a year's time his child had grown big.

Year's holiday we killed a pig, and Harelip Feng came ᵐmove the bristles. He stayed over for dinner and some liquor, and as he was about to leave, Granddad told him to take a handful of the large steamed buns with him. He tucked them into his waistband and left. People were always poking fun at him by saying:

"Harelip Feng now has an heir."

Usually, when Harelip Feng did some work for us, whether it was grinding half a peck of beans to make bean curd or grinding a couple of pecks of the best red beans to make cakes, Granddad would have him come over to the house for a meal. Once, while we were eating, the old cook said in front of everyone:

"Harelip Feng, you'd better eat a couple less buns so you'll have more to take home to your heir . . ."

Harelip Feng wasn't the least bit annoyed by all this, not really feeling that he was being mocked.

"He's got plenty to eat at home," he said solemnly. "He's got food at home."

When the meal was finished, Granddad said:

"Why don't you take some home anyway?"

He picked up a few, but didn't know where to put them, since they were too hot to tuck up under his waistband and might drop out if he put them up his sleeve.

"Carry them in your cap," the old cook volunteered.

So Harelip Feng went home carrying them in his cap.

If someone in the neighborhood was having a funeral or a wedding and Harelip Feng was one of the banquet guests, as the meatballs were served, someone would say:

"Harelip Feng, you'd better not eat those. Don't forget, you have an heir at home."

Then someone would pick up Harelip Feng's share of meatballs with his chopsticks and place them on a small plate beside him. The same thing happened when the braised pork was served and when the dried fruit was put on the table.

Harelip Feng was never embarrassed by all of this, and when the banquet was over, he'd wrap the things up in his handkerchief and take them home for his son.

VII

Harelip Feng's son was like everyone else's, cutting teeth at seven months, crawling at eight, walking at a year, and running at two. In the summer the boy went naked except for a stomacher around his middle, as he tried to catch little frogs in the ditch in front of his house. His mother sat by the door embroidering another stomacher for him, while his father was in the mill striking his wooden clappers and watching over the little donkey as it turned the mill.

VIII

Two or three years later, when Harelip Feng's second child was on the way, he was in such high spirits that a grin was constantly on his face. When he was outside, people would ask:

"Is it going to be another boy, Harelip Feng?"

He'd just laugh, trying hard to conceal his elation.

When he saw his wife carrying a big basin in the house, he'd say to her:

"What do you think you're doing? Can't you let me handle that for you?"

He also stopped her if she was carrying a bundle of firewood:

"Can't you let me handle that for you?"

And yet Big Sister Wang daily grew thinner and more gaunt. Her eyes seemed bigger, her nose more pointed.

Harelip Feng said that she'd be all right if she'd only eat a few more eggs during her lying-in period and get her strength back.

Harelip Feng's home was a happy one then; in front of the window he even hung a white curtain that he'd bought in town. There hadn't been a curtain at Harelip Feng's window all these years—this was the first time. He bought two catties of new cotton filling, several feet of printed cloth, and twenty or thirty of the best eggs. He worked the mill as always, while Big Sister Wang cut and sewed baby clothes out of the printed cloth. The twenty or thirty eggs he'd bought hung from a rafter in a basket that swayed in the breeze every time the door or window was opened. Whenever an egg peddler passed by their door, Harelip Feng would say to his wife:

"You're not well, and I think you ought to eat a few more eggs."

But though he always wanted to buy a few more eggs, his wife would never let him.

"You never got your strength back after the first baby was born, so what's the harm in eating a couple more eggs this time? I can go out and sell a few extra catties of rice cake to make up for it."

When Granddad went over to his place to pass the time of day, Harelip Feng would talk about his wife:

"She's so thrifty," he'd say, "she won't burn a single straw more than is needed. She won't even eat an extra egg, even though she's about to have a baby. You wait and see, she's going to put our family on its feet." A look of contentment was on his face.

IX

As August turned into September, the crows came. Actually, there were already some crows in the sky in August, but not nearly as many as in September.

The clouds at sunset in August were as red as fire, forming unusual shapes: tigers, big lions, the heads of horses, packs of dogs. But by September these clouds appeared no more. We were no longer treated to the sight of skies filled with bright red, golden yellow, purple, or cinnabar-hued clouds. None of them appeared in the sky again, either at dawn or at dusk—they were all gone. The September skies were quiet and empty; the black clouds of July and the red clouds of August were gone when September arrived—even the rains and winds ceased. During the day there was only the bright yellow sun, at night only the snow-white moon.

As the weather turned cold, people began putting on their lined jackets, and since no one went out to cool himself off after dinner, the yard appeared quiet and lonely. The chickens and ducks went to roost, pigs bedded down in their pens, and dogs curled up in their dens; in the absence of any wind, the mugwort in the yard stood motionless; in the absence of any clouds, the evening star shone as brightly as a little lamp.

On one such night, Harelip Feng's wife died. The following morning, as flocks of crows flew overhead, they buried her.

The crows flew over only at dusk and at dawn. Where did they come from? Where were they headed? They came flying from some distant place, darkening the sky like a huge black cloud and shattering the stillness with their loud caws; then, passing overhead, they were gone as quickly as they'd come. Perhaps the grownups knew where they flew to, but none of the children knew, including me.

I'd heard that the crows flew to the willow grove on the southern bank of the Hulan River, but I doubted this, because there didn't seem to be anything they could do over there. The willow grove was a dark, gloomy place. I had no idea just what was in there, nor did I know what there was beyond it. Standing on the bank of the Hulan River and looking over at that dark, gloomy grove of trees, which stretched for several li, I saw several large white birds circling overhead. Besides those birds, I hadn't a clue as to what else might be there. I'd heard that's where all the crows went, but what they did and where they flew to from there no one could say.

Harelip Feng's wife had died in childbirth, and legend has it that women who die that way can be accepted neither in large temples nor small ones, thus being doomed to become homeless spirits.

I wanted to go to the shed and take a look, but Granddad wouldn't allow it, so I waited at the gate. I saw Harelip Feng's son walking in front of his mother's coffin carrying a funeral banner. The banner went ahead, the coffin followed, and Harelip Feng led the procession toward Great Eastern Bridge.

The funeral banner, cut out of white paper, was shaped like a web and was honeycombed with holes, streamers trailing from it. It was held aloft on a pole resting on the boy's shoulder. He neither cried nor showed any emotion, although the weight of the banner seemed too much for him.

Heading east, they walked farther and farther as I watched them from the gate, until they crossed Great Eastern Bridge. I remained standing there looking into the distance even after I could no longer see them.

Caw caw. Crows flew overhead. One flight passed, then another. The crows were still flying by and screeching as we walked back into the house.

X

Now that Harelip Feng's wife was dead, no one gave him any chance of making it. He had been left with two small children, a four- or five-year-old and a newborn baby. Now let's see how he's going to manage this! "Now we'll see some fun," the old cook said. "Harelip Feng will start hitting the bottle soon, and he'll sit on the millstone and wail."

Everyone else in the neighborhood agreed that this time he was done for. All those people eager for some entertainment began preparing themselves for the excitement Harelip Feng's predicament would create.

But Harelip Feng, rather than completely lose heart, as everyone around him anticipated, lived not as one in the throes of despair, but as a man with a firm grip on life. The sight of his two children had a steadying effect on him, for he knew that he had to plant his feet solidly and make something of his life. It didn't matter to him whether he had the ability or not; he just saw what others did and knew that he'd have to do the same. And so he lived on as usual, assuming whatever responsibilities fell to him.

He began feeding his newborn baby, starting unsuccessfully with chopsticks, then switching to a spoon. He fed the baby and minded the older boy. When it was time to fetch water, he did so; when it was time to work the mill, he did so. When he got up in the morning and opened his door, if he saw one of his neighbors fetching water from the well, he'd invariably say:

"Out getting water, are you?"

If he met a bean curd peddler, he'd say:

"Out selling your bean curd pretty early, aren't you?"

He was blissfully unaware that in the eyes of others he was considered a hopeless case; he didn't know just how difficult they considered his position to be. He didn't realize that he was done for. It simply never crossed his mind.

Admittedly, he felt his share of grief, and tears sometimes welled up in his eyes, but the sight of his older boy leading the little donkey to water immediately brought a smile to his tear-filled eyes.

"He'll soon be a real help to me," he'd say.

Day after day he fed his younger son, but the boy's eyes kept growing bigger and bigger, his arms and legs thinner and thinner. In the opinion of others, this baby had no chance of surviving, but to everyone's amazement, he held on tenaciously. Eventually, the people grew bewildered by this young son of Harelip Feng's who just would not die—they were appalled: How could such a thing happen on the face of the earth?

Whenever Harelip Feng finished his work, he held this child of his, and when the weather was too cold, he lit a fire to warm him. The child's smile was a fearful sight, with something of laughter in it, something of crying. In fact it looked like neither, but rather a mixture of the two. But it pleased Harelip Feng no end, and he'd say:

"The little rascal's playing with me."

or:

"The little rascal really knows what's going on."

The child didn't know how to clap his hands until he was seven or eight months old, an age when other children were already crawling and sitting, and on the verge of learning to talk. But Harelip Feng's child could do none of these things. He could only clap his hands.

Yet Harelip Feng beamed when he saw his son clapping his hands.

"The child's growing faster every day," he'd say.

In the eyes of others, not only was the child not getting any bigger, he actually seemed to be getting smaller, for the thinner he grew, the larger his eyes appeared. Seeing his eyes get larger, and nothing else, it seemed to observers that he really wasn't growing at all. The child looked more like a clay doll than a living person; there was no apparent difference in him even after the passage of two months. No one who saw the child for the first time in a couple of months would be amazed by a sense of how quickly time was passing, for although adults don't appear any older in that period of time, a child is supposed to have changed a great deal.

No one would be conscious of the passage of time by looking at Harelip Feng's child. Adults like to measure time by their children, but they could get no such satisfaction from looking at Harelip Feng's child, for there was no observable growth even after the passage of a couple of months. Far better to go out and look at the cucumbers in the rear garden: planted in April, they threw out tendrils by May, grew flowers in June, and by the end of June, there were cucumbers ready to be eaten.

But Harelip Feng didn't see things this way; in his eyes, the child grew bigger every day. The older boy could lead the little donkey out to the well to drink, while the younger one knew how to laugh, how to clap his hands, and how to shake his head. He would reach his hand out to take food and was already cutting a tooth. When he opened his mouth to laugh, that little baby tooth of his gleamed white.

EPILOGUE

The little town of Hulan River, in earlier days it was where my Granddad lived, and now it is where he is buried. When I was born, Granddad was already in his sixties, and by the time I was four or five, he was nearly seventy. As I approached the age of twenty, Granddad was about eighty. Soon after he reached the age of eighty, Granddad was dead.

The former masters of that rear garden are now gone. The old master is dead; the younger one has fled.

The butterflies, grasshoppers, and dragonflies that were in the garden may still return year after year; or perhaps the place is now deserted.

Cucumbers and pumpkins may still be planted there every year; or perhaps there are no more at all.

Do drops of morning dew still gather on the flower-vase stands? Does the noonday sun still send its rays down on the large sunflowers? Do the red clouds at sunset still form into the shape of a horse, only to shift a moment later into the shape of a dog?

These are things I cannot know.

I heard that Second Uncle You died.

If the old cook is still alive, he'll be getting on in years.

I don't know what has become of any of our neighbors.

As for the man who worked the mill, I haven't the slightest idea how things have gone with him.

The tales I have written here are not beautiful ones, but since my childhood memories are filled with them, I cannot forget them; they remain with me—and so I have recorded them here.

December 20, 1940
Hong Kong